FROM PLATO TO LUMIÈRE:
NARRATION AND MONSTRATIC
AND CINEMA

André Gaudreault
Translated by Timothy Barnard

With this lucid translation of *Du littéraire au filmique*, André Gaudreault's highly influential and original study of film narratology is now accessible to English-language audiences for the first time. Building a theory of narrative on sources as diverse as Plato, *The Arabian Nights*, and Proust, *From Plato to Lumière* challenges narratological orthodoxy by positing that all forms of narrative are mediated by an 'underlying narrator' who exists between the author and narrative text.

Offering illuminating insights, definitions, and formal distinctions, Gaudreault examines the practices of novelists, playwrights, and filmmakers and applies his theory to the early cinema of the Lumière brothers as well as to more recent films. He also enhances our understanding of how narrative develops visually without language – monstration – by detailing how the evolution of the medium influenced narratives in cinema. *From Plato to Lumière* includes a translation of Paul Ricœur's preface to the French-language edition as well as a new preface by Tom Gunning. It is a must-read for cinema and media students and scholars and an essential text on the study of narrative.

ANDRÉ GAUDREAULT is a professor in the Département d'histoire de l'art et d'études cinématographiques at Université de Montréal.

TIMOTHY BARNARD is a film historian, publisher, and translator based in Montreal.

ANDRÉ GAUDREAULT

From Plato to Lumière:

Narration and Monstration in Literature and Cinema

Translated by Timothy Barnard
Preface by Paul Ricoeur
Preface to the English-language edition
by Tom Gunning

UNIVERSITY OF TORONTO PRESS
Toronto Buffalo London

Originally published in 1988 as *Du littéraire au filmique*
© Les Presses de l'Université Laval / Méridiens Klincksieck
Revised edition © Nota Bene / Armand Colin 1999
Translation © University of Toronto Press Incorporated 2009
Toronto. Buffalo London
www.utppublishing.com
Printed in Canada

ISBN 978-0-8020-9885-6 (cloth)
ISBN 978-0-8020-9586-2 (paper)

Printed on acid-free paper

Library and Archives Canada Cataloguing in Publication

Gaudreault, André
    From Plato to Lumière : narration and monstration in literature and cinema /
André Gaudreault; translated by Timothy Barnard; preface by Paul Ricoeur;
preface to the English-language edition by Tom Gunning.

    Translation of: Du littéraire au filmique.
    Includes bibliographical references and index.
    ISBN 978-0-8020-9885-6 (bound). – ISBN 978-0-8020-9586-2 (pbk.)

    1. Motion pictures – Philosophy. 2. Motion picture plays – History and
criticism. 3. Narration (Rhetoric). I. Barnard, Timothy II. Title.

PN1995.G3813 2009   791.4301'5   C2008-906172-1

This book has been published with the help of a grant from the Canadian
Federation for the Humanities and Social Sciences, through the Aid to
Scholarly Publications Programme, using funds provided by the Social
Sciences and Humanities Research Council of Canada.

University of Toronto Press acknowledges the financial assistance to its
publishing program of the Canada Council for the Arts and the Ontario Arts
Council.

University of Toronto Press acknowledges the financial support for its
publishing activities of the Government of Canada through the Book
Publishing Industry Development Program (BPIDP).

For Éliette and Adrien

Cinema and literature: shadow plays, simulacra that resist all wisdom … except that of understanding how they work.

Gilles Thérien, 'Le cinéma québécois,' 114

Whence the vulgar temptation for the writer to write intellectual works. Gross unscrupulousness. A work in which there are theories is like an object with its price-tag still attached.

Marcel Proust, *In Search of Lost Time: Finding Time Again*, 190

Contents

List of Illustrations

Preface

André Gaudreault has asked me to introduce his book to his readers. I gladly accepted, not only because I expected to find in this book a confirmation of my own working hypotheses concerning narrativity, but also to see those hypotheses developed and transformed through contact with an art that no longer allows us to limit the categories of narrative and narrator to literature, even if we consider literature to encompass both the novel and the theatre. I have not been disappointed. The author has given us a veritable treatise on film narration.

The main virtue of this work is that it puts the *cinema* on an equal footing with the *stage*, while at the same time putting the *stage* on an equal footing with the *text*, thus taking film criticism out from under the thumb of literary criticism, that older discipline to which it has involuntarily been submitted. The title of the original French edition of this book, *Du littéraire au filmique*, seems to suggest that this analysis moves in only one direction, 'from the literary to the filmic.' In fact it expresses an emancipation of the latter from the former (which includes both literature and the theatre). Now, if there is to be any legitimacy in speaking of film *narrative*, from the outset, from within the field of literature itself, the categories of 'narrative' and 'narrator' had to be taken beyond their investment in literature and theatre. It was his success at this highest level of abstraction that first interested me in the work of André Gaudreault. But this rigorous abstraction had its counterpart: he needed, with equal cogency, to demonstrate what is specific to the generic categories of narrative and narrator in literature, theatre, and film. In other words, he had to show that the difference among these three fields is not simply a difference of medium, having nothing to do with these categories, but rather a difference of *kind* of narrative within the *genre* of narrative. Just as he has succeeded in making this distinction – and his success here is complete, since his recomposition of the categories of narrative in the area of film forms a *system*, as the book's subtitle in the French-language edition ('Narrative System') indicates – he has succeeded equally well in bringing to light the difficulties inherent in a general narratology. These difficulties have to do with the fact that what we call narrative can designate both the genre and the kind of narrative. In this regard the work of André Gaudreault represents a remarkable tool with which to *remove ambiguity*.

The author demonstrates that this ambiguity is not to be blamed on narratologists, but that it has to do with the very nature of the problem. This is why the reader should not consider the rereading of texts by Plato and Aristotle to be nothing more than a quaint antiquarianism. There, for the first time, two different ways of identifying the basic narratological categories were laid out. The author's explanation of Plato and Aristotle, which he performs with exemplary precision, brings us right back to the source of the ambiguities that continue to affect contemporary narratology. It is from this source, from these ancient texts, that we need to begin the fundamentally analytical task of establishing a hierarchy of concepts. For here is where the problem lies: how to establish a proper *hierarchy* of our principal categories in such a way as to make it possible to redistribute them over several *co-ordinated* areas: texts, the stage, and film. I venture to say that it is not just narratologists who have much to learn from this exegesis of texts from Plato dealing with mimesis and diegesis, but also Hellenists and philosophers. Henceforth it will no longer be possible to mix these two models, even if one might attempt, as does André Gaudreault, to construct a higher-level model that integrates these two dissimilar contrivances.

This makes the chapter 'Early Narratology' much more than just an archaeological detour. However, in order legitimately to propose a complex model, the author first had to restore to these two ancient schemas their originality. In Plato diegesis – narrative – is the genre to which are subordinated 'simple' narrative, where the poet is the narrator who relates events, and narrative 'with imitation,' where the poet expresses himself through his characters; here mimesis means personification. In Aristotle, on the other hand, Mimesis is the genre, but in the very general sense of poetic or artistic representation, and thus distinct from the Platonic use of the term, where it is a separate kind of narration. In Aristotle diegesis is thus subordinate to the representation of human action in a *creative* way, while the Platonic distinction between exposition by the narrator and imitation-personification by the characters participating in the action is downplayed. Here mixed forms are acknowledged, opening the door to new art forms, the cinema among them.

This clarification, rigorously carried out in the chapter 'Early Narratology,' leads us to the ultimate question: what is the *narratable*, seen independently of whether we are talking about *written, staged, or film* narration?

What allows us to speak of narrative in each case without confusing kind and genre? If we take for a moment the example of literature, what remains of narrative if you take away the *textual* element and the *performative* element, that is, narration and monstration by characters in action? There remains the *énoncé* of the ordered sequence of the transformations undergone by the characters. The minimalist position that the author defended in the past, and which he tempers here, would seem to me to be less open to the accusation of laxity were it buttressed by the category of 'emplotment,' or configuring action within time. The reader will recognize here the *muthos* of Aristotle's *Poetics*, an element that has not been taken into account in Gaudreault's complex model derived from the two narrative systems, which order mimesis and diegesis in different ways. With the concept of emplotment, succession and transformation within a recounted narrative are clearly linked. This is what André Gaudreault assumes when he writes: 'any message through which a story is communicated, whatever that story may be, must by rights be considered a narrative' (chapter 6).

We must in any event maintain the notion of narrative at a very general level if we are to be able to speak of textual, staged, and film narratives without abusing the concept itself. Obviously, the price we pay is to distinguish, beginning with textual narrative, between the general form of the narrative, as set out above, and the spoken or written narration that a narrator uses to recount events. In other words, we should be able to distinguish the *narrative-énoncé* in its two forms: *narration* (which becomes a kind of narrative genre); and staged *monstration*. If we are not willing to pay this price, we will have to pay an even greater one: the inability to speak of film narrative in any way other than by vague analogy with and ultimately disguised borrowing from literary criticism, which is tantamount to denying film art its autonomy. André Gaudreault has opted for the first choice and its high price. But it is not as high a price as that imposed by the second option. This is the risk he has run and the gamble he has taken from the beginning of this book to the end.

Basing himself on this generic definition of narrative, the author can construct what he calls the filmic system: cinema's ability to combine and make to work together a range of operations having to do with film shooting and editing, and which together give film narrative a legitimacy equal to that of textual or staged narrative.

The fact that film appears, on first examination, to be closer to theatre than to the novel is easily ascertained. Both *show* rather than tell, in the non-generic sense of narration as opposed to monstration. This provisional assimilation of film narrative to staged narrative presupposes that there is already a clearly established distinction between narration and monstration, with staged narrative being defined as a narrative communicated through characters in action. We thus again evoke the Platonic pair made up of 'simple' narrative and narrative 'with imitation,' where imitation means personification.

The resemblance between theatre and cinema stops there. Filmic monstration follows its own distinct destiny, one that André Gaudreault has had the fortuitous idea of reconstituting by concentrating on 'early cinema.' I am in no way competent to judge this strategic decision. According to Gaudreault, this period was a time when a *procedure*, the cinema, encountered a *process*, film narrative. He locates the arrival of film narrative in the passage from the tableau shots of early cinema to a cinema proper in which the shot loses its autonomous unity. The author pursues this progressive narrativization on two levels, corresponding to the two stages of filmmaking, shooting and editing. In the first stage he identifies narrative as latent in the very mobility of the image and thus defines a sort of innate and spontaneous narrative, that of the articulation of frames, or photograms, within a single shot. He can thus subdivide each level, the initial profilmic level and a cinematographic level. In the former the recording of the image includes mise en scène – in the most physical, material sense of putting before the camera – and enframing. This first articulation proper to filmic monstration already distinguishes it from the staged monstration of theatre, where the spectator experiences the scene in the present. In cinema the recording of the image casts film mise en scène into the past. The difference between theatre and cinema becomes even greater when we superimpose the explicitly narrative operation of editing onto the monstration of recording of the image. This means that in film production narration is tied to monstration. Now, in theatre there is a single monstration, unique each time, with each performance, whereas in the cinema monstration, after having been stripped of all its 'here and now' quality by the recording process, is followed by another operation, editing, a narrative locus par excellence. The narrative operation of editing so closely resembles textual narration that film critics do not hesitate to speak of 'writing with film.' Yet, since it is tied to monstration – itself a very special genre – it differs from textual narrative so much that any subordination of the filmic to the literary is forbidden for all time.

On the basis of this well-ordered linking of common narrative genre with the three narrative species – textual, staged, and filmic – the author takes on the pre-eminent question, namely the question of the *narrator*, or rather the enunciative *agent* of the narrative; here film narrative is privileged. For anyone who has considered the complexity of film's narrative structures, a simple answer to the question 'Who sees?' is no longer plausible. The agent responsible for communicating film narrative is harder to identify than is the case with textual narrative – even though literary narratology has lost its way by identifying too many narrative agents. But – and here we have yet another example of cinema's originality – the film narrator exists to an even lesser extent than the narrator of textual narrative, who already is not a flesh-and-blood author, a unique personage, even on the level of the printed page. The film narrator has no proper name, but rather assembles a number of image-makers. And yet you need a grand narrator if there is to be a successful ordering of monstration and narration and, within monstration, as has been said, of mise en scène and enframing. Here, André Gaudreault acknowledges his debt to Albert Laffay, the inventor of that narrative agent called the 'grand image-maker,' the equivalent of the textual narrator. This grand narrator exercises its power in particular through the temporality of the narrated. It does so by linking the temporality that is created by editing with the temporality already established by the recording of the image. Thus, Laffay's 'great image-maker,' who is both monstrator and narrator, becomes, in André Gaudreault's hands, a 'mega-narrator.' So be it!

In sum, the great contribution of André Gaudreault's book is in the way he fights equally well on two fronts: that of the *generic* unity of narrative communication; and that of the *specificity* of film narrative, when ranged alongside textual and staged narrative.

PAUL RICOEUR

Preface to the English-language edition

Gaudreault's Blasts from the Past: Tracking the Filmic Narrator

Like many important works on cinema originally written in French, it has taken some time to get André Gaudreault's first book into English. The wait has certainly been worth it, and the delay also provides us with a historical perspective on this work. Published originally in 1988, it was the book version of a doctoral dissertation that Gaudreault began at the end of the seventies. Gaudreault's original work emerged, then, from a moment of excitement and transition (indeed foundational) in the academic study of film. Serious scholarship in film, while a long tradition in France where Gaudreault had done graduate work, was still a newcomer in North America (with the first doctoral programs in the United States dating from the early 1970s). To rehearse a well-worn tale of origin, film studies in North America (and Great Britain as well) gained academic respectability (and a degree of autonomy) partly through the prestige brought by imports from France. While the debt the field bears to this inheritance remains unexhausted, in recent years it has been more decried than celebrated.

The new seriousness that academic film studies gained in the seventies came first largely from the intersection between film studies and semiotics or semiology, the science of signs, especially from the applications of semiology to film made by French film theorist Christian Metz, under whom Gaudreault had studied. Although the strictly semiological phase of film studies was relatively brief, it had an enormous effect. Semiological analysis converted the study of film from a topic dominated by what many people saw as little more than fandom or journalism into a discipline based on a novel, yet apparently rigorous, science. With its own terminology and modes of analysis, such as Metz's grand syntagmatic, film semiology had both the feel of a discipline and the romance of unfamiliarity. (A Brazilian friend of mine described an early conference on film semiology in São Paulo in which an attendee listening to the new method responded that it sounded like a combination of 'algebra and Macumba.') Suddenly a popular form of art, entertainment, or persuasion that had gained power over mass audiences (and suspicion from cultural elites) because of its apparent immediacy had been rendered scientific, complex, and sometimes obscure. All of this allowed film studies to gain an academic foothold.

But if one can now recount this systematization of film studies with the cynicism of hindsight, and a new sense of its ultimate limitations, the new method had the great virtue of dealing with the actual processes of film texts in detail. I no longer find the actual categories of Metz's grand syntagmatic useful tools, but the way it raised the issue of temporal and spatial segmentation in film narrative seems to me a fundamental contribution. With semiological methods film studies could approach films not simply as aesthetic masterpieces or campy entertainment, but as *texts*, complex operations of signification. Semiology offered film studies methods of analysis, which could also relate film to other forms of signification, whether verbal or pictorial. The nearly universal assumption that films were primarily a narrative medium – or at least a means of telling stories – could now be probed with some precision, and if semiology did not answer all possible questions, it nonetheless allowed one to formulate them more precisely. Semiology interacted with older forms of narrative analysis and generated a new sub-field of film narratology, eventually triggering as well non-semiological approaches such as those of Edward Branigan and David Bordwell.

Anyone who participated in this dawn of academic film studies in the early seventies remembers not only the excitement and energy this burst of complex and powerful theory had on film studies, but also a certain narrowing of the nascent field that seemed to follow in its wake, as historical research, discussions of film styles and genres, and other elements that had only recently begun to develop scholarly methods, suddenly seemed not worth the effort, naive if not reactionary undertakings. Theory reigned in academic film studies, and what was often termed in contrast (if not disdain) 'empirical' research played a secondary and increasingly marginal role. (One European scholar told me that, when he pointed out to a fellow enthusiast of the new semiology of film that the theory he had evolved could only apply to a handful of existing films, he was told, 'That's immaterial!') Polarization between theoretical and historical approaches seemed inevitable, and historical research seemed to be an endangered species. But at the end of the seventies two new elements arose that again changed the intellectual terrain. The first arose within film theory as the all-embracing claims of grand theory encountered a critique from feminist writers such as Laura Mulvey, Mary Ann Doane, Kaja Silverman, Gaylyn Studlar, and Miriam Hansen and from journals such as *Camera Obscura*. The second impulse came from an unexpected direction, triggered more by film archives than academics: the (re-)discovery of early cinema as a topic for research and – indeed – theorization. Feminists recognized that the semiotics and theories of spectatorship of cinema offered rich ground for rethinking the nature of the relation between the subject and discourse – an issue of importance not only for cinema but for a political rethinking of the way texts operate. The move in film studies towards psychoanalytical models of the spectator created a rich new field for speculation, although it occasionally involved a move away from the specific attention to textual problems that had made semiology such a powerful tool of analysis. But feminist models offered ways of conceiving the process of text reception as varied rather than universal, constituted by the actual forces of social organization as well as subject formation, such as gender, and, increasingly, class and ethnicity.

The other alteration supplies my essay with a different sort of blast from the past: the discovery of early cinema. Here too difference and variation replaced a reliance on assumptions of universality, only the difference was diachronic. In 1978 in Brighton, England, a series of screenings were held as part of the annual conference of the International Federation of Film Archives (FIAF). For a week the FIAF archivists projected their holdings of fictional films made between 1900 and 1906 for a group of scholars. These film historians (including a rather youthful André Gaudreault and myself) saw this newly accessible corpus as a place where the theories of spectatorship and narration that had emerged over the last decade from the new semiological film studies could be tested. Viewing these neglected films from the early period of film history triggered an interaction (rather than a mutual exclusion) between theory and history.

Thus, at the time that André Gaudreault was writing this book, the field of film study had fairly recently sought to place the new discipline on a firm, even scientific, foundation through the methods of semiological analysis. But equally important, this foundation was also undergoing its first challenges: critiquing its methodology through an acknowledgment of the role that differences might play in the reception of films, and endowing theoretical concepts with a historical dimension that might render some of its claims more relative. Gaudreault used the historical perspective supplied by a careful investigation of the fictional films made before 1907 (a process facilitated if not created by the FIAF project, for which Gaudreault assembled an annotated filmography, as well as an additional project helmed by Eileen Bowser at the Museum of Modern Art) to rethink the narrative processes of cinema. But Gaudreault has also pursued the theoretical roots of narratology further back than the early part of the twentieth century to the foundational discussion of narrative in the West in the work of Plato and Aristotle. Indeed, one of the great contributions of Gaudreault's book lies in his careful rereading of Plato and Aristotle's concepts of diegesis and mimesis. As the original preface to this book by the late eminent philosopher Paul Ricoeur stresses, this rereading made an essential contribution to our understanding of narrative theory, both historically and philosophically, that goes beyond the domain of film studies.

Through both these moves, rather than viewing the past as an already established source for a fixed tradition, Gaudreault revealed how the historian's task lies not in simply establishing past events, but in approaching past practices and concepts as potentially destabilizing the conventional wisdom of the present. As Gaudreault's work demonstrates, history is always changing and that change stimulates rather than replaces theory. Not the least of the riches offered by Gaudreault's book comes in its careful, theoretically inflected accounts of issues in early film history, from his fascinating discussion of the way early copyright lawsuits debated the legal nature of film, to the role the lecturer played in film during the era of its increased narrativization, to his concluding discussion of the intermediality of early cinema. These chapters offer not only deeply researched historical accounts within Gaudreault's carefully argued theoretical arguments, but models of how these discourses can interact and transform each other. Yet Gaudreault in this work does not explore the narrative form of early cinema in order to produce a piece of historical research. Rather, he believes that a broad historical approach reveals the range of narrational practices and deepens the theoretical insight he pursues. Thus, this book also supplies a careful consideration of the role of a voice-over narrator in a film from the late eighties (*Dark Eyes* by Nikita Mikhalkov from 1987) and the way the various levels of filmic narration interact, including the soundtrack.

What, then, are the key issues that Gaudreault raises in the narratology of film and that film poses as a challenge to narrative theory? Gaudreault, like most narratologists, makes an analytical distinction between the story and the act of storytelling. He divides narratology into two areas of focus based on this distinction. Following the terminology of linguist Louis Hjelmslev, Gaudreault calls the approach that focuses on story the narratology of content. Here issues of medium are secondary to defining the nature of what constitutes a story (or to use Gaudreault's term, a 'narrative'). The other focus, which Gaudreault calls the narratology of expression, deals specifically with the textual discourse of the narrative and foregrounds the medium. I think it is correct to say that the main emphasis of Gaudreault's book lies in the narratology of expression and especially the specifically filmic aspects of narrative. I would add, almost as an aside, that I find Gaudreault's discussion of the content side of film narratology – specifically his claim (dependent on the definition of narrative by Claude Bremond) that because film is a temporal medium it is naturally geared towards narrative – while theoretically consistent, one of the more debatable positions taken in this book. (I would argue for a stronger definition of narrative, involving the role of characters, which is partly why I prefer the term 'story' over the more vague 'narrative.')

Gaudreault centres the most original aspects of his theory, however, on rethinking the expressive aspect of narrative in film. His dual blasts from the past – early cinema and Ancient Greece – provide a new slant of illumination onto filmic narration. A tradition had evolved, solidified by the brilliant narratology work of Gérard Genette, that characterized the Greek discussion of poetics in terms of a dichotomy between mimesis and diegesis. Mimesis became identified with the theatrical form of presentation, in which actions and characters are presented to an audience, and diegesis was identified with the narrative poem, in which a poet speaks in his or her own voice. Gaudreault, returning to the original Greek texts, showed that this dichotomy represented a modern reworking, and indeed distortion, of the original texts, in which these two forms had never been systematically opposed. In Plato diegesis was an overarching category that included the recounting of events and actions in the voice of a narrator (simple diegesis) as well as the portrayal of action through representation on stage (diegesis by means of mimesis) and a mixed form in which the voice of the poet and inserted dialogue spoken by characters alternated. Crucially for Gaudreault, Plato does not exclude theatrical presentation from the role of narrative, but rather sees it as an alternative method of telling a story. That theatre can play a narrative role forms a cornerstone of Gaudreault's narratology, from his discussion of Plato to his polemic against Jean Mitry's understanding of early film as a movement from theatricality to narrativity that concludes this book. We run here up against the basic dilemma in describing filmic narration. The concept of narration derives from literary texts, and therefore traditionally refers to a strictly linguistic fact. Is narration therefore applicable as a concept only to verbal texts (a position basically endorsed by Genette)? Or is it a more broadly semiological concept, transferable to other media or to their mixture in such forms as theatrical spectacle, graphic novels, film, or television? The common-sense recognition that all these forms can tell stories argues for their being in some sense narrative. But what are the tools for the description of storytelling in media other than the strictly verbal? In Gaudreault's reading, Plato includes theatrical presentation as a form of diegesis, but this does not involve a discussion of the process of narration or a narrator. Can theatrical and filmic stories be said to have a narrator?

Here Gaudreault introduces his most original concept, an important addition to the realm of narratology generally and to filmic narration especially: the monstrator. Although not a word commonly in use in the English language (there are archaic instances of it), its meaning is clearly defined by Gaudreault. A monstrator *shows.* (The term derives from the root *monstrer* in French, from *monstrare* in Latin, which means *to show*, the same root contained in the common English word *demonstrate* and, most likely, in *monster*, a curiosity worthy of being shown, or in *monstrance*, a device used in the Catholic Church for displaying the consecrated wafer.) If the narrator's fundamental role lies in conveying a story through a verbal account, the monstrator shows a story, presents it to an audience (in a clear parallel to Plato's mimesis as a form of diegesis). The monstrator denotes the storytelling agent behind a visual presentation of a story, the parallel agent to the textual narrator. However, by avoiding the term narrator, Gaudreault stresses the difference in medium and mode of this form of storytelling. An important new concept, Gaudreault's highlighting of an agent of showing causes me to wonder whether the monstrator has more than just a narrative role, and whether we can speak of film's monstrator displaying other visual attractions, rather than exclusively telling stories.

Thus, the mode of verbal narrative and the mode of mimetic narrative receive theoretically distinct agents: the narrator and the monstrator. I believe this distinction allows a very clear distinction between narrative modes while still allowing us to see them both as modes of the task of narration. For Gaudreault these two different agents correspond to two different media, verbal storytelling and theatrical presentation. Although he stresses the range of practices each mode can have, they remain distinct. The verbal narrator may aspire to the objectivity of a scenic presentation, as in the late novels of Henry James described by Percy Lubbock, and seem to adhere to a principle of showing. Yet the narrator remains irrevocably tied to verbalization and can only be described as 'showing' by analogy. Likewise, the theatrical monstrator may introduce a battery of devices that stress the mediations by which the stage action is presented, such as Brecht's epic theatre, but the presentation of the action to the audience remains paramount. Gaudreault's main focus is, of course, on film, and the issue immediately arises to which mode of narration film corresponds. His answer allows for a complex process of analysis of film narration, because Gaudreault claims that film narrative combines both these two modes, monstration and narration. I find this claim both productive and questionable.

Gaudreault's position is subtle. He realizes that a theoretical discourse cannot claim the status of a scientific description of an object. We might clarify this by saying that any theoretical model illuminates aspects of the object it treats and (I at least believe) may obscure others. The issue becomes which theoretical model produces the greatest degree of insight. I have no doubt of the benefits of Gaudreault's division of filmic narration into these two agents, although I will also indicate what I feel are the weaknesses of making these differentiated aspects into distinct theoretical entities. The strengths of this theory of filmic narration, I believe, are analytical. Gaudreault provides a guide, especially useful in pedagogical situations, to the breakdown of the variety of means the filmic narrator uses to tell a story. Thus, in his most complex analysis of an instance of film narration, his treatment of *Dark Eyes*, the difference between the monstrative role of the fundamental narrator and the verbal role of the delegated narrator is made clearer by this differentiation. Although in many ways these means correspond to the basic aspects of film style (mise en scène, composition, editing), to stress them not simply as aesthetic tools but as means of narration is an illuminating way to approach film analysis. Thus, Gaudreault's theory stresses the various modes of filmic narrative, its intertwining of monstration and narration aiding the analyst in a complex account of how filmic stories are told.

I am less sure about the value of breaking the three levels of film discourse that Gaudreault describes (and which I also used in my discussion of filmic narration in my book on D.W. Griffith) into three separate narrative agents, then linking them together by a synthetic meganarrator. I fear this multiplying of narrative agents complicates matters unduly, creating an intricate Ptolemaic system in which sub-narrators are hypostasized in ways that actually obscure the synthetic aspect of filmic narration. I prefer approaching narration as a task that uses a variety of stylistic means that need not be hierarchized (or that should be hierarchized only within individual texts, so as to privilege one means of narration over another, say, camera movement for Jansco, editing for Eisenstein, or mise en scène for Yevgenii Bauer). I think the same narrative task can be accomplished by editing or camera movement or even complex blocking of actors' movement within the frame (see the way Eisenstein blocked out the murder in *Crime and Punishment* within a single static shot as an exercise for his seminar in film directing). These different approaches create different stylistic systems, but I don't feel they differ as narrative modes in the way novels and theatrical productions do.

I am least convinced by the need to restrict the term 'narration' in film to the realm of editing, since it seems evident to me that camera movement can indeed create the sort of relations Gaudreault ascribes to editing (including temporal distinctions that are occasionally expressed through camera movement, as in films by Resnais, Visconti, or Wajda). Indeed, the creation of different temporal levels is not unknown even to theatre (think of the flashbacks in *Death of a Salesman* and many other plays). I see no reason to privilege the role of editing in filmic narration, though traditionally editing was certainly the most thoroughly discussed form of filmic narration. In our present era, however, dominated as it is by the complex sequence shots of Hou Hsiao-hsien, Abbas Kiarostami, Bela Tarr, and Jia Zhang Ke, to continue to see editing as the privileged tool of film narration seems unduly limiting.

Indeed, I wonder, had Gaudreault been writing his original book during the nineties, when scholars such as David Bordwell, Kristin

Thompson, Ben Brewster, Lea Jacobs, and Yuri Tsivian had moved from considering the period of early cinema to an investigation of the stylistic of the teens, whether the figure he calls the filmographic monstrator would be seen as secondary to the filmic narrator dependent on editing. Directors in the teens, such as Yevgenii Bauer, Victor Sjöström, and Franz Hofer, created a complex and powerful narrative style through their use of deep staging. History, we see again and again, inflects theory, in terms of both the immediate context in which theoretical work is undertaken and the models that historical investigation supplies. I firmly believe that Gaudreault's book offers not only a historical document, but also a guide to thinking how theory becomes renewed by an awareness of its immersion in history.

If the founding era of academic film studies sometimes pursued a somewhat unrealistic goal of establishing a scientific basis for the study of film, nonetheless the detailed precision of the analysis it spawned still, in my opinion, provides us with methods of complex description and a systematic consideration of the variety of things a film does. In contrast to the more thematic analysis of film that seems to dominate film studies today, this approach produces not only a way to consider films as complex texts, but also a basis of debate over the way film operates, rather than simply evaluating whether films align with the critic's ideological positions. Gaudreault's important work on the intermediality of early cinema that concludes this book shows how the interaction of film theory and history continues to expand and bear fruit. Perhaps particularly in the areas in which I question some of Gaudreault's system, I feel that this work is still alive, still has much to tell us about the unfinished task of truly accounting for the way films affect us, and about the possibilities film holds as it continues to tell the stories of the modern world. Clearly, like a chapter in a film serial (which Gaudreault references as this book ends), this work is to be continued ...

TOM GUNNING

Acknowledgments

The issues raised in this book are the fruit of funded research begun in 1977 when I started teaching in the Département des littératures at Université Laval in Quebec City,[1] and which continued, from 1977 to 1983, when I was preparing my doctoral dissertation.[2] The ideas found here owe a great deal to all those who played a part in this research and study, or who were associated with them in one way or another. I cannot adequately thank all those who, after reading my work, took the trouble to give me their comments and criticisms and who thereby helped me maintain my enthusiasm for research and theoretical inquiry. I thank in particular my two dissertation directors, Michel Marie and the late Michel Colin of Université Paris III. They trusted my instincts and helped me a great deal, as did François Baby and Tom Gunning, who, each in his own way, helped me develop and refine some of the ideas found in this book. The many discussions I have had, since my dissertation defence, with Jacques Aumont, David Bordwell, François Jost, Roger Odin, Dana Polan, Marc Vernet, Paul Warren, and, especially, Denis Saint-Jacques, have been very exciting and have helped to give form to some of my new hypotheses. The late Paul Ricoeur, once he learned about my hypotheses concerning Plato and Aristotle, encouraged me to publish them and generously agreed to write the preface to this book. I am also grateful to Gérard Genette, who wrote to me (see chapter 2) in response to some of the questions I posed in my dissertation, and to the late Christian Metz who, initially in his writings and teaching, and then in our discussions together, helped me to clarify some of my ideas. I repeat my thanks to those who, while I was writing my dissertation, discussed it with me or even read and commented on parts of it, helping me more than they know:

Anne Bienjonetti, Louis Francoeur, Gilles Girard, Jacques Goimard, Joseph Melançon, Pierre Ouellet, Esther Pelletier, the late Marie-Claire Ropars-Wuilleumier, and, especially, the late Ernest Pascal, professor of Classical Studies at Université Laval in Quebec City. He was passionately interested in the questions I raised at the time with respect to the Plato text I eventually wrote about. I cannot adequately express my gratitude to Eileen Bowser, Robert Daudelin, David Francis, and Madeleine Malthête-Méliès: it was thanks to them especially that I was able to get a foothold on that 'lost continent' that is early cinema.

I also thank the Social Sciences and Humanities Research Council of Canada for the fellowship they awarded me during my doctoral studies and for their financial support during my subsequent research for this book. In addition, I thank Jean Châteauvert and Andrée Michaud for their judicious comments on the manuscript of the original French edition of this book and the Département des littératures at Université Laval, which made my task easier in so many ways.

The afterword was written, and subsequent work on the manuscript carried out, under the aegis of GRAFICS (Groupe de recherche sur l'avènement et la formation des institutions cinématographique et scénique) at the Département d'histoire de l'art et d'études cinématographiques of Université de Montréal. GRAFICS is funded by the Social Sciences and Humanities Research Council of Canada (SSHRC) and the Fonds québécois de recherche sur la société et la culture (FQRSC) and is a member of the Centre de recherche sur l'intermédialité (CRI) at Université de Montréal. The ideas presented in the afterword are the fruit, in part, of research conducted while I was the recipient of a Killam Grant (1997–8) from the Canada Council for the Arts, to which I am deeply grateful. I thank Fernand Roy of Université du Québec à Chicoutimi, with whom I had such useful conversations when I was writing this part of the book, thus enabling me to refine my argument.

Finally, for this English edition, I thank Frank Collins for his initial translation of several chapters, some of which found its way into the final translation presented here; my translator, Timothy Barnard, who knows that one cannot translate a scholarly book without reflection, research, and invention; Marco Santos for his help in locating the English-language sources quoted here; and Tom Gunning for his preface to this edition. My thanks also to GRAFICS, where some of the work of preparing the manuscript for publication was carried out, and in particular to Louis Pelletier, for his research around the book's illustrations, and Lisa Pietrocatelli, who once again demon-strated her great publishing skills.

I also thank all those at the University of Toronto Press who believed in this project, including Ron Schoeffel and Jill McConkey and those who read, evaluated, and in some cases commented on my manu-script. My thanks finally to professor Paul Perron of the University of Toronto, who was the prime mover behind the project of publishing an English-laguage edition of my book. If it had not been for him, this book would not exist, and I am especially grateful to him.

FROM PLATO TO LUMIÈRE:
NARRATION AND MONSTRATION IN LITERATURE
AND CINEMA

Introduction

And our lack of surprise demonstrates that we had always been aware, without openly speaking of it, of that tutelary genius which, with a wave of a wand, opened up extraordinary cinematographic vistas to us, projected onto the magical walls of movie houses.

Albert Laffay, *Logique du cinéma*, 82

One of the initial hypotheses that brought this book about is that film narratology demonstrates a lack of consensus with respect to such basic notions as the 'narrator,' by which we mean the narrative agent responsible for communicating film narrative. We must quickly add that in this respect film narratologists are in good company. Even within the 'mother theory,' literary narratology, there is no consensus on this question. Of course in literature the problem is much less thorny because in textual narrative[1] it is not uncommon for an agent to manifest itself from the outset as being responsible for the narrative that follows; in other words, to identify itself as the narrator ('I am going to tell you a story ...'). Textual narratives thus enjoy a relative advantage, or so it seems, because their narrator often *explicitly* carries out its role. This probably explains why there is a certain common denominator to the many definitions we find, in various works of narratology, of the textual narrator's activities, roles, and functions. But by no means is there unanimity on this question. Far from it. This is especially so with regard to the various ways in which a narrator's intervention can be limited. In the case of textual narrative, should we attribute to the narrator responsibility, or 'paternity' (narratological, at least), for all the narrative activities which are not, on the one hand, the work of the actors (that is, the characters) nor, on the other, the work of the real and concrete author who wrote the text? This question never fails to give rise to biting debates and to arouse great passions in the field of literary narratology. Thus, whereas the most famous narratologist of textual narrative, Gérard Genette, thinks that we can sort things out just fine narratologically without there being any intermediary between the explicit narrator (identified as such) and the author (real and concrete), other theorists believe that we should conceive of the former in a much narrower way and attribute to another agent some of what has traditionally been seen as being the work of the narrator. This other agent might be an *abstract author,* or an *implicit* (or *implied*) *author,* or even a *supra-diegetic agent.*[2] Many narratologists believe this should be the case, from Wayne C. Booth to Jaap Lintvelt by way of Mieke Bal, for instance. Indeed, almost innumerable theoretical attempts have been made to locate, somewhere between the narrator and the author, an agent more concrete than the former but less real than the latter and which might account for certain intermediary narrative activities that narratologists sometimes have trouble attributing to the narrator or author without violating certain canonical givens of narratology.[3] However, and quite paradoxically, this is a hypothesis that, despite the amazing frequency with which it is raised (and, if I can reveal my true colours, despite its being so obvious), has still not become dominant in literary narratology. Not so long ago, Genette slammed the idea quite hard. In one of his narratological studies he states, with some irony:

> In narrative, or rather behind or before it, there is someone who tells, and who is the narrator. On the narrator's far side there is someone who writes, who is responsible for everything on the near side. That someone – big news – is the author (and no one else), and it seems to me, as Plato said some time ago, that that is enough.[4]

But is it really? If we think of the remarkable staying power of hypotheses which suggest that there exists, in literature, one or more intermediaries between the author and the narrator, we might well think otherwise. In any case we will see, in this study, that Genette's position is certainly not sufficient in the case of cinema, for reasons that have to do, first of all, with the very nature of the medium. Between the real and concrete author (here the filmmaker) and the explicit narrator identified as such in certain film narratives, we will note, as our study progresses, certain intermediary agents, most of which will be specific to the whole contraption that is cinema. But we will also see that part of the problem at hand will also touch upon the domain of literature and will serve to support those hypotheses that, in literary studies, postulate the existence of some intermediary agent between the author and the narrator. This is one of the 'lessons' that film narratology can give to literary narratology. After all the incursions into literary narratology taken by film narratologists, maybe it is time for literary narratologists in turn to take a detour into the cinema; it might well prove to do them some good.

Even though the question of the film narrator has only rarely been clearly posed, the basis of the problem has for a long time been part of film theories, even pre-narratological ones. The writings of Jean Mitry and Christian Metz often raise the various problems posed by film narrative and make valuable contributions to the question. But the true precursor to film narratology probably remains Albert Laffay, in an incredibly perceptive book published in the early 1960s. This work, entitled *Logique du cinéma*, anthologized articles he had published over the course of several years.[5] In the chapter 'The Narrative, the World and Cinema' Laffay established the discipline's first basic principle: 'All film is ordered around a virtual linguistic focal point that lies outside the screen.'[6] Laffay was also the one who proposed, in the same work, the old but magnificent (and how very poetic!) expression *great image-maker* to designate the agent I will call, for now, the *film narrator*, that 'virtual presence hiding behind *all films*.'[7] All film narratologists owe it to themselves to reread this chapter and thus reacquaint themselves with its main lessons. Laffay, who did not possess any of our narratological tools, had what I venture to call the prescience – pre-science – to define with great theoretical precision and adroitness the figure that stands in the background of all film narrative works, although he did not yet dare call that figure the 'film narrator.' For Laffay, this figure is a

> fictive and invisible character, brought forth by the joint efforts [of the film's director and technical crew]. Standing behind us, it turns the album pages for us, directs our attention with a finger pointing discreetly to a detail, and at just the right moment quietly tells us what we need to know. Above all, it gives rhythm to the unfolding of the images.[8]

One of the problems I will try to resolve here is actually easily described: to determine whether, like Laffay, we can postulate the existence in film narrative of an *underlying* agent – his great image-maker –

that would be the cinematic equivalent of literature's textual narrator. This problem, in the case of cinema, is overdetermined by the fact that a given film, and there are many examples, might include a speaking narrator, who in due course becomes a narrator we occasionally see on the screen. The role and function of this narrator seem quite like those of that other speaking narrator we have been calling the textual narrator. This cinematic speaking narrator initially appears to have a paradoxical status: at times we can confuse his or her activities with those of the great image-maker, and at others there are signs and pointers here and there throughout the film that lead us to think that this is definitely not the case. This will raise many questions. This speaking narrator in film narrative who undertakes to recount, *verbally*, certain events: is he or she an 'assistant' to the great image-maker, or are we to suppose that they are on the same level, a seemingly primary level, as the equally verbal narrator of textual narrative? Just what is the relationship between this speaking narrator and the great image-maker of film narrative? Is the great image-maker the equivalent of the so-called 'implied author' in textual narrative? These questions can be arranged as depicted in table 0.1.

The problem can be very simply described, as I said above. While it is easily posed, the answers are not self-evident, especially if we truly want to take into account the insights of literary narratology and the present state of these questions in film narratology, which is what I propose to do here.

As the reader will discover, I shall follow a winding path. First, I will try to situate film narrative in relation to those two other narrative forms: textual narrative and what I call *staged* (or theatrical) narrative.[9] While it is true that film narrative offers narrative structures that can be likened to those of textual narrative, it is also the case that film narrative 'stages' characters in action, as does staged narrative. Even if we discount discussions that lump together film narrative and textual narrative, many texts still link film narrative with staged narrative. But what is at stake here is not to try to identify the cinema either with the novel or the theatre. Instead, it is a matter of setting out and aligning a limited and identifiable number of parameters that are common to different forms of artistic practice and that all have to do with narrativity – that faculty certain texts have, in Mieke Bal's words, for 'allowing themselves to be decoded as a narrative text,'[10] that is at play in any text (textual, staged, filmic, or any other) that includes a story told by any sort of agent. The three forms of narrative we will discuss here

Table 0.1

Textual narrative	Film narrative
Author (writer)	Author (filmmaker)
Implicit author, abstract author, etc.	The Great Image-Maker (primary agent?)
Textual narrator (primary agent?)	Verbal narrator

represent three possible forms of narrativity. We will attempt to define the ways each functions as a narrative, and this will be based upon distinguishing, as clearly as possible, among each of the semiotic vehicles involved: writing, the stage, and film. This study should thus make it possible (at least that is my hope) to identify the precise 'narrative frontiers'[11] of textual, staged, and, finally, film narratives. These frontiers will not be conceived of as necessarily impassable, but rather as the dividing lines between the respective fields of action of the various agents responsible for the types of narrative communication[12] under discussion. For me, as we shall see later, the existence of various narrative-producing agents is a result of the semiotic vehicle (of the nature of the means of expression put into play by that vehicle).

The ultimate goal of my research is to identify and define the way, or ways, in which film narrative functions and thus to contribute to the establishment of a narratological theory of the cinema. This is why I think it necessary to discuss the two forms of narrative that, with film, are the most common in our society: textual and staged narrative. But there is another, more fundamental, factor behind this decision: film is a seemingly *more complex* narratological object than textual or staged narrative, and this is because it is the product of a *combination* of the narrative possibilities of the other two. More precisely, it is the product of a *linking* of the two basic modes of narrative communication: *narration* and what I call *monstration*. Moving from the textual and the staged to the filmic, that is, 'from the literary to the filmic,' *narrative* becomes a *system*;[13] hence the title of this book in its original French-language edition. Film's ability to combine is thus the basis (at least in part, and only in relation to the other two narrative arts in question) of its narrative specificity, since textual and staged narratives are apparently limited to a singularity of means, at least at their primary communicative levels.

True enough, this reference to textual and staged narrative will not always be easily carried out. Of the two types of narrative, to date only the first has been the subject of a 'full narratological examination' (in the same way as one refers to a complete medical or physical examination). Indeed, the state of studies on staged narration is such that even a specialist in the theatre was prompted to express surprise, not that long ago, at the 'backwardness and poor quality of narrative study of the theatre.'[14] The situation has changed little since then. It thus appears to me to be necessary, and even indispensable, to begin by attempting to respond to certain narratological problems posed by the theatre, even before opening the door to film narratology proper.

At the same time, my desire to clarify the relationship between narrative and these two 'representational' arts, theatre and cinema, requires me to turn back and reconsider some of the hypotheses of modern narratology. This, in my view, is a field with at least one obvious shortcoming: its overemphasis on textual narrative (an emphasis that can occasionally yield to verbal narrative but rarely to other narrative forms). This dominance of the written is probably linked to the semantic shifts and distortions to which, in my view, the conceptual pair mimesis/diegesis has been subjected. These concepts have been inherited, we should recall, from a tradition in which the textual was not in a dominant position. The concepts in question, bequeathed to us by Plato and Aristotle, need today to be adapted to this (new) reality in which the textual has taken precedence over the oral. This is precisely what I propose to carry out here. Since Genette, an opposition has been created between mimesis (imitation) and diegesis (narrative), and I will try to account for the reasons for this. This opposition is the hole in the net of narratological theory that even recourse to the Ancients cannot fix. Because for Plato mimesis was not, contrary to what is too often claimed, in opposition to diegesis. Rather, it is simply one of the forms that diegesis can take. We will also see that mimesis and diegesis are not opposite categories in Aristotle either. Aristotle, with inverse reasoning to Plato's, saw diegesis as one of the forms of mimesis. We will thus demonstrate that this contemporary dichotomy unwittingly borrows one of its terms, mimesis, from Plato and the other, diegesis, from Aristotle, thereby ignoring much of what is to be found in book 3 of Plato's *Republic* and in Aristotle's *Poetics*.

The questions raised will allow me better to establish my definition of staged and film narrative. They will also allow me better to discern what is specific to these two narrative arts, arts that share a systematic use of characters in action. Going back to the Ancients will also allow me to test the theoretical value of mimesis and diegesis, concepts that are almost always evoked in studies of narrative problems – hence the importance of a good understanding of the ways in which they work. In studying film as narrative we will also test the theoretical universality of these two concepts. These concepts have indeed not been applied to the theory of cinema in a way at all equivalent to their application to literature by Genette, who appears to be the first to have revived them (hitherto, they had only been sporadically used since they were first developed).[15]

I will, moreover, offer a new interpretation of the way these two concepts are linked, and show my preference for Plato's ideas over those of his pupil. And this only incidentally, within a study in which cinema occupies a front-row seat; we must give Plato his due, even if that is not the primary purpose of the exercise. I find it particularly interesting that Plato, one of whose texts (the famous myth about the cave) prefigured the mechanisms of film projection, proposed a theoretical framework whose strictly narratological purposes will allow me better to understand the narrative mechanisms of the cinema.

This return to 'early' narratology (or even to its prehistory!) is not the only return to the past proposed in this book. Even though the strictly cinematic hypotheses I am about to formulate will not be limited to any specific corpus, since they claim to be valid for all film discourse, and although all historical periods are cited, a special place will be accorded to what will henceforth be described as 'early cinema.' There are several reasons for this. First, this field is one of the author's areas of specialization. Further, in terms of method, it more easily allows for taking issues one at a time: the primary importance of the image in early cinema makes it possible to study an object that is less complex than sound film, a form that blithely mixes audio-visual and verbal narratives, thus multiplying primary and secondary narrative agents. It is not unthinkable that the level of confusion apparent in the field of narratology today is a result of the desire on the part of many authors to solve every problem at one blow.

This dividing up of phenomena, I hope, will enable me to offer narratological propositions applicable, first of all, to 'silent'[16] film (which is no small matter, since this form represents a third of film's lifespan). It may seem unfortunate to limit ourselves initially to this earliest stratum of the object under study,[17] but my propositions will be applied to sound films and 'talkies' later on in the book. The last part of this book,

unlike the doctoral thesis on which it is based, will continue this narratological questioning, integrating problems of narration raised by the
sound track and, especially, those raised by the later arrival of a verbal
narrator. This narrator evokes the film lecturer of the turn of the century in the way he or she draws together the threads with which film
narration is woven.

There are two other reasons that justify or explain even more directly
why I have chosen to focus on early cinema. First of all, and this we
should all be able to readily agree upon, the heuristic value of this period, when cinema and narrative first met, appears self-evident. It is by
no means certain that the 'film narrator' was born with the Lumière
Brothers' invention. What then could be more interesting than to identify this narrator's first appearance?

The other reason is more personal, although it is not necessarily a
product of chance. If it were not for my coming to know early cinema,
towards the end of the 1970s, I doubt that the hypotheses I present here
would ever have attained their present state of development. While the
narratological theory I propose can be considered, despite the distance
I sometimes maintain from him, a *Genettian* theory of film narrative,[18]
it is equally true that it can also be considered (please excuse the play
on words) a *genetic* theory of film narrative, because the theoretical
concepts and system I propose will in large measure flow, as we shall
see, from the developments I identify in film expression between 1895
and 1915.

1 Early Cinema and Narrativity

With the cinematograph too [you have to tell stories]. And these stories can be much more lavish, much more wonderful than stories told
in the theatre.

Georges Méliès, in Malthête-Méliès, Méliès l'enchanteur, 166

What has become known as 'early cinema'[1] is becoming a field of study
whose value to scholarly study goes beyond its simple status as a 'period' in film history. And it is probably not paradoxical that we are dealing with the only period of film history in which many proven
specialists are theoreticians rather than historians. Because of the issues
its place in history raises and the context in which its recent rediscovery
has taken place, this period, willingly or unwillingly, poses as many, if
not more, theoretical questions as it does historical ones. This is why
current discussion of early cinema interests theoreticians as much as it
does historians; in its magnitude this is a new phenomenon in the history of film history.[2] We thus see a strong propensity on the part of theoreticians working on this period to 'do some history,' and an equal
propensity on the part of historians to 'flirt' with theory. This has been
the case since the late 1970s, when the current rediscovery of the period
began, and is the result of the novel issues the period presents. In fact,
right from the outset early cinema has been used to discuss theoretical
and often narratological issues. For some, notably Noël Burch, working
on early cinema has not really involved doing historical work, but
rather has meant questioning the apparent 'naturalness' of what would
soon be seen as 'the' cinematic language. Burch demonstrated that this
language was not inherent to the medium and that the first filmmakers

and camera operators went about things differently (they used other 'codes' and had recourse to a different 'language' in order to filmically 'address' their contemporaries).[3] Although they are not entirely absent from Burch's work, narratological concerns proper are more clearly visible in the writings of other scholars present at the Brighton conference on early cinema, especially Tom Gunning and the present author.[4] For them it was, and is, a matter of tracing early cinema's development so as to enquire into its relationship to a current that runs right through it and that was soon to dominate film practice: narrativity. They also seek to understand how narrative met cinema, which Christian Metz rightly described as having 'narrativity built into it.'[5]

The questions thus raised were and continue to be of great importance: they encouraged the rise of a whole new point of view among scholars towards films made before 1915. This new point of view gave rise in turn to a new way of conceiving the relationship between filmmakers of the period and their films, especially with regards to narrativity.

From this perspective, the most important contribution of this new research seems to me to have been the primordial 'discovery' of this early period's prevailing view of the shot (or 'tableau,' as was said at the time, in a way quite consistent with what I am trying to explain here). For early filmmakers, the shot seemed to function as an *autonomous* and *self-sufficient tableau*. This is a foundational hypothesis with especially important ramifications, as I shall attempt to demonstrate.

The privileged 'mode of film practice'[6] of the early years promoted an aesthetic of the moving photograph (the singular is important here). The Lumière cinematograph was, in the beginning, a machine that produced multiple photograms[7] (needed to form a *single shot*) and not, at least back then, a machine that created a *series of shots*. In those days, and this remained entrenched for a very long time (as much among filmgoers as filmmakers), each look 'cast' by the camera produced a *view* or *tableau*. And that was a *film*. It was only bit by bit that pluripunctiliar or multiple-shot films[8] took hold (for numerous reasons that would take too long to describe here). The invention of 'cinema as we know it' was, in fact, the result of a combination of two different 'language systems,' and it seems to me that film theory generally does not adequately take these two strata into account, even though each has its own history. 'Film language' is the product both of the invention of a *procedure* (the camera that creates shots) and the development of a *process* (the assembling and editing of different shots, with the idea of creating a single entity, a film). Now, in early cinema, a film was a shot or, if you prefer, a tableau. At the phylogenetic level, we must distinguish at least three main periods in the development of the mode of film representation that would ultimately prevail: (a) the period when films were made up of just one shot – filming only; (b) the period when films contained several non-continuous shots[9] – filming and editing, but the filming was not done in a truly organic manner, or determined by the editing; and (c) the period when films contained many continuous shots – filming determined by editing.

It is difficult to date phenomena that overlap and cross each others' paths, especially since these different periods were not established by decree. Indeed these 'periods' interpenetrate each other to such a degree that it would perhaps be preferable to see them as different and concurrent *modes* of film practice (especially as concerns the first two periods) rather than as *periods*. Be that as it may, it is possible to situate most punctiliar or single-shot films in the period ending in 1902, to identify 1903 as the year in which the race to include multiple shots began (a limited race, but a real one: that year a film rarely contained more than ten shots), and, finally, to discover filmmakers truly dividing up their *scenes* and thus shooting with a view to editing only in the early 1910s.

This attempt at periodization might appear an empty exercise to anyone unaware of the primordial 'language' effects that are set into play, at the level of filming the shot, when one moves from the second 'period' to the third. The act of filming changes radically when carried out with the next stage, editing, in mind. This periodization makes it possible to better understand, at the narratological level, the position we should assign the various ways of linking shots when the basic unit, the single shot, was seen as having an *autonomous unity* (despite the fact that, after 1902, it began to be joined to other autonomous shots). It was a period, in other words, when a *singular* object, the shot, was tacitly considered to be autonomous and absolute and was not really required to *communicate* with other shots.

Several scholars have tried to explain the origin of this conception of the shot as an autonomous tableau. There is no doubt that other popular media of the time (magic lantern shows, vaudeville, etc.)[10] had a hand in this. It is difficult to imagine how it could have been otherwise. Only retrospectively does it seem strange that at the time people so strongly felt a punctiliar or single-shot film to be the norm or that filming any given action required only one *point of view*, only one shot. It seems reasonable to suppose that initially it was sheer chance that led to films becoming pluri-punctiliar, or made up of several shots. Because of the pressures and constraints imposed by the subject being filmed, among other reasons, filmmaker-operators gradually changed their 'narrative enterprise' and came to see film as a *juxtaposition* of *singular* shots. Certainly, it would be difficult to stick strictly to a punctiliar view if one suddenly decided to recount the story of the 'Life and Passion of Christ' or to depict the most recent boxing match on film. In fact these were two extremely popular subjects at the turn of the century, subjects that seem to have played an important role in the movement from punctiliar to pluri-punctiliar films. Both presuppose a temporal development that greatly surpassed what could be recorded on one strip of raw film stock. The 'Passion Play' was by definition already 'scripted' into scenes, before any 'cineastic' treatment, and each scene is separated from the next by a lapse in time, sometimes a very long one, which therefore had to be omitted (creating an ellipsis). As a 'profilmic'[11] subject, a boxing match is also already segmented, into rounds, and generally lasted too long to be shown in its entirety, again forcing filmmakers to make cuts, first in time and then, eventually, in the film itself.[12] In any case, the germ of pluri-punctiliar or multiple-shot films is already found in the first catalogues of the Lumière brothers, at least as far as actualities, or short news items, are concerned. There is nothing to prevent us from thinking, despite the lack of any formal proof, that the many 'views' describing, for example, the visit of the czar or some other VIP to Paris, or the visit of the French president to some other country, were shown successively, without interruption, after having been glued (and thus edited) together.

And yet, the progression inherent in the various elements of pluri-punctiliar or multiple-shot film production, after 1902 when it began to establish itself, remained subordinate to that mighty conception of the shot as an autonomous tableau, a truly centripetal unit that found its narrative equilibrium in the action going on before the camera, between the moment when the operator began to turn the crank and the moment he decided to stop.[13] In the beginning, any idea for a film ideally had to envision a single spatio-temporal site within which the action would unfold. This, of course, led the filmmaker-operator to extreme forms of mise en scène – to a continuous manipulation of the profilmic. *L'arroseur arrosé* (*Waterer and Watered*, Lumière, 1895) – also known as *A Joke on the Gardener* – is a good example of this. First, let's recap the story. A young scamp steps on a gardener's hose. The gardener, surprised that the flow of water has stopped, imprudently peers

Figure 1.1 *La Vie et la Passion de Jésus-Christ*, Pathé, 1903 (Cinémathèque québécoise)

into the nozzle to see if it is blocked. Right then the boy removes his foot from the hose and the gardener (the 'waterer') is ... watered. The gardener chases the boy, who runs towards the left edge of the frame, and then drags him back to the centre of the frame and administers a good spanking.[14]

All of this action is played out and presented in just one shot, in one continuous take. There is no temporal or spatial interval or cutaway: the action is 'gathered together' on this 'stage,' this 'set' – the garden at which the camera is pointed. Definitely no cutaway, but almost! The boy flees to the left and almost escapes from his pursuer. His pursuer, as the on-screen 'stand-in' for the great image-maker responsible for film narrative, delegates this role to himself by grabbing the boy right at the moment when he is about to escape the camera's field of view and thus disappear from our view. He grabs him and quickly brings him to the centre of the frame in order to carry out the spanking before the film runs out! The whole thing comes close to a chase film, a genre whose glory days ran from 1904 to 1907 and which played a major role in the development of film narrative.[15] Right from the start *Waterer and Watered* contains all the elements of that soon-to-be 'classic' genre of early cinema: a peaceful initial situation is disturbed by the introduction of an actor who commits some misdeed and flees. In this film, however, made when the Lumière cinematograph was only one year old, the invitation to continue that flight beyond the borders of the initial frame was not taken up, for lack of an awareness of the possibility of making pluri-punctiliar films with multiple shots. Pluri-punctiliarity is thus an essential condition for the chase film, whose time had not yet come. This film belonged to a time when the single moment still reigned. In the beginning cinema was seen only as a *punctum temporis*, an enlarged *punctum temporis*, of course, but one whose segmented nature (its *segmentum temporis* quality) could not really come to the fore before pluri-punctiliar or multiple-shot films, with their juxtaposing of segments, became the norm. Is it not in fact true that 'moving images,' when they are not part of a pluri-punctiliar film, display a temporal unity that is just as indivisible as the temporal unity that inescapably constrains the 'language' of still photography?

This conception of the tableau as autonomous and absolute was complemented by the peculiar aesthetic ordering the 'show' and giving it direction and meaning. While the dominant aesthetic of later cinema would be an aesthetic of *narration*, the aesthetic governing the work of early filmmakers was an aesthetic of *attraction*.[16] For a long time the cinematograph was a fairground phenomenon, as much on exhibit itself as it was a means of exhibiting and showing. Cinema's first viewers came to see the projector and the screen onto which it cast its images as much as they did to see the steam engine bearing down on them in *L'arrivée d'un train à La Ciotat* (*Train Entering a Station*, Lumière, 1895). The 'attractions' of the 'hardware' of the apparatus[17] (which was, in a sense, the signifier) were just as important as those of the 'software,' of the image's content (the signified). The simple act of movement was in itself an attraction, which could be augmented by the attractional qualities of a train, a baby eating, or a watered waterer.

We know that for the Soviet filmmaker Sergei Eisenstein an attraction was a spectacular phenomenon of the highest degree, one that made it possible to address the spectator directly in his or her seat; to 'go get 'em' if you will, in order to provoke a reaction. Jacques Aumont has identified precisely what an attraction was for Eisenstein:

The attraction is originally the music hall number or sketch, a relatively *autonomous peak moment* in the show. It draws upon techniques of representation that do not belong to dramatic illusion; it draws upon more aggressive forms of the performing arts (the circus, the music hall, the sideshow).[18]

Everything is here! Even the sideshow! Thus what *Uncle Tom's Cabin* (Edison, 1903) gives us are the peak moments, the highlights, of the show on which it was based; what *What Happened on Twenty-Third Street, New York City* (Edison, 1901) shows, after a wait lasting longer than its title, is the precise moment when a passing woman walks over a blast of air from below, making her skirts billow; the special moment created by *Train Entering a Station* is the instant when a locomotive seems about to run right over the spectator. And dozens, even hundreds, of stage, circus, and acrobatic acts were filmed between 1895 and 1908. Aumont, perhaps unwittingly, even accords Méliès and his imitators a special place in his description of the attraction: 'The most fully developed example of [an attraction] is the "trick," that is, any kind of special performance.'[19]

Even the mighty chase film, despite the inexorable progression of its shots, might be seen as an assemblage of distinct attractions. Rarely are there shots in a chase film whose only purpose is to show the simple passing of pursuers and pursued. On the contrary, most such films, despite the linear progression inherent to their subject, retain something of the strictly centripetal specificity of the self-sufficient unit so characteristic of films composed of just one shot. Each shot presents an isolated attraction: in one shot, the pursuers take turns bumping into some obstacle, ending up together in a heap; in another a group of women are the chief attraction, displaying their ankles with the help of a fence obstructing their path; in yet another, it is a shot of a river that has to be crossed on stones just slippery enough for at least one of the characters to tumble in. And finally there is the famous *Great Train Robbery* (Edison, 1903), several of whose shots demonstrate obvious attractional qualities: the explosion in the mail car (shot 3), the murders of the mechanic (shot 4) and the passenger who tries to escape (shot 6), the dance in the saloon (shot 11), the gunfight with its sensational clouds of smoke (shot 13) and, of course, the final shot (or opening shot, as the case may be),[20] in which the outlaw leader shoots at the spectators, an exemplary attraction if ever there was one.

Hence the view that between 1900 and 1915 cinema demonstrated a tension between two divergent modes of film spectatorship (each, of course, being linked to a specific kind of production): the first was based on a relationship of 'exhibitionist confrontation' between the screen and the viewer; and the second presupposed, quite to the contrary, the viewer's 'diegetic absorption,'[21] where the screen acts as an intermediary between the viewer and the narrative. Two quite distinct modes, and yet somehow they have coexisted throughout film history. They are modes that give rise to two kinds of viewer, to viewers with different expectations, and do not predispose the viewer towards the narrative possibilities of the medium in the same way.

The reader will immediately grasp that the two modes of film practice inferred by these two spectatorial positions do not have the same kind of relationship with the current that runs through film history and that is the subject of this book: narrativity. Where does narrativity fit into this? Could a film, fresh from the Lumière brothers' laboratory, be seen as always and already, essentially, and even ontologically, narrative? Under what conditions did cinema meet narrativity?

These are the crucial and pressing questions that bring together two phenomena, film and narrative, so often associated with each other. But before we can answer our questions adequately we will have to take a short detour beyond cinema in order to clarify certain problems concerning narrative. This will allow us to establish certain basic principles without which we couldn't hope to establish a narratological theory that might ultimately be applied to cinema.

2 Narrative Problems

We currently use the word narrative without paying attention to, even at times without noticing, its ambiguity, and some of the difficulties of narratology are perhaps due to this confusion.

Gérard Genette, *Narrative Discourse: An Essay in Method*, 25

One of our tasks is to define clearly what we mean by 'film narrative.' First we need to ask ourselves: after which date, in cinema, can we say we are dealing with narrative? Are all films, of whatever kind, narrative films? What is it that, properly speaking, makes film narrative? Has film always been narrative? If this is the case, just what is it that gives film this 'natural' inclination? And, if not, what route did this relatively young medium take in order to set out on the 'narrative road' that the 'feature-length film of novelistic fiction' represents?[1] How are we to explain Christian Metz's comment that 'even supposedly non-narrative films (short documentary films, educational films, etc.) are governed essentially by the same semiological functions that govern "feature films"'?[2] Should narrative, in cinema, be confined to a genre? How indeed are we to understand a statement such as this: 'In the realm of cinema, all non-narrative genres – the documentary, the technical film, etc. – have become marginal provinces'?[3] Is the documentary non-narrative? Why? How? Beyond which threshold must a film pass before it is considered narrative? Put another way: where does narrative in cinema begin, and where does it end?

These are the questions to be asked if we are to grasp the fundamental properties and parameters of film narrative. There is a first step, however, a preliminary question that must first be answered: *what is narrative?* It goes without saying that to answer this question we must turn to the principal narratological theories that have developed in recent years and consider their application apart from cinema. This circling back, this detour, will allow us, to a certain extent, to gauge these narratological theses in the light of a new medium, a medium that, in the twentieth century, made us all avid consumers of narratives. It is important, moreover, to bring cinema into narratology's bosom, especially since modern authors, as Tzvetan Todorov has remarked, have forsaken the 'narrative road' of literary expression in all its forms: 'Today, it is true, it is no longer literature but cinema that creates the narratives that every society seems to need in order to live. Filmmakers recount stories while writers set words at play.'[4]

It is the lot of narrative to be the shared legacy of these two great arts, the novel and the film. But before inquiring into this legacy, we need to ask another question that will act as a catalyst for our topic here: *Can we, or can we not, speak of narrative with respect to a play?* This is a digressive question with respect to our final goal, that of bringing to light the principles of film narrative, but it is an essential one just the same. Why not attack the chain of narratological problems precisely at that link where, from the perspective of the present study, it appears to be the weakest? And the theatre appears in some respects to be the blind spot of narratological theory. Even Plato and Aristotle, as we shall see, did not see theatre in the same light ontologically: for Plato tragedy (and even comedy) was one of the forms of diegesis; whereas Aristotle appears to refuse to grant it any strictly narrative status. If it is possible to translate 'diegesis' as 'narrative,' Plato would undoubtedly not hesitate to accept the expression *theatrical narrative*, or even *staged narrative*, terms Aristotle would likely reject.[5] As surprising as it might seem, things have not changed much twenty-three centuries later: if we read the major works of contemporary narratology, the uncertainty that reigns with regard to the narrative status of theatrical discourse becomes immediately apparent. One could even say that narratological theory has forged no unanimity as to the ultimate narrative status of theatrical discourse, although signs of change are on the horizon. There are narratologists who affirm the narrative status of the magic formula[6] and the kitchen recipe,[7] but the art of Shakespeare and Molière has not yet been dealt with successfully by narratology. Several basic problems thus remain unresolved. Although many of today's leading narratologists believe that theatre really does present a narrative, others refuse to accept this, for reasons they see as fundamental and to which I shall return. Here the old opposition between Plato and Aristotle is being rehashed, in a somewhat modified context.

This vexed question of the narrative status of theatre becomes, at least implicitly, even more crucial when we recall that the narrative status of cinema, that other 'representational' art, is so readily agreed upon. How to explain some theorists' refusal of narrative to an art that uses flesh and blood actors on a stage to present a series of events, when those same theorists are generally much more conciliatory towards the cinema, which also uses actors?

There is no denying that hardly anyone would object to the expression 'film narrative.' It is clear, plain, and precise. It seems to cause no confusion and few dispute its legitimacy.[8] It fits well enough into the paradigm, alongside such common expressions as 'fictional narrative' or 'literary narrative,' and it carries the same connotations as these. On the other hand, the expression 'theatrical narrative,' or 'staged narrative,' is, for some, totally unacceptable. How are we to explain this difference in the treatment of two arts that, while the literary monody covers its inert pages with a continuum of abstract signs, share what Roland Barthes called the 'density of signs' found in semiotic media that join, in a necessarily 'polyphonic' manner, several expressive 'languages'?[9]

On the other hand, cinema shares with the novel a 'prerecorded' structure that confronts the auditor with a fait accompli, while the theatre unfolds in the present. It is also true that the novel and the cinema, the former more so than the latter, can throw off the spatio-temporal constraints to which theatrical discourse is inescapably bound. Both also depend for their transmission on a solid and uniform physical medium, the book and the reel of film, something that assures them a durability that is irremediably denied, in its fleetingness, to the theatre. But are these sufficient conditions for refusing narrativity to the theatre, when common sense has never hesitated to grant that status to cinema and the novel? What profound difference, at the narrative level, distinguishes these arts?

It should be said that the great question of theatre's narrativity has only rarely been asked explicitly. Unequivocal positions on the subject are rare. Algirdas-Julien Greimas, for example, speaks of 'theatrical works' as a 'kind of narrative,' but only parenthetically, in a study devoted to other problems.[10] The same is true of Anne Ubersfeld's comments on 'theatrical narrative'[11] and on the theatre as a 'form of narration.'[12] But these are isolated occurrences in the works of authors busy frying other fish. One of the few theatre specialists to ask this question is Patrice Pavis, for whom 'narrative is the most visible layer of the theatrical system.'[13] His work illustrates an entire tradition, which goes back to Aristotle, in which narrative genres stand in opposition to dramatic genres, thus setting *narrative* and *theatre* at odds with one another. This view holds that drama cannot be narrative. So what is it about theatre that justifies its exclusion from the category of narrative? In his *Dictionary of Theatre* Pavis spells out the problem :

> Narrative analysis ... dealt first with simple narrative forms (folktale, legend, novella), then with the novel and multiple-code systems such as comic strips or motion pictures. Theatre has not yet been analysed systematically, no doubt because of its extremely complex nature (given the number and variety of its different signifying systems), but perhaps also because it is associated by critics with mimesis (imitation of an action) rather than with diegesis (narration by a narrator). The main reason may be that theatrical narrative is only one specific case of a narrative system whose laws are independent of the kind of semiological system used.[14]

Mimesis versus diegesis: a simple opposition that emphasizes the apparently insuperable difference between these two kinds of discourse. On the one hand, *imitation without a narrator,* and on the other, *a narrator but no imitation.* The complex ramifications of this opposition constitute the problem, as we shall see. In fact those narratologists who refuse theatre all narrativity are unanimous on the question of the narrator's absence.

This absence has always concerned theorists who work on the problem of theatrical discourse. In their book *L'univers du roman,* Roland Bourneuf and Réal Ouellet offer a fairly widely accepted opinion that, without being entirely explicit (the work is about the novel, not the theatre), sets out one way to think about the differences between literary narrative and the theatre:

> The novel is thus above all a *narrative:* the novelist places him- or herself between the reader and the reality being described and interprets that reality for the reader. In the theatre the spectator is placed directly before events unfolding on the stage.[15]

It is this very absence of a mediator, this immediacy, which is usually invoked when refusing narrativity to the theatre. In the theatre, according to this hypothesis, a story is not *recounted*, it is *represented*. There is no narrator. It is curious to note that, for their part, the authors of *L'univers du théâtre* (including the same Réal Ouellet) also tackle this question, from another angle, heating up the debate even more: 'Representation consists in playing out a fiction on a stage, whereas narration is the action of *recounting* that same fiction.'[16] Then, a little further on, they remark: 'In its own way theatre thus takes on the telling of a story. It is not recounted by an intermediary, the narrator, but is displayed directly, in the language of the theatre: through decor, lighting, sound, gestures.'[17]

The authors are well aware of the problem of the narrative status of the theatre, especially if we stick to the generally accepted definition of narrative. Their approach to the theatre resembles that of Claude Bremond, for whom 'recounting can only ever be limited to describing what happens to someone or something, to stating the attributes of his or her development.'[18] They conclude by recognizing a certain resemblance between dramatic unity and other kinds of narrative unity, leading them to state that 'recounting and representing are thus the same thing.'[19] Just so: if we follow Bremond's definition to the letter, how could we refuse narrativity to the theatre? But this is not the view of Tzvetan Todorov, for whom, if the narrative comes to the receiver in any way other than through a mediator, an intermediary, a 'narrative focal point,' we cannot truly speak of narrative. Dialogue, for example, is not a narrative because here the narrative is 'contained' in the dialogue, and because the 'narrative is not reported.'[20] The narrative ambiguity of the theatre thus lies in the fact that plays present a series of events through a discourse that, unlike even the most 'objective' literary narrative, does not appear to be proffered, at the moment it is communicated to the public, by anyone other than the actors. Other literary genres, as we know, pose practically no problem for the narratologist. This is the case with certain kinds of poetry, lyric poetry in particular, which is the inverse of theatre: here, more so than in the novel, the narrative agent leaves traces of its activity behind, so much so that readers sometimes perceive its presence in the very poetic fabric. However, unlike a play, this kind of poetry often, according to Todorov, 'recounts nothing, describes no event, but contents itself … with musing, with expressing an impression.'[21] The enunciating agent is thus not a recounting agent because it recounts nothing. There can be no question, then, of narrative, or of narration.[22]

But what do we ask of a text for it to be deemed a narrative? This is a very controversial question. There is a certain 'tradition' in narratology that would have us disregard the quality of the semantic content when identifying narrative. This means that, for a text to be considered a narrative, all it has to do is give us information concerning the development of this or that subject. No more and no less. Here the only necessary condition is to establish a 'sequential development' among units in a 'transformative relationship.'[23] When we consider this 'requirement,' it is clear that every play, and even more so, every film, can (and must) be considered a narrative. In fact, such a 'minimalist'[24] position raises some problems: some scholars think it loses all by embracing all. The major problem arises above all from the fact that we cannot use it to define the limits beyond which a text might no longer be considered a narrative. So minimalist is this position that any *segment* of a narrative, any segment at all, can in the final analysis also be considered narrative!

The other frequently adopted path to defining narrative is well enough known that we needn't dwell on it here. It has a greater number of requirements than the first position, which I qualified as minimalist. That first definition asked that we consider only quantitative questions, and held that if there is *no transformation* whatsoever, there is *no narrative*. Conversely, if there is *at least one transformation* (any transformation at all), *there is narrative*. Any transformation at all? It would seem so – as long as there is one (quantity), it makes little difference what it is (quality). In contrast, the second position has qualitative as well as quantitative requirements. Here, in order for there to be narrative, a minimum of *two* transformations must be present, and not just any transformations: first, something must disrupt the given situation; then, a new and possibly final situation must be established, once all the peripeteia provoked by the perturbance have played out.

Any 'message' that delivers only part of this sequence (a sequence we will henceforth call the *minimum narrative sequence*) cannot be considered a complete narrative. This, of course, would not prevent that segment ultimately from being considered narrative in nature.[25]

There is a factor beyond simple (narrative) content and its structuring that, implicitly at least, is sometimes invoked by narratologists when defining narrative. This, as I mentioned earlier in passing, is the question of the delivery, of the means of communicating the narrative. Genette, as we have seen, wants to limit the label 'narrative' to texts delivered by a narrator using spoken or written language to address potential auditors.[26] This position, as he indicates, most closely resembles Plato's *haplē diēgēsis*, as we will discuss later. Thus narration alone can communicate a narrative.[27] Plays and films are not narrative because they do not *recount*, they *display*. Todorov seems to be of the same opinion when he writes that 'the theatrical story is not *reported*, it unfolds before our eyes ...; there is no *narration*, the *narrative* is contained within the characters' lines.'[28] If there is no narration, it is because there is, instead, representation. This is true of cinema and theatre alike. How then are we to understand this mode we call *representation* in terms of the form we call *narrative*? Are they mutually exclusive, as Genette and Todorov would ultimately have it? If representation is not suited to producing narrative, what then does it produce? Todorov's statement that 'the narrative is contained within the characters' lines' may perhaps be valid for theatre, whose characters truly do talk a lot. But is the same true for silent film, for example? Speech, words; perhaps there are ways of *recounting* without literally *speaking*, without *narrating* ... Well before speech arrived in film in the form of intertitles or the lecturer's commentary, some filmmaker-operators were working towards some sort of narrative project. This much is clear. As early as 1894 a patent application for a moving picture camera refers to 'telling stories by means of moving pictures.'[29] Before setting out on our study of the modes of narrative communication, it is probably worth analysing some of the mechanisms of film narrative and then describing the context in which the *cinema* encountered *narrative*. That encounter, the subject of our next chapter, was by no means a product of chance.

3 In Search of the First Film Narrative

Unlike a language, an image is unable to signify grammatical person and its constituent elements cannot be pinpointed in the same way. How then can it engage in narrative? We will not be able to claim it can until we clarify just what we mean by narrative in a series of moving and silent images.

François Jost, 'Narration(s),' 194

The title of this third chapter, although metaphoric and somewhat ironic, can in fact benefit from being taken literally. Here, following upon questions raised in the first two chapters, we will try to identify the necessary conditions for film narrative and to define with the greatest possible rigour what narrative in the cinema is. We will thus almost inevitably have to confront the great question of cinema's 'encounter' with narrativity. This is a considerably puzzling matter, as these comments by Christian Metz some years ago suggest:

To be sure, it has often been justly remarked that, since film has taken the narrative road ... it could only be the result of a positive development in the history of film ... There was nothing unavoidable, or particularly natural, in this. Yet even those who emphasise the historical aspect of this growth never conclude that it was meaningless or haphazard. It had to happen, but it had to happen for a reason; it had to be that the very nature of cinema rendered such an evolution if not certain at least probable.[1]

The hypotheses underlying such a statement seem just as puzzling today. There is nothing *natural* about cinema setting off on the narrative road, but the *nature* of cinema was a contributing factor just the same (we will see how such a paradoxical claim can in fact turn out to be true). The vista opened up by these questions will now become our starting point in an attempt to understand the various ways in which narrative in the cinema functions.

In order to do this we will use a body of work made up of the earliest films. To answer the question 'are the first Lumière films narrative?' we will have to make certain distinctions from the outset. Even if *La sortie des usines Lumière* (real title: *Sortie d'usine* [*Workers Leaving the Lumière Factory*], 1895) and *L'arrivée d'un train à La Ciotat* (*Train Entering a Station*, Lumière, 1895) are narratives, they do not appear to be narrative to the same degree as *Arroseur et arrosé* (*Waterer and Watered*, Lumière, 1895). The action of the first film is easily summed up: the doors to a factory open and a large group of workers exits the building.[2] This is a simple action and appears to offer no significant disruption. We could, of course, assert that the various elements of this action meet the conditions for what in the previous chapter we called the *minimum narrative sequence*. Metaphorically, one might indeed posit an initial situation (the closed doors of the factory just before mealtime), a disruption (the workers coming out), and a final situation (the re-establishment of the initial situation when the doors are once again closed). We might go even further and scrutinize more closely the various parameters structuring the film's action, taking into account the protocol governing its presentation or even the underlying intentions of what we might call the 'mise en film.' Marshall Deutelbaum did something of the sort when he wrote this about the film:

> Less obvious, though even more intriguing is the way in which the film nearly returns the scene before the camera to the state at which it was when the film began. Both at the beginning and at the close, the cinematic image offers only the exterior of the factory seen from the same point of view. So similar in appearance are these opening and closing images to one another, in fact, that if one were to loop the film into a continuous band, the action would appear to be a single periodic event.[3]

This analysis brings Deutelbaum to the conclusion that the Lumière films are clearly set apart from the simple and naive Edison films of the period. By analysing their production we can see interventions in the Lumière films that Deutelbaum believes qualifies them as being more narrative than the Edison films.

But can we really consider *Workers Leaving the Lumière Factory* a narrative? As we saw at the end of the preceding chapter, there are at least two answers to this question. For some narratologists it is clear that this film, despite its brevity, simplicity, and relative incompleteness, has an uncontested right to the label narrative. The only criterion they require for any given *énoncé* (utterance) to qualify as *narrative* is that it *narrate*;[4] that is, that it be an *énoncé* that orders its constituent elements according to the two fundamental principles of narrativity: sequence and transformation. According to this view, any *énoncé* that relates acts, movements, or events in 'sequential development' and that develops a 'transformative relationship' can be considered a *narrative*.[5] On the basis of these principles, not very demanding ones at that, we can conclude, as I have elsewhere,[6] that any film, indeed any shot (at least any changing shot), can rightly be considered a *narrative*. According to this view, then, these three Lumière films can automatically be considered true narratives.

Opponents of this position have other requirements, as we have seen. Their definition of *narrative* is different even when, as is most often the case, they do not adhere to a different concept of *narrativity*. They simply refuse the status of *narrative* to an *énoncé* that does not offer *every one* of the various narrative phases that are supposed to exist in a *minimum narrative sequence*. Thus, of the three films under consideration here, only *Waterer and Watered* meets the test. One might even say that this reel, truly a little 'narrative gem,' is a borderline case. A film showing any less of a narrative structure than *Waterer and Watered* would never, in this view, be considered narrative. The film might even serve as a yardstick in this sense. It meets the standard of the *minimum narrative sequence* perfectly (the film and the concept seem made for each other!). The film's story moves from an initial state of equilibrium (the gardener peacefully carrying out his work) to a state of disequilibrium (the young scamp disturbs the gardener's tranquillity) and then to a final equilibrium (after he takes action, the gardener, now free of the intruder, returns to his work).

It is easy to see that it is a different matter for films such as *Train Entering a Station* and *Workers Leaving the Lumière Factory*, despite the latter's 'full circle' structure. In the case of the former we note from the outset a certain incompleteness:[7] the train arrives at the station and stops, but the film ends before it leaves again. This question of incompleteness remains secondary, however, because in the final analysis even a film whose action seems as complete as that of *Workers Leaving the Lumière Factory* could also be refused the status of narrative. Despite its apparent total conformity to the *minimum narrative sequence* (the 'opening and closing *images*'[8] evoke that sequence's 'initial and final *situations*'), we could make the most of the fact that there is no real disturbance (and no agent of disturbance).[9] One would be justified then in arguing that, in the final analysis, these two films give us only simple *situations* of an embryonic narrative. These situations could just as easily be the initial or the final moments of this possible narrative. For *Workers Leaving the Lumière Factory* to be a narrative, in this view, the scamp of *Waterer and Watered* would have to escape from the universe of the film to which he is confined (for eternity!), position himself on the wall enclosing the yards of the Lumière factory, and from there, let's say, hurl firecrackers at the workers who, outraged, would chase him to the local railroad station where the practical joker would flee on board the first train he could catch, heading, say, for La Ciotat!

While it is legitimate in the end to confer the label 'narrative' only on narrative *énoncés* that conform to the *minimum narrative sequence*, it is clear that we are still dealing with a principle that runs the risk of serious attack (if this is not already the case). Roland Barthes, Tzvetan Todorov, and A.-J. Greimas, to mention only those three, do not hesitate to equate 'narrative' with 'narrative *énoncé*.' This is yet another duality to be reckoned with in connection with the word 'narrative.'[10] For this reason, in this book I will avoid as much as possible any inopportune use of the word 'narrative.' Instead I will use (with some exceptions) 'narrative *énoncé*' when I am not referring to a 'complete narrative' or one that meets the criteria of the *minimum narrative sequence*.

One of the things that demonstrates the ambivalence – oops, the polyvalence – of the word 'narrative' is the fact that narratology plainly lacks terminology for designating the many different phenomena it wishes to distinguish from each other. It is as if this young discipline has developed too rapidly to allow its lexicon to expand at the same rate and meet the demands imposed on it. This state of affairs is exacerbated by the fact that there are two autonomous and distinct schools of narratology, each with its own aims. One and the same term can designate different phenomena in each of the schools. One can imagine the problems facing the narratologist who moves between schools in a single study. The two schools are easily identified and distinguished from each other, and it would be useful to do so here, since their dual existence is not unrelated to the problems just raised with respect to the definition of narrative.

First, there is the school we might call the *narratology of content*, whose principal practitioner is undoubtedly Greimas. This school privileges the study of narrative content (the story told), *entirely independently* of the medium through which it is recounted. Most of the theoretical conclusions arising from Greimas's work, for example, deal with the question of structuring events. This approach does not concern itself with the medium (images, words, etc.) through which the auditor discovers that the hero did or did not have blue eyes or whether he was bored to death. It is interesting to note that an analysis of the acts in the 'Life and Passion of Christ' carried out using these theories is just as valid for the textual narratives found in the Gospels as it is for the different film narratives they have inspired: *Jesus of Nazareth* (Franco Zeffirelli, U.K.-Italy, 1977), *Il Vangelo secondo Matteo* (*The Gospel According to St Matthew*, Pier Paolo Pasolini, Italy-France, 1964), *The Robe* (Henry Koster, U.S., 1953), or indeed any of the *Passions* produced at the turn of the twentieth century.

The other school, and most of the present book's concerns lie here, is the *narratology of expression* (to preserve Louis Hjelmselv's content/expression dichotomy), whose leading practitioner is Gérard Genette. Narrative expression (the discourse of telling), for this school, is more important than the content (even if, of course, it is difficult to study one without at least some concern for the other). The principal concern here is the means of expression (such as the written word in textual narrative, moving images, sounds, words, official documents, or the music used in film narratives) by which a piece of information is communicated to the auditor. Conversely, the great questions of the narrative agent (who speaks? who sees?) and of the different modes and systems of narrative communication are posed here only in a circumspect manner.

Narratologists will not necessarily have the same starting points, and their approach to a problem will depend on which school has had more influence on them. Some definitions may even lose their relevance, acuity, and even validity when transplanted from one approach to the other. This is true of the definition of narrative as a *minimum narrative sequence*. We should grant that this definition *in no way takes into account the medium* through which the story is told. When we tried to gauge the extent to which Lumière films meet this definition, the questions we asked would have been just as relevant if we had been dealing with *textual* adaptations of these *énoncés* of *film* narrative.

But what does this mean? That narrativity can exist according to two different criteria? This appears to be the case: at bottom, there exist two

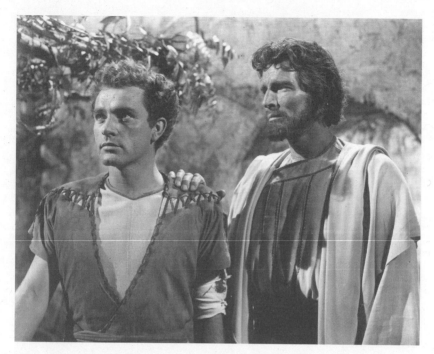

Figure 3.1 *The Robe*, Henry Koster, 1953 [Still] (Cinémathèque québécoise)

kinds of narrativity, or in any event two ways of thinking about narrative form, depending on the medium through which the narrative is communicated. We might call one kind of narrative *extrinsic*: it deals solely with *narrative content*, independent of its means of expression. The other kind could be called *intrinsic* narrativity in that its narrative quality derives directly from the means of expression. The cinema, as we shall see, is one of these. Is not a film such as *Waterer and Watered* narrative both in an extrinsic and an intrinsic sense? With respect to the former, the story it tells, regardless of its medium, meets the conditions of the *minimum narrative sequence*, and, with respect to the latter, moving images, as the rest of this chapter will be devoted to demonstrating, are intrinsically narrative, regardless of the degree to which the action they present is structured.

We would thus be justified in considering a film's message as being assailed on all sides by narrativity, and the cinema as an exemplary narrative art. For, if the linguistic *énoncé* (which is the basis of textual narrative) can easily be something other than narrative (some linguistic *énoncés* are injunctive, dubitative, descriptive, etc.) this is not the case for the filmic *énoncé* (or utterance), which is the basis of film narrative. One of the fundamental hypotheses of this book is that cinema, as Metz said, has 'narrativity built into it': that the filmic *énoncé* can only abstain from narrativity with great difficulty and in exceptional cases if it is not to deny its very nature.

What then is generally required of a text for it to be considered, in the widest sense, a narrative? What makes one 'message' narrative and another not? For Claude Bremond, in order that a given message be seen as narrative, it is sufficient 'for some animate or inanimate subject, through this message, to be placed in a given time, t, then t + n, and that we be told what happens, at the moment t + n, to the attributes that had prevailed at the moment t.'[11]

Bremond's requirements are in complete agreement with Todorov's: sequence ('time t' then 'time t + n') and transformation ('what happens to the attributes'). Seen in this light, we recognize immediately that a film shot, any shot, is run through and through with this ability. Film can dodge or neutralize this narrativity only with great difficulty. Bremond's definition, however, presents a problem that seems, more than anything else, to be the result of a fault in his formulation. Although elsewhere Bremond is explicit and precise in noting that for him transformation represents an essential condition of narrativity, the text quoted above allows us to believe the contrary, since it in no way says that the attributes prevailing at the moment t + n have to be *different* from those prevailing at the moment t. We can therefore conceive, for example, of a sequence of two still photographs, one of which presents a subject in a posture of waiting in an immobile setting (say, an old man sitting on a bench), while the other presents the same character, a few moments later, with nothing having happened, to the point that the two photos seem to be identical.[12] This sequence would in all respects satisfy the criteria formulated by Bremond: photo #2 (moment t + n) shows us *what has happened* to the subject's attributes in photo #1 (moment t): *they have remained the same.* The old man, pensive in #1, is still pensive in #2, only moments later; at moment t + n he is in the same sitting position as at moment t, etc. And yet it seems that Bremond would not include this sequence in his 'big narrative family.' One could certainly propose, and here we can quote the author himself, that 'to recount or tell is to enunciate a development, and to do that is to adopt a position with respect to a possible change, either to confirm it or to deny it,'[13] and we might then claim that our sequence most certainly enunciates a development in relation to a possible change, which in this case did not (or could not) take place. However, we would end up in an untenable position: we would have to negate in the second moment what hadn't been enunciated in the first.[14] We must not forget that Bremond, a few lines after his definition, clarified it a bit by adding, 'To recount the story of S amounts to stating that S kept attribute b and replaced attribute a with attribute á.'[15] He also, even further on, adds that for him change is the minimum condition for narrativity: 'without [change], no narrative is possible.'[16] His definition is thus poorly drafted, allowing for a meaning not intended by its author. We should add a brief amendment so that this misreading is prevented. The definition might read as follows: a message is narrative (or communicates a story, for Bremond) when it presents any subject in a process of *transformation*, and the subject is then placed within a time t, then t + n, and we should be told what happens at the moment t + n to the attributes that prevailed at the moment t.

It thus seems that we can now propose that any shot, according to this amended definition, is a narrative *énoncé* (that any shot is a narrative, given its intrinsic narrativity), since by definition any shot presents a series (*sequence*) of images in motion (*transformation*). But is this really the case? Is any shot truly a narrative *énoncé*? Are there not exceptions to this? We said above that sequence and transformation are the sole essential conditions for establishing the narrativity of an *énoncé*. But what do we mean exactly by 'transformation'? We must be careful.

'Transformation' must not be understood in the sense of 'substitution,' or there is nothing to prevent us from viewing any syntagm composed of two photographs (whatever they might be) a narrative *énoncé*. Now, for two photographs to be 'promoted' to this 'rank,' they must fulfil two conditions. First, they must not be completely *alike*: if they are, there is no narrativity, as we have already shown, since there would be no *change* (a decidedly much less ambiguous term than 'transformation'). Second, they cannot be entirely different from each other: the subject of the transformation in question, or, rather, of the change in question, must be assured a certain degree of *continuity*, or else narrativity cannot be demonstrated.

In other words, there must be, in the two essential phases (t and t + n), both some commonly shared and some distinctive elements. Narrativity requires, as Todorov points out, that certain features be

different and others alike. It is 'in the tension of two formal categories' that narrativity is constituted: the exclusive presence of one of
them brings us into a type of discourse that is not narrative. If the
predicates do not change, we are not yet within narrative, but in the
immobility of psittacism; yet if the predicates do not resemble each
other, we find ourselves beyond narrative, in an ideal reportage entirely consisting of differences.[17]

Todorov is careful to clarify what we should understand by 'transformation':

> Now, transformation represents precisely a synthesis of differences and
> resemblance, it links two facts without their being able to be identified ...
> It is an operation in two directions: it asserts both resemblance and differ-
> ence; ... it permits discourse to acquire a meaning without this meaning
> becoming pure information; in a word, it makes narrative possible and
> yields us its very definition.[18]

Transformation thus provides us with the very definition of narrative. We should try to identify the full import of this proposition: transformation (in the sense of change or modification) could conceivably
be the sole and unique condition for narrativity because, being by definition a process, it implies an ever-present sequence.[19]

We must conclude, therefore, that there are at least two kinds of
'shots' in cinema (or, to be more precise, two kinds of sequences of photograms) that cannot be seen as narrative énoncés. One because of its
lack of difference: the freeze frame or motionless shot (where both the
subject and the camera are immobile).[20] The other because of its lack of
continuity (but would this be a shot?):[21] a series of images (hypothetical
but easily obtained – examples of this exist) wherein each image is distinct and depicts a new object.

On the question of intrinsic narrativity, the narrativity inherent to
a medium and its language, we can posit right from the start that the
cinema was a machine for producing narrative énoncés, narratives in
a sense. Every shot (with certain exceptions) is thus a narrative énoncé that presents an action. Only its incompleteness (we saw this with
the rather crazy ending we came up with for Workers Leaving the
Lumière Factory) prevents us from considering it as extrinsically narrative. Thus, if we follow our reasoning through to its logical conclusion, every shot would be either a narrative or a segment of a
possible narrative.

As a corollary, every shot in a multiple-shot film, taken in isolation, would be (apart from the exceptions mentioned above) a narrative. What does this mean? Would a film made up of seven hundred shots contain seven hundred narratives? What happens then to the film's overall narrative? The necessary hypothesis thus seems to be: on the level of intrinsic narrativity alone, there exist two levels of narrative in cinema. The first of these narrative levels corresponds to the micro-narrative communicated by each shot, as a photogrammatic énoncé. The second, higher narrative level is generated from this first level. It is produced by juxtaposing the micro-narratives communicated by each shot. A multiple-shot film is thus a second-level narrative énoncé, made up of several first-level narrative énoncés (as many as there are shots). These two levels, which we should see as two superimposed layers of narrativity, correspond to each of the two 'articulations' found in the cinema's dual changeability:[22] the *changeability of the subjects represented*, which is the basis for the *sequence of photograms*, and the *changeability of the spatio-temporal segments*, made possible by the *sequence of shots*. The first layer of narrativity produces first-level narrative énoncés that are attributable to 'moving iconic analogy' (Metz),[23] deriving from the *process* at the basis of cinema, that of *creating a sequence of photograms*. The second layer, which sequentially comes second, produces narrative énoncés of the second level (but which are dependent upon énoncés of the first level) resulting from the *procedure* of *creating a sequence of shots* (editing).

Thus, when we say that cinema, at a given point in its history, 'took the narrative road,'[24] the narrativity we refer to is not the 'innate' narrativity that we have just been describing, but the second level, this second layer of narrativity that until now we have only touched upon but which is really the level that interests us most. This is the level that does not settle for 'perceptual analogy alone,' which as Metz observes 'makes it possible in a pinch to avoid any properly linguistic codification.'[25] And it is in light of this division of film's narrative abilities that we must henceforth view this other observation by Metz:

From the moment that the cinema encountered narrativity [for us, the *second* level of narrativity] ... it appears that it superimposed over the analogical message [for us, the first level that is *already narrative*] a second complex of codified constructions, something 'beyond' the image, something that has only gradually been mastered (thanks to Griffith in particular).[26]

These two narrative layers are rarely identified clearly and separated from each other, but their dual presence is felt just beneath the surface throughout the whole history of thinking about the cinema. This should not surprise us, because it is possible to connect each of them to one of the stages necessary to produce a film: shooting and editing. One author, however, Yuri Lotman, has clearly distinguished between them and his observations fit completely with what I have been describing here:

> Joining chains of *varied shots* into a meaningful sequence forms a *story* ... *The second type of narration* involves the transformation of *one and the same shot* ... The chain of alterations of the face is, of course, a narration. At the same time it is not the joining of a number of signs into chains, but the transformation of *one and the same sign*. Recall one of the first steps of the cinema, a film strip from Demeny's photophone: twenty shots of an actor pronouncing the words 'Je vous aime.' ... The iconic sign can be transformed into a narrative text because it contains several mobile elements.[27]

At an initial level it is thus the *changing* aspect of the image that provides an 'innate' and 'spontaneous' narrativity, the truly intrinsic narrativity that produces the sequence of photograms which makes up a shot. And, Lotman says, it is 'joining chains of varied shots into a meaningful sequence' that constitutes, at a second level, the *meta*-narrativity that results from editing. The source of this narrativity is in the 'primary' narrativity of each shot. This primary narrativity underpins the secondary narrativity and contributes to the development of its 'supra-punctiliar' plot. This is because, in order to ensure its own functioning, the second layer of narrativity tends (at least within certain aesthetic systems) to cover over the first layer of narrativity and 'recycle' it for its own ends. Here lies the importance, for example, of attempts to do away with autonomous shots around 1910. The film viewer does not experience (should not experience, we might even say if we base our argument on the norms that have governed the history of cinema) the sensation of being placed before a multitude of narrative *énoncés* of the first level that accumulate bit by bit to produce the narrative *énoncé* of the second level, the film's narrative as a whole. On the contrary, the meta-narrativity being discussed here results more from the systematic obliteration of the narrative *énoncés* of the first level (the obliteration of their individuality) than from their accumulation.[28]

Of course we can also ask whether the production of these two levels of narrative, of these two layers of narrativity, presupposes the same kind of semio-narrative operations and if this production is the work of one and the same narrative agent. We should ask then if it is possible to impute the production of these two levels of narrative to a film 'narrator.' If that is the case, we have to conclude that each level is communicated in the same manner: by narration. But is the simple transfer onto film of a profilmic reality enough for us to speak of *narration*? In other words, if we have a film made up of just one shot that presents, in the manner of the theatre, the performance of characters in dramatic action (as in, say, *Waterer and Watered*), one shot that is thus limited to the first level of narrativity alone, *does such a film deliver its narrative message in a different way than the theatre delivers its own?* And does *editing* in cinema, which gives us the second level of narrativity we have just established, *allow film to change narrative systems?* This would indeed be the case, according to the view taken in this study. In this regard, one of our basic hypotheses, as mentioned above, is that there are two basic modes, two distinct systems of narrative communication: monstration and narration. The first is the product, at least in part, of characters in dramatic action (whether in the theatre or in the cinema). The second emerges from a higher level of abstraction and goes beyond the concreteness inherent in all cases of 'representation' (in the sense with which the term has been used until now in this book).

These two modes of narrative communication are 'as old as the world' and are rooted in an era, that of Ancient Greece, during which the narrative text was necessarily fleeting, since the privileged means for delivering a narrative was its *direct* communication to its auditors (which is still the case today for theatre actors and traditional storytellers). In order successfully to understand the place of film narrative in relation to textual and performed narratives, we will now have to examine the narrative practices of Antiquity. These are all the more important because they gave rise to a whole body of thought (that of Plato and Aristotle) which is the very foundation of narratology; narratological interpretations today constantly use and sometimes misuse this legacy.

This 'detour through the direct,' through narrative communication offered *directly* to the auditor by a flesh-and-blood speaker, will be all the more useful to us for the way in which the character/auditor relationship it rests upon is relatively analogous to what we find in the cinema.

4 Early Narratology: Mimesis and Diegesis[1]

In his myth of the cave, Plato tells the fantastic story of the Greeks, chained to the spot, watching unfold on the wall of the cave the spectacle of what they believe to be reality. The philosopher (or wise man) who is able to avoid such a situation can by the same token confirm that this reality is in fact only the shadow, the reflection of an arranged *mise en scène* behind a small wall where objects lit by fire are moved about.

Gilles Thérien, 'Le cinéma québécois,' 114

One of the most fundamental questions in narratology concerns 'narrative modes' and thus, in the words of Tzvetan Todorov, 'the way in which [the] narrator tells us [the story], the manner in which it is presented to us.'[2] This is a most important question, and has given rise to a number of theoretical systems (most often binary in nature) whose goal is to account for the distinctions that can be made between the various 'regimes' of narrative communication that narrators of every stripe can call upon (or are bound by?). This issue has given birth to conceptual pairs as familiar and useful to us as mimesis and diegesis, showing and telling, and representation and narration.

The first of these pairs dates back to Plato and Aristotle who, as we know, were in a sense the precursors of narratology. Here, in the first of three chapters devoted to the different modes of communicating narrative, we will examine these two concepts. We will come to see important differences of meaning between the terms of these dichotomies, allowing us to distinguish, on the one hand, between diegesis and narrative telling and, on the other, between mimesis and representational showing. For these are not, contrary to popular belief, conceptual systems whose respective terms can be freely interchanged. While narration and representation, for example, are, in Todorov's words, 'those narrative modes' to which 'we refer when we say that a writer "shows" us things, while another only "tells" us,'[3] mimesis and diegesis can in no way be considered their respective equivalents because, as Paul Mazon explains, 'the Greek epic was oral literature' and 'was never meant to be read.'[4] The reason for this is that, *like every other literary form of the time*, it was produced above all for *listeners*. These listeners, moreover, were also called upon to be *spectators* as much as mere listeners, even in cases where speech was not truly rendered theatrically. Mimesis and diegesis are thus categories that apply to a kind of *spoken narrative* that shares with *textual narrative* the fact that it too is a verbal narrative, but one that radically distances itself from textual narrative because it makes possible, through its potential for 'spectacle,' the birth of a highly specific form of narrative, *staged narrative* (which did not necessarily always take the form of theatre). As Paul Vicaire remarks, 'Reciting bards, and later rhapsodes, prefigured theatrical performance.'[5] Back when books were not widely in use, the principal forms of literature always and already presupposed an immediate physical contact between the poet (or his delegates, the bards or rhapsodes who declaimed the text or the actors who performed it) and the audience who received it. In this sense, we can state that every form of literature of the day was connected in some way to staging (whether a stage was truly present or not) and, by this very fact, to spectacle. It was in such a live[6] setting that Plato was led to propose his theoretical system founded upon two categories, mimesis and diegesis. These categories were thus not originally conceived of as applying to textual narrative, unlike the categories showing and telling, which only truly apply to textual narrative, as we shall see in the following chapter.

What, then, are we to make of these categories bequeathed to us by the Ancients? And, above all, how might these categories, dating back twenty-two hundred years before the invention of cinema, be of use to those of us who study this art form? As I have said, the reasons for returning to the Ancients are many. The most important has to do with the fact that, paradoxically, the literary context of the era in which these categories were founded shares at least one thing in common with our own: in each case, the dominant manner of transmitting narrative involves characters acting out the story. Back then, there was theatre (and also, as we have seen, every other form of literature that involved some sort of performance); today, we have the cinema. Of course, the cinema is not theatre, and in many respects what it presents us resembles textual narrative more than it does staged narrative. But above all we must not forget, as Christian Metz remarks, that 'the cinema is first of all a *dramatic* art,' that the story it tells 'is told through action ... is acted out by its participants themselves and not narrated by an external narrator.'[7] Now, there is a world of difference between transmitting a story through a narrator and acting it out by characters playing the roles. This is one of the things that Plato and Aristotle have taught us. One of the basic hypotheses of this book is that the cinema has succeeded in creating a mode of transmitting the narrable that is completely specific to it because it easily and organically combines, using its own resources, the filmic equivalent of the modes proper to textual narrative (narration) and staged narrative (monstration). A film, like a play, is founded upon the performance of characters acting out the narrative. But by using various techniques, including, most importantly, editing, film succeeds in suffusing in the gaps between the images the figure of a narrator that, even if it is completely different from its textual counterpart, appears to share the majority of this latter's attributes. Because it is also true, as Metz remarks, that 'the imaged discourse [is] to a certain extent the equivalent of the story spun by the words of the novelist.'[8]

While Plato and Aristotle don't use the terms mimesis and diegesis in the same way as each other, their ideas on the matter will be highly useful to us in our search for the basis of the modes of transmitting the narrable. The two Ancients don't look at the problem from the same angle, but that will only serve to add to the wealth of issues at stake. For, despite appearances, the two systems they offer us are not contradictory, even if the mimesis of one is not the same as the Mimesis of the other. In neither thinker is mimesis contrasted with diegesis, despite what the *modern* contrast between these two terms might lead us to believe (an opposition found nowhere in Plato or Aristotle). In fact, to contrast mimesis with diegesis the way we do today, and this will be the first problem we will discuss, is without realizing it to contrast a Platonic concept (mimesis) with an Aristotelian one (diegesis).[9] It is true that each of these terms is present in both the (*avant la lettre*) narratological works of these two Ancients,[10] but they are never directly contrasted in either of them. If we refer back to the original texts, we can see that Plato and Aristotle used the same words for different concepts. There are thus two forms of diegesis and two forms of mimesis, giving us four distinct concepts that, moreover, and this may come as a surprise, do not enter

Figure 4.1

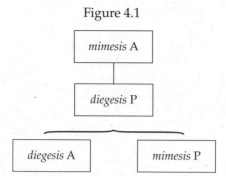

into any real contradiction with each other! On the contrary, the two systems of thought bequeathed to us by Plato and Aristotle actually complement each other quite well, so well that we might imagine them superimposed, in the simplified version depicted in figure 4.1, in which the letter P refers to Plato and the letter A to Aristotle.

As we shall see, there is absolutely no contradiction between what I describe here as mimesis A and Mimesis P[11] because these are simply two different usages of a word that, like many others in every language, carries more than one meaning. As for the different way in which diegesis is used, we will find a way to reconcile the terms of this apparent contradiction, even if how we will do so seems less evident now. In this case the apparent contradiction is due to a shift in meaning rather than a simple case of polysemy. But first, let's look at Plato's famous *Republic*.

The standard interpretation of the argument Plato has Socrates expose in book 3 of the *Republic* is as follows. After 'conclud[ing] the topic of tales,' Socrates proposes to examine with his pupil Adeimantus '[the topic] of discourse' (*lexeōs*) (392c; Shorey).[12] To do so, Socrates demonstrates that a poet, in his lexis (392c) and his diegesis (392d) may or may not resort to *imitation*, to mimesis (392d). Poets recount events – *narrate* – 'either by simple narrative – *haplē diēgēsis* – or by narrative expressed through imitation – *dia mimēseōs* – or by a combination of the two – *di'amphoterōn*' (392d; Griffith).[13] Socrates then cites Homer as an example of a poet who resorts to *imitation* in some passages, while in others he uses 'simple narrative' (Griffith) or 'narration, pure and simple' (Shorey) instead. Figure 4.2 (below) depicts this line of reasoning.

Looking at this figure we can see that diegesis and mimesis are not contrasted with each other but that the latter is one of the possible

Figure 4.2

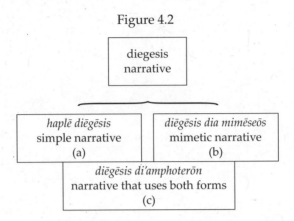

forms of the former. While no Plato scholar today explicitly denies that the three 'genres' given above are internal divisions of diegesis, most modern scholars forget to take this into account and content themselves with contrasting diegesis and mimesis. This is the product of an annoying lexical habit that confounds in a single term, 'narrative,' the two Platonic concepts *diēgēsis* and *haplē diēgēsis*. Here is one example, taken from Gérard Genette: 'There are, therefore, at the origins of the classical tradition, two apparently contradictory divisions, in which narrative is contrasted with imitation, either as its antithesis [in Plato] or as one of its modes [in Aristotle].[14]

Genette's claim that, for Aristotle, narrative is one of the modes of imitation is quite correct (but we will soon see how the 'imitation' in question has practically nothing to do with Plato's mimesis). However, Plato's text does not permit us to say that, for him, narrative is the *antithesis* of imitation. Narrative is not 'contrasted with *imitation*,' but rather with what Plato calls '*haplē diēgēsis*,' or *simple narrative*. We should also see in Plato the same kind of 'contrast' Genette finds in Aristotle, but in the opposite direction, because for Plato mimesis is a form of diegesis.

A few lines later, Genette adds: 'For Plato, the realm of what he calls *lexis* … is divided theoretically into imitation proper (*mimēsis*) and simple narrative (*diēgēsis*).'[15] Here Genette contrasts *simple narrative* with *imitation*, which is perfectly in keeping with Plato's text, but his parenthetical indications contrast *mimēsis* with *diēgēsis* (and not with *haplē diēgēsis*) and thus lead him, through the omission of a crucial word, to confuse two distinct concepts.[16] .

This omission is harmless only in appearance. It is also, unfortunately, all too common, and not only in the work of narratologists. Roselyne Dupont-Roc, for example, a Plato scholar and a recent translator into French (with Jean Lallot) of Aristotle's *Poetics*, writes that narrative 'can use modes of expression that are diametrically opposed or that, when they intermingle, give rise to hybrid genres: a) *simple narrative* … b) *imitative narrative* … and finally c) the epic, which alternates *narrative* and *dialogue*, mixing the two genres.'[17] She seems to forget for a moment that the two genres she had just described are not *narrative* on the one hand and *dialogue* (or, of little consequence here, *imitative narrative*) on the other, but rather *simple* narrative and dialogue (or imitative narrative). The term 'narrative' on its own is reserved for the 'family of genres.'

We should also remark that this fuzziness may be the source of the fuzziness in our standard classification of genres, in which *dramatic* genres are contrasted with *narrative* genres. The very terms of this classification seem to refuse any narrative status to drama, which, as we can see, cannot be reconciled with Plato's ideas. Isn't the theatre, for Plato the model par excellence of the dramatic genre (and thus of staged narrative), one possible form of diegesis?

It is difficult to understand how book 3 of the *Republic*, which in another connection is the source of more than one difficulty,[18] could have given rise to such a widespread reading in which mimesis and diegesis are contrasted and, on that basis, in which theatre is excluded from the realm of diegesis. Because Plato's original text cries from the rooftops that, first of all, there are at least two ways for poets to create diegesis, to recount events: either this diegesis never resorts to imitation (in which case it is *haplē diēgēsis*); or it resorts to it exclusively (in which case it is mimesis, which, let me stress, is and undeniably remains a form of diegesis, a *narrative* – a *diēgēsis dia mimēseōs*, Plato described it, or a *narrative told by means of imitation*, to which we will return). Thus, we find in Plato the following remarks:

> 392d (Griffith): Aren't all stories told by storytellers and poets really a *narrative* – *diēgēsis* – of what has happened in the past, of what is happening now, or of what is going to happen in the future?
> 393b (Griffith): But it's all narrative – both the individual speeches he delivers and the bits he says in between the speeches.
> 393c (Griffith): In passages like this, apparently, Homer and the rest of the poets use imitation – *dia mimēseōs* – to construct their *narrative* – *diēgēsis*. –

Yes. – If there were no passages where the poet concealed his own person, then his whole work, his whole *narrative*, would have been created without using *imitation*.

394d (Shorey): We must reach a decision whether we are to suffer or not our poets to narrate – *diēgēsis* – as imitators – *mimoumenous* –.

396c (Griffith): I think the decent man … in his *narrative – diēgēsis – …* will not be ashamed of an *imitation – mimēsei –* of this sort.

Let's return for the moment to Socrates and Adeimantus as they continue their conversation and arrive at a discussion of the concrete manifestations of poiesis in Greek society. Socrates reminds Adeimantus of the three genres of 'poetry and storytelling' (394b–c; Griffith), which he classifies as: (1) the dithyramb, defined here as a *'di'apangelias autou tou poiētou' poiēsis*, a *story* (a *narrative*) that the *poet himself* recounts (thus without ever giving the floor to anyone other than himself and always remaining the narrator of his own story and never resorting to imitation) – this, then, is *haplē diēgēsis* (393d); (2), tragedy and comedy, defined as a *'dia mimēseōs holē' poiēsis*, which proceeds by means of imitation alone (thus giving the floor to imitators, or actors); and (3) epic poetry, defined as a *'di'amphoterōn' poiēsis*, which uses both methods. This gives us our figure 4.3, which complements the previous figure.

Beginning at 394d, Socrates pursues his argument and expounds the advantages and disadvantages of imitation, pronouncing himself opposed to the imitation of the vile and base things that ignoble men are led to commit and in favour of a selective imitation, to which decent men are led, by restricting imitation to subjects with the same nature, or better, than such men. He concludes that decent men (or noble men or men of the right sort, etc., depending on the translation) will have a 'form of speech' or will create a *narrative* (*diēgēsis*) of which the 'literary form' (*lexis*) will 'be one that partakes of both, of imitation and simple narration, but there will be a small portion of imitation in a long discourse' (397e; Shorey). The 'style' (*lexis*) of the ignoble man, on the contrary, will 'consist entirely of *imitation*, in word and gesture, with maybe a small amount of *narrative*' (397b; Griffith).[19] Next comes a very short passage (397b–c) on a quality seen to be essential to the two genres of *lexis* under discussion: the unity of tone in the former compared to the plurality of tones in the latter. Here Socrates arrives near the end of his argument and asks (397c; Griffith): 'Do all poets, then, and storytellers of all kinds, hit upon one or other of these styles, or some combination of the two?' There follows the crucial question I

Figure 4.3

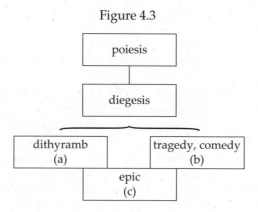

have already referred to and Adeimantus's famous response, which has given rise to the diverging translations I have quoted here.

From the outset, then, and if we leave aside the long exposition on morality, there exist for Plato two fundamental modes of narrative communication, two ways to transmit the narrable, which take the form of two kinds of narrative: on the one hand, a 'narrative without imitation' (*haplē diēgēsis*) and, on the other, 'a narrative by means of imitation' (mimesis). But this way of summarizing the question (see the two previous parentheses) is somewhat prejudicial: by contrasting *haplē diēgēsis* with mimesis in this way, we risk losing sight of the importance of the word *haplē* in the former term and, given the absence of any reference whatsoever to diegesis in the latter, we also risk erasing it completely and creating a direct contrast between diegesis and mimesis – the way everyone else has! We might also note the importance of the relationship of these two contrasted terms to imitation: it is through direct reference to imitation, to mimesis, that *haplē diēgēsis* is, precisely, said to be *simple* (*haplē*). At one point (393c), Plato quite clearly describes *haplē diēgēsis* as *aneu mimēseōs … diēgēsis* (literally: a diegesis without mimesis, a narrative without imitation). For this reason, we must stop simply contrasting *haplē diēgēsis* with mimesis and be more explicit. Since *haplē diēgēsis* is a form of diegesis without imitation, it would be preferable to speak of it as a non-mimetic diegesis and, in the case of mimesis, for obvious reasons, to refer to it as mimetic diegesis. In the end, this is simply a literal translation of Plato: *diēgēsis dia mimēseōs* (= narrative through imitation). This new way of naming and especially of describing the two contrasted terms (non-mimetic diegesis vs. mimetic diegesis) appears to be more respectful of Plato's dichotomy and should cause less confusion. With this system it becomes possible to produce, in figure 4.4, a new version of figure 4.2 and to sum up Plato's ideas on the modes of narrative communication.

The conceptual pair mimesis and diegesis has thus enjoyed the success it has as a dichotomy because of a confusion of meaning and a shortcoming in the translation. And also, perhaps, because Aristotle's theses would soon achieve supremacy over Plato's. The use Aristotle makes of the concept of diegesis has surely gone unnoticed: for Aristotle, diegesis is in no way contrasted with mimesis. Moreover, Aristotle uses the term diegesis only rarely (five times in his entire *Poetics*) and he *never* uses the term mimesis to describe a specific mode of communicating a narrative. What Aristotle offers in reality is an implicit (implicit because it is never made explicit) critique of and commentary on Plato's vision of poiesis. In his own fashion, Aristotle adopts Plato's generic classification system and gives us his own version, at the outset of his book, in order to use this to think about the various problems of poetics. As we shall soon see, Aristotle's generic classification system, despite some misleading appearances, can be made to fit Plato's in its entirety. The misleading appearances reside simply in the fact that Aristotle, for reasons that can be easily explained, does not use the same words as Plato to describe similar phenomena. A shift in accent has taken place from one thinker to the other. While the fundamental question Plato attempts to answer in book 3 of the *Republic* concerns above all *lexis* and diegesis (which forms of *lexis* are available to poets who wish to tell a story, to create a diegesis), the question Aristotle addresses is entirely different in nature. He comes at the issue by way of what we might call 'artistic imitation (or representation)' or 'poetic imitation (or representation)' in general (in the very specific sense in which we say that art 'imitates' or 'represents' reality). The problem is that the Greek word for designating this reality is *mimēsis*, a polysemic word par excellence, as we saw with Plato. But this shouldn't surprise us, because the exact same situation holds in English, where the two most important equivalents used to render the meaning of the word mimesis[20] are 'imitation' and 'representation.'[21] Isn't Plato's mimesis the same as what we in English describe as 'theatrical (or staged) representation (or imitation)'? And, as far as Aristotle is concerned, doesn't Aristotelian Mimesis correspond, on another level, to what we denote with the expression 'poetic representation (or imitation)'? This polysemy explains why the first figure in this chapter, 4.1, had the term

Figure 4.4

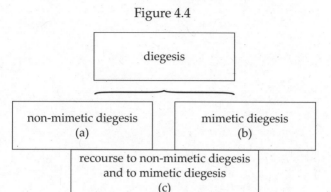

mimesis at its head: this was Aristotelian Mimesis (which I designate with a capital M to distinguish it from Platonic mimesis). Let's return then to that first figure, in order to complete it in light of our discussion thus far.

Let's look now at Aristotle's proposals concerning the two lower boxes (a and b) in figure 4.5 and identify what distinguishes them from Plato. Aristotle's ideas on this matter are found in a very brief text. Unfortunately, this text presents a major difficulty that it would be pointless to dwell upon here, because what is at issue in it is much more philological than narratological in nature.[22] In any event, no matter which interpretation we privilege here, the result will be about the

Figure 4.5

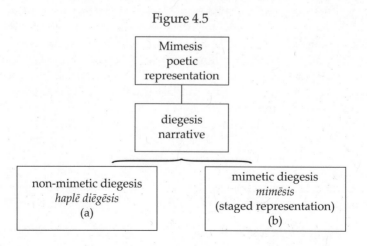

Figure 4.6

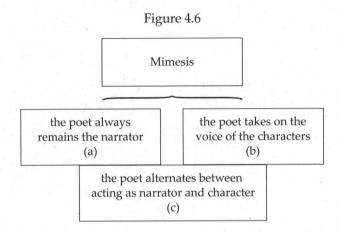

same for us. Here then is how Aristotle sees the problem of the modes of what he calls Mimesis, or 'representation' (1448a 19–23):

> A third difference in these arts is the manner in which one may represent each of these objects. For in representing the same objects by the same means it is possible to proceed either partly by narrative and partly by assuming a character other than your own – this is Homer's method – or by remaining yourself without any such change, or else to represent the characters as carrying out the whole action themselves.[23]

We thus have three genres that, in particular, correspond term for term to the three genres of Plato's diegesis: (1) 'partly by narrative and partly by assuming a character other than your own': this is Plato's *diēgēsis di'amphoterōn*, which consists of resorting to the two other forms (Aristotle, moreover, remarks that this was Homer's method, which Plato had also said in book 3); (2) 'or by remaining yourself without any such change': this, in Platonic terms, is *haplē diēgēsis* – the narrator remains the narrator and refuses to become on occasion another character by imitating that character, refuses all recourse to mimesis – in the Platonic sense of the term, of course; and (3) 'or else represent the characters as carrying out the whole action themselves': in resorting, in this case, to Platonic mimesis alone, to mimetic diegesis, wherein the actors have a role to play ('carrying out the whole action themselves') in recounting the story. Hence figure 4.6, which compares favourably with figure 4.2 and whose lower part (boxes a, b, and c) is even superimposed on it.

Figure 4.7

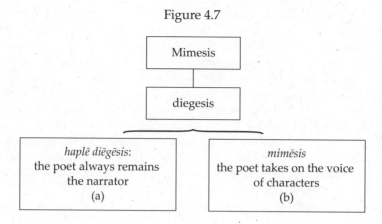

We can now carry out an initial fusion of Plato's and Aristotle's ideas. We thus obtain a new figure 4.7, that functions like an echo of the 'representation' (this word truly is polysemic!) we made in figure 4.1, whose goal was to join the two Ancients' systems before proceeding to a case study.

This fusion can be made the product of an even more perfect communion. But before carrying out any new operation, we must solve a problem arising from the different uses to which Plato and Aristotle put the word diegesis. For Plato, this word designates, as we have seen, a 'family of genres,' but for Aristotle it is a lone genre. Indeed, for Aristotle it is only when poets act as narrators (either constantly – box a of figures 4.6 and 4.7 – or intermittently – box c of figure 4.6) that we can claim the category diegesis to be present. This way of posing the question, however, puts it in a false light from the outset, because there can never be a question of 'claiming' whenever the axiology of Aristotle's ideas on the subject is concerned. Because, at bottom, the strict question of narrativity (in the sense I've used this word until now) is completely secondary in Aristotle. This is quite apparent in the way he places Mimesis at the head of his theoretical system and in the way he isn't affected, on this topic, by Plato, who sees the phenomenon from a very different perspective. What Plato calls *haplē diēgēsis* Aristotle simply calls, without any spirit of opposition or emotion (there is no hint of this), diegesis. What could be more normal? What could be more normal than not to feel the need to qualify as *haplē*, or simple, a phenomenon that knows no other form? For Aristotle, diegesis is the work of the *apangellonta*, of the narrator. When this narrator expresses itself, its product is 'diegetic' (which may explain why diegesis is present only when the narrator is present, whether constantly, in a, or intermittently, in c). The eventual 'dieget-icity' or not of a literary text is not one of the main concerns of the *Poetics*, because Aristotle's argument is located on another level. He only pays lip service to the concept – the word diegesis or one of its derivatives[24] appears on only five timid occasions in a book dozens of pages long (twenty-six chapters, some of them admittedly quite short). Moreover, his necessary equivalence between diegesis and *apangellonta*, as we said above, probably explains why we have, since this date, traditionally contrasted dramatic and narrative genres, thereby excluding theatre from the field of 'narrative' because it has no narrator,[25] no real *apangellonta*.

Despite this fact, it remains possible to carry out a true fusion of the hypotheses of these two precursors of narratology. This is what I propose to do in figure 4.8, which, let us hope, reconciles in practice the ideas of two philosophers whose narratological thought can be seen as in no way contradictory.

This figure, let us hope, clarifies the question of the relationships to establish between two categories of such importance in narratology, diegesis and mimesis. Above all, it makes it possible to gain an overall view of a series of proposals that are of fundamental importance to anyone interested in the underlying problems posed by the manner in which the narrable can be transmitted. At the same time, this figure does not, of course, resolve every problem, and it raises a number of questions. But it makes it possible to look at the necessary distinction between staged and textual narrative from a different perspective, as the following chapter will attempt to put into practice.

Figure 4.8

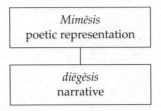

1. non-mimetic diegesis	1. mimetic diegesis
2. *haplē diēgēsis*	2. *mimēsis*
3. *diēgēsis aneu mimēseōs*	3. *diēgēsis dia mimēseōs*
4. narrative without imitation-personification	4. narrative told through imitation-personification
5. the poet always remains the NARRATOR	5. the poet takes on the voice of CHARACTERS
6. dithyramb	6. tragedy and comedy

1. combination of non-mimetic diegesis and mimetic diegesis
2. *haplē diēgēsis* + mimesis
3. *diēgēsis di'amphoterōn*
4. narrative combining both forms
5. the poet alternates between acting as a NARRATOR and as a CHARACTER
6. epic

Key: 1, new English term proposed for Platonic categories; 2 and 3, the textual form of these categories in Plato; 4, near-literal translation of 3; 5, definition of the mode as found in Aristotle; and 6, the genre used in artistic practice.

5 Textual Narrative and Staged Narrative

… Dramatic poetry, for both Plato and Aristotle, was a perfect example of effacing the author.

Jean Lallot, *'La "Mimésis" selon Aristote,'* 15

Originally, then, two basic modes of narrative communication existed. The first was non-mimetic diegesis, which necessarily brought the services of a narrator into play. In a setting like Ancient Greece, where textual narrative did not have the importance it has today, this mode was the one inevitably chosen by poets who, by refusing imitation and the personification of their fiction's characters (Plato's *mimēsis*), were themselves obliged to recount the story they were telling (Plato's *apangelia*). They were this story's sole teller, its sole narrator (Aristotle's *apangellonta*) for its entire duration. The second mode was mimetic diegesis, which, on the contrary, brought 'imitators' into play (Plato's *mimēsis*): characters who acted out the story (Aristotle's *prattontas*), stage actors who are so adept, precisely, at passing for narrators. Of course, there is a third mode, one that arises when the narrator resorts, within a single work, within a single performance (and the work was always a performance, even in the case of non-mimetic diegesis, which is something we should not forget), to each of these two modes: a third way that brings into play both a narrator (the *apangellonta*) and characters (the *prattontas*), even if, in some cases, this required both a narrator and the characters to coexist under the same 'hat.' Here the bard or rhapsode, like a veritable one-man band, 'speaks in person' (Plato, *Republic* 393a) rather than remaining himself and speaking for himself (Plato, *Republic* 393c and Aristotle, *Poetics* 1448a19). As Plato demonstrates quite well at the beginning of book 3 of the *Republic*, the line between mimetic and non-mimetic diegesis, from a Platonic perspective, was very easy to cross during this period. It was enough for a poet of the non-mimetic school suddenly to quote the speech of one of the characters in his story, as if these characters had spoken the words themselves, rather than reporting it through indirect discourse, for him to engage all at once with the other system, that of mimetic diegesis. It was enough, then, in order to change systems at least momentarily, for a single 'I' spoken during the performance not to refer to the primary story-telling agent, the poet himself, for this breach to succeed in introducing Plato's famous mimesis, mimetic diegesis, into a diegesis that had hitherto been non-mimetic.

Is it then the case, and this is the question we must now confront, that all textual narrators, which normally operate within a non-mimetic system, can enter into the realm of mimesis, of mimetic diegesis, simply by adding a colon and quotation marks to their story? Not in the least. Because, unlike the bard or the rhapsode, the textual narrator, *while narrating*, is not at the same time *giving a dramatic performance*. The term mimesis has to be understood in its true sense: when he formulated his critique of Homer, Plato was not thinking, premonitorily, of those who might eventually read the *Odyssey* in the form of a book; he was thinking of those hundreds of young Greeks who attended performed declamations of the story. He wanted to avoid exposing them to storytellers who allowed themselves to resort to imitation (or, at least, to imitating vile and base people and situations). Mimesis, mimetic diegesis, is *imitation*, it is *personification* – there, in front of you on the stage (or wherever the story was acted out), on the part of the poet or his assistants. The most concentrated form of mimesis was comedy and tragedy – that is, the theatre. Today's textual narrator may well want to imitate this mode by opening up some quotation marks, but this is not enough. What is required of it, rather, is to *open its mouth*, in order to succeed in speaking in person – because, basically, this narrator isn't imitating, it's *quoting*, purely and simply. Gérard Genette expressed this quite well when he wrote that imitation in verbal narrative is 'perfectly illusory,' 'for this sole and sufficient reason, that narration, both verbal and written, pertains to language, and language signifies without imitating.'[1] As astounding as it may seem at first sight, a work that contains such radically mimetic sections as the *Odyssey* is entirely denied the status of mimetic diegesis *in the version found on our library shelves*, because it does not have the same *expressive substance* as the

Odyssey to which Plato was referring. This is why it is important to make the distinction, as we will throughout this book, between a play in the form of a book and the same play as it is staged. This is a position that has been adopted, moreover, by theoreticians of the theatre, although only fairly recently.[2] On the one hand, a written account, a *textual narrative*, is limited to non-mimetic diegesis alone, while on the other *staged narrative* is capable of giving rise to mimetic diegesis.

Naturally, since moving back and forth between mimetic and non-mimetic diegesis was common and easily negotiated in Plato's day, each influencing the other, we can assume that such a 'tradition' was not eliminated overnight. Indeed, at a time when Ancient Greece is no more than a distant memory, we have seen more than one textual narrator attempt to give 'his' – and in order to render the narrator both gender-neutral and non-anthropomorphic, I will henceforth refer to 'him' as 'it' – to give its necessarily non-mimetic diegesis (necessarily non-mimetic because it is textual) the airs of mimetic diegesis by concealing its role as a narrator (Plato 393a) and dissimulating its presence behind the presence of its fictional characters, leaving as few traces of its narrative activity as possible. In other words, by attempting to make us believe that, like the theatre, the story has been emancipated from any 'narrative voice,'[3] that the story has come to us directly without an intermediary such as the narrator. How does the narrator do this? By systematically resorting to the techniques Percy Lubbock has described as *showing*, while avoiding as much as possible those techniques associated, for the same author, with *telling*. The associations of these terms (positive in the case of the former, negative in the case of the latter) can immediately be ascertained in this commentary by Lubbock on Henry James's *The Awkward Age*:

> There is no insight into anybody's thought, no survey of the scene from a height, no resumption of the past in retrospect. The whole of the book passes *scenically* before the reader, and nothing is offered but the look and *the speech of the characters* on a series of chosen occasions. It might indeed be printed *as a play*; whatever is not dialogue is simply a kind of amplified *stage-direction*, adding to the *dialogue* the expressive effect which might be given it by *good acting*.[4]

Let us agree, then, that despite all their effort such works remain, it goes without saying, within the realm of non-mimetic diegesis alone. It remains no less true, however, that these works presuppose the existence of a narrator that is much more discreet than the sort that expresses itself in blow-by-blow fashion through *telling* or even, to adopt one of Genette's expressions, through *talking*.[5] By *showing*, the narrator attempts to attain a state of self-effacement in favour of its fictional characters, deciding not to take on all the possibilities at its disposal. This is a narrator that *acts as if* it isn't able to enter into the inner world of its characters (who are nonetheless, in a sense, its own creation), which acts as if it can't loom over the field of action or organize the elements of the story it is telling along a temporal order of its own choosing. A narrator that 'shows' the characters from without – something like the way theatre directors and filmmakers are obliged to work – and that, just like them, once again, doesn't hesitate to endow its characters, as much as possible, with speech.

The opposite approach can be found in the omniscient narrator which, as Otto Ludwig described over a century ago, 'is the absolute master of time and space ... It can think, it represents without being limited by any aspect of reality, it stages unhindered by physical impossibility; it has all the powers of nature and all the faculties of the mind.'[6] Thus, the narrator, as has been demonstrated many times over, can be present as a narrative agent to varying degrees. The more it intervenes 'personally' in the reality continuum of the fiction it is recounting, the less the world being narrated will appear to the reader as something autonomous and unmediated. On the contrary, all elements of this world will be perceived as emanating from this intermediary, from the intervention of this mediator of the narration, the narrator.

But, try as it might to efface itself and to deploy all the techniques of *showing* (foremost among them being the 'stage,' owing to the fact that the stage reveals only a very limited part of the narrator's manipulation of the world and of the objects being narrated),[7] this narrator is unable to call upon mimetic diegesis, a realm that is irredeemably closed to it. Its characters are not living beings, they exist 'only on paper,' as the expression goes. Even frantic recourse at every step of the narrative to that ultimate expression of showing, the quoting of speech supposedly pronounced by the characters (and which I propose to name, in keeping with the vocabulary introduced above, *quoting*), is not enough to admit the narrator into the realm of mimetic diegesis. The narrator can take its transitiveness and transparency to their limit all it likes, it will still be present, like a thin plastic sheet that renders an image in soft focus, or a translucent pane of glass, or a magnifying glass, according to the situation. Through an imperative of the text, the narrator will always be situated between the narratee and the world being narrated. And yet it is upon and through this plastic film, this pane of glass, this magnifying glass, which are the true focal planes of the work, that the elements of the world being narrated come to be inscribed and refracted, to be filtered by the narrator, which is necessarily limited to a process of trans-semiotization (it translates into words – into text to be precise – non-verbal events, gestures, attitudes, actions, etc.). Or, at the very least, the narrator is limited to a process of transcribing (it transfers into text that which, in the world being narrated, is presented as being verbal). Although the *story* being told may very well be more prominent than the discourse that makes me retain it, it is first and foremost a story that is, precisely, *told*.

At this stage of our discussion, it is impossible not to think of the work of the linguist Émile Benveniste, who proposed a typology that commands our attention here.[8] Benveniste sought, above all, to identify the degree of subjectivity in language (and not necessarily in narratives), to identify the subjectivity of the agent responsible for linguistic enunciation. He set himself the task of understanding how this agent marked (or didn't mark) its *énoncés* with its presence (meaning its presence as a subject, with its subjectivity). Benveniste proposed, in keeping with the way purely linguistic and grammatical units (the deictic 'shifters')[9] function, that we categorize speech acts as 'belonging to one or another of two distinct sub-groups,'[10] 'story' and 'discourse.' *Énoncés* of the former category are *story énoncés*. These are characterized by the absence, on the level of the linguistic and grammatical units in question, of traces or marks (the marks of *énoncé*) of the agent that has produced and offered up these *énoncés*. This makes possible the preeminence of *what* is said (in the sense of the matter being discussed, of what is being talked about) over *who* is saying it. This is the preeminence of the *énoncé* over the enunciation and, therefore, over the enunciator. On the other hand, those *énoncés* that are classified as 'discourse' are *discourse énoncés*. This category presupposes that the speaker, the enunciator, appropriates language's formal devices and marks his or her *énoncés* with his presence, thereby leaving as much or even more room for his or her own subjectivity (as an enunciator) than for the question of what is being related. Discourse *énoncés* are held in place by shifters, whose most visible kind is, precisely, 'I.' From the moment an *énoncé* is braced with an 'I,' as Émile Benveniste remarks, 'a human experience is restored and reveals the linguistic instrument behind it.'[11] 'I,' by virtue of its *self-referentiality*, its reflexiveness, can only refer to the very person who utters it, to the enunciator him- or herself: 'This term can only be identified as what we have called elsewhere a discursive agent which refers only to reality.'[12]

Benveniste's intuitive analysis has enjoyed great success, and much effort has been expended since to discover other ways in which subjectivity is inscribed upon language. Genette, who was probably the first to take up this question, opened new lines of enquiry by re-examining a passage from Balzac's *Gambara* that Benveniste had offered as an example of 'pure' story, as a concentrated expression of a story *énoncé* that appeared to be free of any discursive patronage.

In order to demonstrate his ideas, Genette had to go beyond the level of grammatical units alone and take into account the narrative aspect of the text in question. He was thus able to show that some segments of this passage from *Gambara* demonstrate a concerted quality (a discursive quality) of narration – how some elements of this text reveal and attest to the presence, beyond the story itself, if not of an enunciator, at least of some agent responsible for organizing the narrative signifiers and capable, for example, of passing judgment on the diegetic universe that constituted the story that was produced.[13] Genette was thus able to conclude that 'the essence of [story] and of discourse ... are almost never found in a pure state in any text ... There is almost always a certain proportion of story in the discourse and an element of discourse in the story.'[14]

On a more strictly linguistic level, the same situation prevailed until quite recently, culminating in Catherine Kerbrat-Orecchioni's remark that 'every assertion carries the mark of the person who enunciates it.'[15] Kerbrat-Orecchioni concludes that 'if we sift through the entire vocabulary, we are forced to conclude that very few words escape the shattering of objectivity.'[16] Indeed, wherever there is speech, *someone*, whether we like it or not, is doing the speaking. Speech, whenever it is the least organized, appears always and already as being produced by some speaker or another (whether this speaker is visible or not), and it will always be a relatively easy task to identify the illocutionary source of the *énoncé* with some degree of precision (or at least to name this source, to give it a name of its own).

This is trans-semiotization, that is plain to see! And that is what, in the end, Kerbrat-Orecchioni argues when she says that 'as soon as a verbal object is converted into a non-verbal object the constitutive heteromorphism of these two kinds of reality creates, without fail, a crevice within which, more or less surreptitiously, linguistic subjectivity will insinuate itself.'[17]

It would also be more productive to view Benveniste's categories as two poles of attraction, towards one or the other of which certain kinds of linguistic and/or narrative production will tend. This would help mitigate the dichotomy of his typology. To do this, we need only adopt an old idea of Tzvetan Todorov's, using the same words – 'story' and 'discourse' – but in a manner closer to common usage than they assume in Benveniste's system. Like Todorov, then, we could adopt the view that 'a work of literature has two qualities: it is simultaneously a story and discourse.'[18] It thus becomes possible to abandon any inclination to force 'all documented forms of discursive production into two distinct sub-groups,'[19] which rapidly begins to seem a fruitless exercise. This, I believe, is a more useful approach to identifying and precisely defining the various modes of narrative, the various systems of narrative communication. In order to do this, we must first come to see narrative, all narrative, as a two-sided phenomenon.

A narrative work (a film, a novel, or another work) would thus be the result of a tension between two poles: on the one hand, the diegetic universe (the story told), and on the other, the agent that organizes this world (the storyteller). All narratives would thus be modulated by these two poles and would, by means of this modulation, become the possible site for privileging one of these two poles over the other. Every narrative is simultaneously a discourse (the discourse of the storyteller) and a story (the story told). When the narrative privileges the story told, it moves towards the side of the story, and when it privileges the storyteller, it moves towards the side of discourse. A narrative is story (more so than it is discourse) when it gives greater prominence to the story told, and it is discourse (more so than it is story) when, on the contrary, it gives greater prominence to the storyteller. In the first case, Benveniste remarks, 'the events are set forth chronologically, as they occurred. No one speaks here; the events seem to narrate themselves.'[20] In the second case, 'the speaker [the narrator, the narrative agent responsible for organizing the narrative] appropriates the language's formal devices [the devices for communicating the narrative] and ... enunciates its status as the speaker [as the narrator].'[21] We thus arrive at the schema depicted in figure 5.1.

Let's look again at Benveniste. He commented that 'events seem to narrate themselves.' Reading this, you might think you were reading Lubbock: 'The story appears to tell itself.'[22] Benveniste is concerned with the narrative énoncé, with the 'story,' while Lubbock is concerned with the *showing* of the textual 'stage.' But we have to be careful not to

Figure 5.1

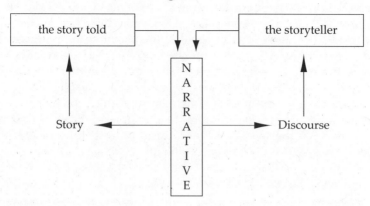

confuse the two: while Benveniste is concerned above all with *enuncia-tion*, and thus takes into account those linguistic elements employed by the *enunciator*, Lubbock sees things completely differently. For him, what counts is *narration*. And he analyses a text by the way in which the elements of the story told in it are presented by the *narrator*.

We have thus seen, to this point, three different ways of looking at the problem of the subjectivity of the narrative agent. These three different positions are those of Plato, Lubbock, and of the 'pair' Benveniste/Genette. For Plato, the 'I' enunciated by the poet should refer to himself alone: there should be no imitation, no assuming of characters. The poet, as a narrator, should not conceal his identity, should not resort to *quoting*, which would result in camouflaging himself as a subject. Please excuse this little rhyme: we might say, for Plato, that 'if you want the vote, you mustn't quote.' It would seem that a poet could, if absolutely necessary, call upon what might, in a verbal narrative, be the equivalent of Lubbock's *showing*, which does not involve dialogue (we mustn't forget, however, that *showing* remains a category applicable most of all to textual narratives). The poet can camouflage his presence – through *showing* – but not his identity – through *quoting*. But this privileged field of action will always be the equivalent of the verbal quality of Lubbock's *telling* and Genette's *talking*, which are a thousand miles from the mimetic.[23] What dooms Plato, as Jean Lallot has well described, is the narrative within which 'the poet conceals his identity … in order to liken himself to someone else … whom he instals in the work as an enunciating subject distinct from himself.'[24]

Lubbock, unlike Plato, privileges our *quoting*, which is one of the forms (he doesn't distinguish among them) of his *showing*.[25] Here it is a question of the narrator concealing itself, concealing its presence (and thus its identity as well) as an agent of the narrative's communication (and this must cause Plato to turn over in his grave). Lubbock does not address the speaker who is able to say 'I' and to proffer other deictic forms ('here,' 'now,' 'my,' 'yesterday,' etc.), whose result would be to reveal the composed aspect of its discourse. Rather, the narrator dormant within that speaker is 'summoned' to present the story told as if this narrator, as the speaker's agent, was not present. (In many cases, although not necessarily, this can automatically have the effect of limiting the number of deictic *énoncés* that can be assigned to a speaker.)[26] In any event, the narrator does not have the 'right' to resort to *telling* nor, of course, to *talking*: here the emphasis is on the *objectivity* of the story told rather than on the *subjectivity* of the storyteller, and thus on *quoting* and *showing*.

Next comes the 'pair' Benveniste/Genette. The former, in a non-normative analysis, looks at the matter from the simple point of view of the subjectivity of language. This is an approach that would soon be shared by Genette, who dedicated himself to demonstrating that the narrator's subjectivity, just like that of the enunciator, can find shelter in (and insinuate itself into) many places, including some where we wouldn't expect to find it. Here, however, we must be careful to distinguish between *enunciator* and *narrator*. Benveniste's and Genette's ideas, when they are applied only to the linguistic substratum (shifters, verb tenses, etc.), address only the subjectivity of the enunciator as a linguistic enunciator. They are not the least concerned with the enunciator's possible role as a narrator. From this we must conclude that, if enunciations have subjectivity, so too do narratives, and that both of them leave traces of the subjectivity that is proper to them. And it would be impossible, without scrupulously transposing and rigorously adapting this system, to attempt to discover the equivalent of these enunciating marks in non-linguistic phenomena such as those that lie at the root of theatrical or cinematic 'language,' even when these are deployed for narrative purposes.

In another sense, an analysis concerned more with the enunciator as a narrator (an analysis found more in Genette but that can also be deduced from Lubbock's remarks), which is to say as a storyteller, is easily transposed onto any form of narrative communication, linguistic or otherwise: theatre, cinema, graphic novels, etc. We could say, therefore, that the 'subjectivity' at the root of the *énoncé* has left *narrative marks* in the text (and not *marks of enunciation*). When, in textual narrative, the narrator uses the techniques of *showing*, it leaves behind very few narrative marks, allowing the story told to take precedence over the storyteller itself. When a textual narrator summarizes, which, as Jaap Lintvelt describes, 'sums up events and speech, giving only an overview,'[27] it places itself at the front of the stage as the person manipulating the story told. As a result, it produces a 'powerful condensation [that] hinders the formation of a mental image of the story,'[28] and thus engages in textual *telling* (and possibly *talking*) rather than in *showing*. The same thing occurs when the narrator, by resorting to iteration, which attempts to synthesize in a single *énoncé* several aspects of the same event, 'destroys the "real" progress of the story and replaces it with an abstract one,' in Danièle Chatelain's formulation.[29] This highlights the way one would with a coloured marker, like a superimposition on the text, a narrative segment that no longer has any semblance of autonomy or immediacy. *Showing* (and, of course, *quoting*) is to the story *énoncé* as categorized by Benveniste what *telling* (and thus *talking*) is to the discourse *énoncé*.

Finally, then, what we are faced with, and what the discussion in this chapter has served to demonstrate, are two fundamental modes of narrative communication: mimetic and non-mimetic diegesis. The latter is achieved through the agency of a narrator and the former through the agency of characters depicting the action. It would thus seem,[30] for the purposes of our discussion, that there exist textual narrative on the one hand and staged narrative on the other. Within the former, various forms, *from talking to quoting*, govern the degree of visibility of a figure present in non-mimetic diegesis alone, that textual being par excellence that is the narrator. In the other, more animated form of diegesis, staged narrative, this narrator disappears and is replaced by characters depicting the action – real, flesh-and-blood characters.

But are things that simple? If, within textual narrative, the narrator is the reverse image of the author, that great extra-textual being responsible for the text, can we be certain that there is no true equivalent of the narrator in staged narrative? Wouldn't it be worthwhile, precisely, to view the theatrical text, whether it be written or staged, as also containing a narrative agent that would be, in this case, the reverse, intra-textual image of that extra-textual agent that is the playwright? This is the question we will attempt to answer in the following chapter.

6 Narration and Monstration

These difficulties are amplified by a second problem, that of identifying the narrative agent. For while in literature this matter is relatively straightforward, this is far from true in the cinema, where critics waver between prenotions of the author and of collective responsibility, without developing or reworking the concept of the narrator.

Jean-Paul Simon and Marc Vernet, 'Avant-propos,' *Communications* 38: 2

If we were to be fairly strict about the matter, neither of the dual uses to which the word 'narrative' is put, as given earlier in this book,[1] would hold. The *Oxford English Dictionary* tells us that 'narration' is 'the action of relating or recounting; a story, narrative, account' and that to 'narrate' is to 'relate, recount, give an account of.' 'Narrative' itself is defined as 'an account or narration; a history, tale, story or recital.' The French *Robert* dictionary adds: 'A verbal or written account.'[2] But this degree of rigour gets us nowhere. After all, the development of a language and its vocabulary is something that dictionaries can only document after the fact. In any event, what purpose is served by excluding cinema, which is neither a verbal nor a written account, from the category of narrative? Even Gérard Genette, who, as I mentioned earlier, has his own good reasons for excluding film from narrative, has left the door ajar, if not completely open. How indeed can we exclude a phenomenon like the cinema from a category such as narrative when common sense tells us straight off and most forcefully that it should be included, from its very beginnings? In this sense, lexical rigour can take us far – too far, because we might be led to exclude even written (or textual) accounts from the category of narrative. This is clearer in

French than in English; in French, 'narrative' is *récit*, a word which comes from *réciter*, a verb that has entered into English – to recite: 'to utter aloud ... to repeat to an audience from memory.' Thus by its very nature the written account contravenes both principles of the word 're-cite': to utter *aloud* and to repeat *from memory*. Hence the importance of the viewpoint, which we can only wish were more widespread, which holds that the terms 'story' and 'narrative' should be understood as one and the same thing: *any message through which a story is communicated, whatever that story may be, must by rights be considered a narrative.*

Moreover, viewing these two entities, story and narrative, as two facets of the same phenomenon[3] yields convincing results and makes it easier to resolve age-old problems that, as we've seen, date back as far as Plato and Aristotle. This approach was already explicitly present in some of the preceding chapters of this book and will continue to be the focus here. It will lead me to establish new parallels between the various possible manifestations and materializations of narrative (text, stage, film). I will thus apply to theatre and cinema the same sort of 'narratological treatment' to which, until recently, only textual narrative had been 'subjected.' Through this relatively comparative approach, I will attempt to identify, and this is a controversial topic, the (necessarily 'narratorial') agents of staged and film narrative; in other words, try to determine if there exists some theatrical or filmic equivalent of the great textual narrator. We will also take the opportunity to enquire into the ways in which staged and film narratives are delivered and attempt to identify whatever might be specific about these forms of narrative with respect to textual narration.

Naturally, it will be difficult adequately to pose the question of the narrative agents of staged and/or film narrative, for the simple reason that there are still a thousand controversies swirling around the textual narrator.[4] First, a little history. The 'first generation' of modern-day narratologists (here I include people like Gérard Genette and Tzvetan Todorov, but also, for example, Wayne C. Booth) advanced narrative science by identifying different kinds of narrative agents, and above all by distinguishing among them. These different kinds, although they were rather few in number, enabled us to become aware of how narrative is structured into various strata or layers. Even if there are very few narratives that employ an unrestricted 'mise en abîme' structure of 'the story of x telling the story of y telling the story of z' variety, *ad nauseam*, it is no less true that any narrative configuration sets into play a series of discursive agents (composed of x number of individuals, where x is not necessarily greater than two). The age-old question of 'Who speaks?' is thus, to my mind, a question of 'Who, of the various narrative agents, is speaking at this precise moment of the narrative?' rather than simply 'Who is speaking in a narrative?' And this because any sentence (or part of a sentence) in a textual narrative can be produced, for example, by a character speaking about (and quoting) another character, or by a character alone (acting out events, let's say), or by a narrator-character, or, yet again, by a narrator. All this without considering the fact that, in the final analysis, any sentence can in some sense be ascribed to the author.

Narratology began to make headway by practising a form of discrimination: all of Genette's work, for example, rests on such discrimination. In the first place, his approach discriminates, in theory at least, between intra-textual agents (narrators, characters, etc.) and extra-textual agents (the author, for example). This is the *implicit* principle behind his 'Narrative Discourse: An Essay In Method,'[5] but it is a principle that has probably suffered from not being, precisely, *made explicit*. Hence the surprise of a 'second generation' narratologist who discovers the following incongruous list of narrators in this fundamental text: Sharazad (the *Arabian Nights*); C. (*Jean de Santeuil*); Odysseus (books 9 through 12 of the *Odyssey*); Marcel (*In Search of Lost Time*); Gil Blas (*Gil Blas*); and Homer (the *Odyssey*).[6] A television game-show host would say, 'Who is the odd man out?' while a specialist in psychometrics would ask 'Which element in this series does not conform to the classification criteria adopted?' The first clue: only one of these so-called narrators has himself, the lucky man, *actually* 'taken a trip.' And it is not Odysseus but … his 'father'! In fact, Homer is the odd man out in this list of narrators. He is the only extra-textual *'flesh-and-blood' being* in this assembly of intra-textual *paper beings*, all of whom belong to the same series, even if they may have been modelled on (and take their name from) real extra-textual prototypes.

The problem that Genette ran up against, and which induced him to invite a 'real being' into his series, is the product of an essential characteristic of textual narrative. This narrative can present itself, can unfold, can come to the reader *without* the apparent help of a narrator that is *explicit* and *identified as such*. This is the case of the *Odyssey*. Who speaks, or who appears to speak, in the *Arabian Nights*? Shahrazad.[7] In *In Search of Lost Time*? Marcel (and not, at this level, Marcel Proust). But in the *Odyssey*? No one with a name. And this is where Genette slipped up (although he himself would probably not look at it this way), leading him to fill in the blank with the name of the author. This is a path we must absolutely avoid taking, at least as far as the cinema is concerned. In a medium in which most narratives are delivered without the mediation of an explicit narrator who is identified as such (and this is the case in the cinema), what good would a theory be if one of its foundational principles brought us – and this would be a 'mortal' sin – to see author and narrator as one and the same? Or if – and this time, perhaps, it would only be a 'venial' sin, but one every bit as disagreeable as the former – it called the former by the latter's name (even if by so doing it suggested that the two are distinguishable?)[8] Where would it all end, narratologically speaking, if we were to decree from the start that the narrator of *The Birth of a Nation* is called David Wark Griffith, or the narrator of *Jules et Jim* François Truffaut? What would be the use of a science that could double so easily as a mere *Dictionary of Filmmakers?*

Can a narratological theory of textual narrative accommodate, any more than its 'sibling' film narrative, such an intrusion of the author into its midst? I don't believe it can. The author might well ornament his text with these intrusions, but he or she has no place, or should have no place, in narratological theory – except, when all is said and done, as the *final agent* (and now is the time to state this). Indeed, it seems to me that narratology can develop in only one direction: that of the greatest possible disembodiment (and 'de-anthropomorphization') of the narrative's agents. It is just as important today as it was some time ago for characters to acknowledge that the textual narrator (*all* textual narrators) also exists, just like the characters, 'only on paper.' In this light, I would like to make two suggestions, which I will only justify and defend later on.[9] First, that we postulate, in the case of textual narratives without a narrator that is explicit and identified as such (books 9 to 12 of the *Odyssey*, for example), the existence of a narrative agent that is thoroughly grounded (narratologically speaking), an implicit 'narrator' with *no proper name* (and to which we must not ascribe the author's name). Second, that we postulate the existence (narratological, of course) of such an agent even in cases where there are, indisputably, one or more explicit narrators identified as such and bearing a proper name. This is the case with books 9 to 12 of the *Odyssey*, a work that is truly of great use to us! For, while Genette believes that there is a narrator with no name operating in the other books of this work (a narrator to whom he has resolved to give the author's name), it is difficult to see how this agent (for Genette, Homer; for us, the implicit narrator)[10] would become indistinct at the moment when one of his characters

Figure 6.1 *Jules et Jim*, François Truffaut, 1962 [Still] (Cinémathèque québécoise)

(Odysseus), taking the stage in books 9 to 12, becomes in turn, and for quite a long section of the book, a kind of narrator. Unless, but this is not tenable, we take the view that any explicit narrator, such as the one Genette calls Homer (or even any delegated narrator, as I will henceforth term an explicit narrator identified as such), only becomes indistinct and loses its function when an agent of a lower level begins to tell some story or another within the other's discourse ... In fact we must acknowledge (and we'll see later on the essential reasons for such a position) that when one agent recounts (level one) that an agent is recounting (level two) that another agent is recounting (level three), then the narrative voice of the final agent is modulated (and controlled and directed) by the second agent, whose voice is modulated by the first. We must also acknowledge that the second agent, coming after the first, is unable to establish its autonomy in relation to the first, which comes before. If I say: 'Peter says: "This is my bedroom,"' not only is 'Peter' (the Peter who is speaking), despite his necessary referential existence, a creation of my discourse (a creation I control entirely), but, in addition, his own discourse is, first and foremost, a product of my discourse.

What is needed, therefore, is first of all to attribute primary responsibility for a narrative's entire content to an implicit agent, which we will henceforth call the 'underlying narrator.' Second, to decree that all narratives, even those that appear to be the work of delegated narrators[11] alone (narrators who are explicit and identified as such, such as Odysseus in books 9 to 12 of the Odyssey, Marcel in In Search of Lost Time, and Meurseault in The Stranger), remain the responsibility of this primary agent we have called the 'underlying narrator.' We might, furthermore, consider this underlying narrator to be the intra-textual image of the real and concrete author, whom we must relegate to the sidelines of the text and forbid from entering into narratology. All narratives, let me repeat ... all narratives, whatever the nature of their semiotic vehicle or, consequently, of the means of expression by which we receive them. It would be worthwhile, in fact, to take the view that all narratives, for example staged or film rather than textual, are 'distilled' by a primary 'enunciator' that can be compared to the figure we identified in the case of textual narrative as the underlying narrator.

Let's turn our attention, then, to the theatre, and try to see what exactly it is about the underlying agent that will make it, there as well, responsible for communicating the story. It is urgent that we address these issues there, on the stage, where it remains possible (at least this is often the case) to show near-equivalents of those explicit narrators the delegated agents, the delegated narrators, who have *much less power* than is commonly believed. Indeed, many plays present their discourse through the figure of a 'reciter,' an 'announcer,' or a 'narrator' who is present on the stage – who thus speaks and acts – or who is relegated to the wings – who speaks, therefore, but does not act – whence he makes his (off-stage) voice heard.

As a 'master of ceremonies,' this figure's role gives it a stature seemingly equivalent to that of the explicit narrator identified as such in textual narrative. It is clear, therefore, that some dramatic activities are prompted by this agent and can be ascribed to it. This is the case, for example, when this agent dictates to the characters – there, during the play, in front of the audience – which gestures they should use. Or when he or she begins to recount, verbally, some story – a different story, because it is included in the original one. It remains no less true, however, that this figure is the product of another agent's discourse (like Odysseus when narrating, or Sharazad, Marcel, and Meurseault) – the product of a kind of *underlying stage 'narrator'* that is responsible, narratologically speaking, for the entire theatrical discourse seen on the stage.

As far as the theatre is concerned, it is entirely to our advantage to identify (and thus to name)[12] this intra-textual agent, which is the *intra-muros* image of the real, extra-textual agent who produced the discourse. This agent will prove to be a more complex phenomenon than is the case in textual narrative. Indeed in textual narrative it is rare for the agent producing the narrative to be collective, or multiple, while in the theatre we have to take into account, in addition to the original author, the person adapting the play, the stage director, as well as, we must realize, the actors and everyone else (from the production manager to the lighting designer) who has some responsibility for the form of the always-in-the-process-of-being-made narrative found in the theatre. Moreover, it is perhaps more urgent in the theatre to acknowledge, identify, and name this underlying organizing agent, because this agent is collective, and thus more fleeting, and because it possesses, for this very reason, much less well-defined borders. For on-stage events are presented in a certain manner and, despite appearances, do not tell themselves. There is an action of communicating the narrative and an agent that performs this action. The role of this agent is of course not identical to that of the textual narrator, but we must succeed in isolating and identifying this agent. This is all the more true when we consider that numerous theoreticians of

the theatre have felt the need for a central figure to which they can ascribe responsibility (narratological, of course) for various aspects of
the performance. It is to this 'stage-manager,' this 'puppeteer'[13] that
we can ascribe, for example, the 'point of view' from which the action
is presented – a point of view that will often not necessarily correspond with the point of view the original author may have inscribed
in his or her text. Each new performance of the work (or at least each
new production) is liable to create a new 'text.' *Tartuffe*'s Marianne is
not really the same character when she is played by a sparkling actress instead of one more restrained. A staged narrative's text is fleeting and transient and bears the stamp of its circumstances. Even a
sparkling actress cannot always match her own performances. The *actors*, then (a category in which I include all those who have a hand in
the work's production, who *interpret* it – in French, I would say its *in-
terprètes*), literally carry out the work of *interpretation*.

What we must do then is to postulate the existence in the theatre of
what Patrice Pavis calls a 'collective subject of enunciation, somewhat
like the narrator in the novel,'[14] an '"authorial" subject [that] is difficult
to identify'[15] – a kind of underlying 'dramatic narrator,' a 'great representer,' we might say, to create a parallel with Albert Laffay's 'great
image-maker' in film. A 'representer' rather than a narrator, because
representation is not the same as narration. For, while we might acknowledge the usefulness of the expression 'staged narrative,' it is essential to acknowledge that the discourse of the stage is not delivered in
the same way as textual narrative. Because while narration is present
every time a character on stage speaks in order to recount, tell, or narrate, the overall discourse (within which this speech is, moreover, the
story told) is not performed the same way – verbally – as this speech itself. Hence our recourse to the term 'representation' to identify the mode
of communicating narrative in a staged performance, a move that is
somewhat desperate, given the inadequacy of this term (something even
theatre specialists acknowledge) for fully accounting for this phenomenon.[16] This is why I once suggested[17] the systematic use of the term
'monstration,' which is already in use[18] (it's even in the *Oxford* English
and French *Robert* dictionaries!). Monstration is beginning to take hold
as a way to describe and identify this mode of communicating a story,[19]
which consists of *showing* characters (in English, monstrance) who *act
out* rather than *tell* the vicissitudes to which they are subjected. Monstration could thus be used to replace the term 'representation,' which is too
specific, too compromised, and far too polysemic. Today the choice of

the term 'monstration' seems to me even more fortuitous, because it made it possible for me to invent the noun 'monstrator,' which I propose to use here again to designate and singularize the theoretical entity, the equivalent of the *underlying narrator* in textual narrative, that is responsible for communicating staged narrative.

We should also understand 'staged narrative' exclusively as 'a narrative communicated by the performance of characters who act it out,' which quickly excludes the written play. Written plays, because of their essentially textual nature, are in no way whatsoever part of the world of monstration (which doesn't prevent them, however, from being perhaps the most accomplished examples of textual *showing*) and are not the product of a monstrator. For we must make a strict distinction between the different media a 'composition' can adopt. Here the book, there the stage. On the one hand, a continuum of written words, removed from the real presence of any speaker, and on the other a continuum of spoken words, enunciated by 'flesh-and-blood' speakers and inscribed onto a 'polyphony of information.' Thus, while it is true, as Ubersfeld remarks, that in the space of the theatre, in which the characters are present, the 'text [of a play] and [its] performance differ the most and the specificity of the theatrical text and the theatrical practice is most obvious,'[20] it is no less true that the same difference prevails, de facto, between textual narrative and staged narrative.

This radical distinction between the written and the performed play is of primordial importance. Because this distinction, if we apply it thoroughly, as I argued in an earlier chapter of this book, justifies adapting the principles of Plato and Aristotle to the new reality of a situation that, unlike their own, grants a (marvellous) place to that inert and frozen object that is the narrative of a book, which, for good reason, the Ancients never really took into account. Just as, in their day, what was not truly a play (a rhapsody, an epic poem, etc.) was nevertheless a public performance and, in a sense, a staged narrative, so too the written play, when it has taken on an autonomous existence (when it is read aloud) is a form of textual narrative communicated by narration rather than by monstration. And thus, in a sense, we might say that narration and monstration (the respective modes of the textual and the staged) are modern-day equivalents, adapted to a new reality, of the Platonic categories of mimetic and non-mimetic diegesis. Equivalents, certainly, but not exact equivalents, because Plato did not conceive of these latter in relation to the text but rather in relation to an always-already staged form of narrative. This is why I propose here to re-equip them, to re-use

Table 6.1

Textual narration	Theatrical monstration
telling	non-mimetic diegesis
showing	mimetic diegesis

them, by not applying them to monstration alone. In this case, non-mimetic diegesis would refer to all cases in which words, speech, and verbal discourse are used within a staged performance to tell a story. We could even use this category to designate the performance of the storyteller, who is called upon, no more and no less, to inscribe verbal narrative within a 'monstrational wrapper.'

We would thus have at our disposal very distinct categories, inherited from both the Ancient Greeks and modern-day Anglo-American scholars, with which to study and identify the related phenomena that make up the two basic modes of narrative communication: on the one hand, textual narration's *showing* and *telling*; and on the other staged monstration's mimetic and non-mimetic diegesis.[21] We would thus arrive at table 6.1.

There are clear advantages to contrasting *textual* narration and *staged* monstration in this way. One of the conclusions we should reach is that there are two basic modes of presiding over a narrative, and that each of these modes is the product of the activity of an underlying agent that is responsible for this communication: the *narrator* and the *monstrator*. These two agents have distinct abilities and powers, as we will discuss in the following chapter.

7 The Narrator and the Monstrator

A story is *told*, but developments are *shown*. These have neither the same
role nor the same tone.

Serge Daney, *Libération*, 23 September 1987, 51

There is reason, then, to acknowledge the existence in the theatre of
some sort of unifying agent, the monstrator, the theatrical equivalent of
the textual narrator. Or rather, the equivalent of the figure that
emerged from our discussion in the preceding chapter (and to which
we will return in greater depth in chapter 11): the underlying narrator.
The monstrator is also an underlying agent, responsible for modulating the various manifestations of 'theatrical language': mise en scène,
set design, lighting, acting, etc. The monstrator, however, is a plural
agent, delegated to so many facets of the production that we cannot
view it as a true 'focal consciousness,' unlike the textual narrator. The
monstrator's seemingly unifying role cannot attain the 'single voice' to
which the textual narrator is confined (or of which it is capable, depending on your point of view). This is because staged narrative, like
film narrative, is presented to the viewer by means of a series of 'demonstrative languages' and a multitude of expressive means. One of
these means, the spoken word, is a close relative of the 'literary monody.' Any information provided in textual narrative can, in the end, be
attributed to the underlying narrator, the – sole – speaker. In the theatre, the narrator's absence, the absence of this stand-in for the author,
prevents us from identifying the staged narrative's mode of communication as *narration* as the term is commonly understood. And if, in the
written work, textual narrative's underlying narrator can appear to be

the author's stand-in, it is probably because it is the only agent among all those that inhabit the text to have preserved a powerful semblance of autonomy and thus of humanity. This phenomenon derives above all from the particular way this agent uses language to tell the story. The various protagonists of staged narrative also use language, but these are precisely the characters whose story is being told. There is no *intermediary consciousness*, no privileged agent to *present* them. They present themselves. Recall that Aristotle said of these characters that they 'represent the characters as carrying out the whole action themselves.'[1] In such cases, the only agents to use verbal language are diegetic: they are necessarily agents in action. And one of the principal characteristics of these agents is that they are confined to the story told and revealed onstage: there, *in front of the viewer*, and in *phenomenological continuity* with him or her – while the textual narrator, for its part, is a veritable *confluence* of significations, a *source* rather than a *target*.[2] Tzvetan Todorov explained this well when he wrote:

> Our vision of the character who takes on the narrative is fundamentally different from that of the other characters ... While the other characters are, above all, images brought into being within a consciousness, the character who assumes the narrative is consciousness itself.[3]

The *narrative* nature of textual narrative is thus completely different from the *acted out* nature of staged narrative: as Todorov remarks, 'the dialogue is characterized, basically, by the absence of a unifying consciousness, one that would encompass the consciousness of all the characters.'[4] This *seemingly* undeniable absence of an encompassing 'unifying consciousness,' as I have said before, most clearly distinguishes the staged from the textual in the way they communicate the narrative. For, when we observe the actors playing their roles, actors who are living matter and thus *autonomous* and *immediate*, we almost necessarily have the impression that no underlying agent exists outside the diegesis – that nothing is responsible for all the 'inflections' of the stage performance. And this is true even if we are ultimately aware that something, somewhere is responsible for the performance. What's more, in the case of stage performance, unlike textual narrative when it is read, no one sees in place of the person for whom the narrative is intended: the person for whom the text is intended sees with his or her own eyes. As Anne Ubersfeld remarks, 'in the theatre, the direction of the gaze is not the product of a previous fabrication ... it is the product

of the spectator's perceptive labour at every moment of the performance.'[5] No one, first of all, has observed on behalf of the viewer: the
viewer is the observer. The 'point of view' is not inscribed in the text
(and here I refer to the 'text' of the performance and not the written
text of the play).

It is, however, no less true – and this is what justifies my attempt to
isolate a unifying figure, the monstrator – that, as Ross Chambers remarks, 'the dramatic material [has] undergone a *de facto* selection process, first when the text was composed and later when it was mounted
on stage.'[6] There thus exists in the theatre an agent that, as Patrice
Pavis describes, takes on the responsibility for 'orient[ing] the meaning
in a linear manner according to a logic of actions toward a final goal:
the *dénouement* and the resolution of *conflicts*.'[7]

The monstrative activity of the monstrator has often been identified
by theoreticians of the theatre, even if it has not been named as such. But
because of the difficulty of categorizing this activity and, ultimately, of
naming the agent responsible for it, and also because of its absolute lack
of a stable identity, they have tarried in including it in the repertoire of
agents responsible for communicating the narrative. As Pavis says,

> This 'authorial' subject is difficult to identify, however, except in *stage di-
> rections*, the *chorus*, or the *raisonneur*. Even these instances are only a liter-
> ary and sometimes deceptive substitute for the dramatist. It might best be
> seen in the organization of the *fabula*, the way the actions are put together,
> the resultant (though it is difficult to trace) of the points of view and se-
> mantic contexts of the speakers.[8]

We can find traces of the monstrator's activity on numerous levels.
Pavis speaks of the organization of the *fabula*, the way the actions are
put together, etc. In other texts, he goes further and, like other theoreticians of the theatre, senses quite well that we must grant the existence of some sort of encompassing agent whose traces can be found
here and there in the stage play. The monstrator, who is usually con-
signed to invisibility, to transparency, to transience, nevertheless has
recourse to certain techniques for bringing its active presence to light.
Chambers comments:

> What's needed moreover is to study the innumerable techniques by
> which the theatre attempts to integrate this narrative perspective, from
> the use of the 'prologue' and the 'epilogue' in classical repertory to the

range of procedures invented by the epic and expressionist theatres of our age: the use of a reciter or, to use Claudel's term, an 'announcer'; placards; linking techniques supposedly 'typical' of dreams; etc.[9]

In other cases, the monstrator's presence can be established 'by a character or a *voice off*.'[10] It is perhaps in such cases, moreover, that the monstrator succeeds in giving us, in the strictest sense, an image of the *narrator*, by means of an *oral* (and thus verbal) imitation of the *textual* (and thus verbal) moorings of the narrative voice. But such an imitation does not render the monstrator a true underlying *narrator*, at least in the sense that I have used the term until now. We must also be very careful about declaring, as Pavis does in his entry on the 'narrator' in his *Dictionary of the Theatre*, that while 'in principle there is no narrator in dramatic theatre, in which the playwright never speaks in his own name, a narrator appears in certain forms of theatre, particularly epic theatre.'[11] For, while it is legitimate to describe as a 'narrator' any character present on stage (whether this character is present in the diegesis or not), or any character who is physically absent but whose voice is heard offstage, this narrator does not have the same status at all as the *underlying narrator* of textual narrative we have been discussing.[12] This agent's role is closer to that of a 'scaffold' than that of a *mediator*. Far from being such a mediator, as Pavis suggests,[13] and far from being a primary agent like the underlying narrator of textual narrative, the monstrator is only a secondary agent. Whereas the textual narrator *makes visible*, the monstrator is incapable of doing this. It can only make *itself* visible (or audible). And it itself is seen (or heard) on the same phenomenological level (that is, with the same degree of 'reality') as the other actors in the play. It is not, it cannot be, a true 'focal consciousness,' whether it is a character or, to adopt Pavis's term, a 'metacharacter.'[14] In this sense, the various acting techniques that have been privileged in order to render the actor autonomous of the character he or she 'represents' (we cannot say in this case that the actor embodies the character), beginning in particular with Brecht, are of course marks of the monstrator's presence. But these techniques do not make the monstrator a narrator for that reason alone.

For, even if they are on the same level, the monstrator of staged narrative and the underlying narrator of textual narrative do not have the same abilities, or the same status. This is exclusively the result of the 'nature' (of the constraints and specificities, I should say) of their respective semiotic vehicles. Earlier we observed that the theatre spectator, like the true observer he or she is, sees the actions of the play's actors directly, without the mediation of a 'focal consciousness,' of a narrative confluence. The reader of textual narrative, on the contrary, sees only abstract signs deposited and arranged on the pages of a book by an intermediary consciousness, the underlying narrator. The monstrator *presents* (direct vision) while the narrator, to use the term very precisely, *represents* (indirect vision). Whatever this latter agent's inclination towards monstration, it can never truly succeed in *showing* its characters. These will always be, to borrow François Baby's expression, detached from their 'situational wrapper.'[15] To return to the terms assigned to these phenomena by Roland Barthes, textual narrative is and always will be 'monodic' and the signs of its expression will never have the 'solidity' of the true monstrative narrative of the stage play, one of whose specific characteristics is that it is a result of a 'polyphony of information.' I believe we should retain this narrow delineation of different semiotic vehicles and stipulate that the textual narrator's 'monstration' is only an illusion. As a corollary, we must also acknowledge that the 'narration' to which the theatrical narrator might aspire is also an illusion.[16] The signs used by the narrator are fundamentally different from those used by the monstrator. And it is the very nature of these signs that stands as an absolutely insurmountable barrier between the two.

Whether we like it or not, when textual narrative (in fact any verbal narrative) is being communicated, there is always 'someone' speaking: the *underlying* narrator. Whether this narrator takes on the trappings of a character-narrator or not (or even of a character pure and simple), this figure 'mills' the speech of the narrative. But we shouldn't let this non-anthropomorphic, properly 'mechanical' image of the mill confuse us: language always appears to be the product of a human subject. It can be used transparently only with great difficulty. As we saw above, and as has been said time and again, it's as if, in the end, it were impossible to neutralize the evidence of the fact that every – linguistic – *énoncé* is moored in an enunciator. It's as if the narrator, as an enunciator, is not able to disappear completely: the signs through which it transmits its message are heteromorphic in relation to the referential objects of its discourse, and this heteromorphy can only 'betray' it. The textual narrator, which seeks as much as possible to disappear as the source of the discourse, can have recourse to *quoting* (in imitation thereby of the monstrator), which has the particularity of placing in relation to each other signs that have a strong resemblance to the referents inferred by its discourse.[17] As Catherine Kerbrat-Orecchioni remarks, 'There is …

one and only one type of linguistic behaviour that can be 100% objective: that is the discourse that reproduces a previous *énoncé* directly and in its entirety.'[18] This takes us back to our starting point, to Platonic mimesis, to mimetic diegesis. But in the final analysis, this objectivity of textual narrative is simply another illusion. For, despite appearances, it is still and always the same voice speaking. Gerald Prince demonstrated this quite well when he wrote that the 'attributive formula' (the way, in textual narrative – this, for me, includes the published text of a play – in which the speaker is named during a verbal exchange) 'is a fundamental weakness of narrative: no matter how diverse the voices brought into play, in the end it's always the same voice narrating.'[19] This is because language can only be a *discursive* tool. Speech is discourse, and discourse is not the whole story. Whatever its degree of transparency, the *focal plane* of verbal narrative remains present over and above the things refracted in it, like the filter of a gaze other than your own: that of the narrator. Todorov remarks:

> It is rare however for literary discourse to be transparent to the point of artlessly filtering the narrative and spontaneously making visible the concepts it transmits. Most often, discourse contrasts its plot and syntactical forms with the imaginary representation of the event. And so, as literary discourse develops, two worlds take shape: the world of the narrative, where beings and objects move about according to specific laws, and the linguistic world, where syntactical rules govern the sentences and impose their own order on them.[20]

'All-powerful' speech (is it not the Supreme Metalanguage?) can discourse simultaneously on the world and on itself, and yet it encounters certain limitations: it cannot render a minimally exact image of the world it so often, just the same, wishes into being. And yet this almost universal ability for bringing into existence, which it owes to its power to detach itself, gives it its strength. But this, paradoxically, is also the source of its weakness: this power to detach itself prevents it from rendering some aspects of reality with exactitude, such as spatial relations and even, to a lesser extent, temporal ones. And this weakness, once it is perceptible, can only 'expose' its concocted nature, can only make visible its human origins and reveal its unnaturalness.

Thus textual narrative, as (seemingly) 'staged' as it may be, will never be able to have regard simultaneously for the topographical and chronometric bases of the event it is recounting. This explains why, for example, it is structurally impossible for the narrator to respect the integrity of the story's chronology, whereas the opposite is true for the monstrator, for whom this is the starting point of its art. Todorov comments:

> We mustn't think that the story corresponds to an ideal chronology. It is enough for there to be at least one character for whom this ideal order becomes extremely distanced from the 'natural' story. The reason for this is that, to safeguard this order, we would have to exit the story every time we switched from one character's dialogue to another's in order to explain what this second character had been doing 'meanwhile.'[21]

What is intrinsic to the narration of a verbal narrative is its complete visibility as narration. The 'natural bent' of verbal narrative is to pretend, always and already, to be the product of a narrator.

The monstrator, on the contrary, is able much more easily (and has a much greater tendency) to produce a substance that presents itself as something 'narrated without a narrator,'[22] to borrow Christian Metz's expression – to present itself as a discourse without an enunciator. Staged narratives are narratives whose centre of interpretation, as we have said, changes and is difficult to identify, to say the least. Indeed, the monstrator works with concrete, human material whose semblance of autonomy literally jumps out at us, unlike the abstract (and thus seemingly artificial and subordinate) material granted the narrator. But this situation has its counterpart in the fact that the 'worldliness' of the material so inaccessible to the narrator is foisted insuperably upon the monstrator.[23] The communicating agent of staged narrative might very well behave out of character and manifest its presence by rendering its base material as 'unworldly' as possible, yet it is still the case that certain powers enjoyed by the narrator will forever be denied it. In this way, for example, the monstrator, at its level of intervention, can never communicate to the narratee (perhaps, if we wanted to be sticklers, we should say 'monstratee') what one of its characters is thinking or feeling.[24] On the contrary, this represents, in Seymour Chatman's view, 'a step further along the scale of narrator prominence.'[25] Narrative, it has often been said, is a discourse on the world. But once it is on the stage, it is a world before it is discourse. When it is moulded by speech, however, it is discourse before it is a world.

One of the consequences of this intrinsic difference between the *narrative*[26] faculties of the narrator and the *demonstrative* faculties of the monstrator is nothing short of fundamental. As Wayne C. Booth illustrated quite well in his discussion of the 'implied author' of the textual narrative (who corresponds, in part, to our underlying narrator), the narrating agent exercises a 'control over the reader's degree of involvement in or distance from the events of the story.' Indeed, a sort of empathy is created, propelling the reader to adopt the same attitude of 'detachment or sympathy felt by the implied author.'[27]

The monstrator, in opposite fashion, is for its part 'condemned' to seeing its 'creation' take on a greater degree of autonomy. The control it is capable of exercising over the narrated (or rather, over the 'shown') and, as a result, over its 'monstratee,' is indeed less *visible* (but not always, necessarily, less effective). Because if a narrator controls our *vision* in a more decisive manner than the monstrator, we might conclude that it can more easily control our interpretation as well. The world shown by the monstrator will thus often be more ambiguous, as a general rule, than the world narrated by the narrator's voice.

The principles I have just outlined involve the relationship between the underlying agents of narration and monstration and their respective semiotic vehicles. It is clear, however, that it remains possible to struggle against the inherent characteristics set in motion by one vehicle or the other. Thus, a narrator is often tempted to give itself the airs of a monstrator. This is the case, for example, in the work of novelists in the United States between the First and Second World Wars. For them, it was of fundamental importance to present a narrative that appeared, to paraphrase Genette's comment once again, to be 'free of any narrative patronage.' Here, we can agree, is a goal that is much easier for a monstrator to achieve on the stage than it is for a textual narrator to achieve on the page, if only because it is easier for the former to succeed in effectively 'covering over' its voice with the voices of others.[28] As Danièle Chatelain points out, there are certainly many factors that might help to neutralize the voice of the textual narrator:

> The importance classical narration grants the storyline and the characters, particularly in dialogue sequences, facilitates this neutralization, because the reader is prepared to forget the narrator if it stands aside and effaces itself in relation to the story. But we must acknowledge that the narrator effaces itself to varying degrees, and the neutralization of its voice is carried out in proportion to the degree of this self-effacement.[29]

We might nevertheless believe, with Todorov, that 'the complete effacement of the narrator is impossible.'[30]

The voice of the monstrator is on the contrary more easily camou-
flaged because it is less moored in place. Even so, various theatrical
practices propel the narrative to the front of the stage, and the *monstra-*
tor can attempt to dress itself up as a *narrator*, can try to find a way to
incorporate into theatrical practice stage equivalents of the text's *telling*
and *talking*. This is something, as we shall see later on, that the *filmic*
monstrator is much better at doing than its counterpart in the theatre.
And what indeed are we to make of this filmic monstrator, about
whom I have deliberately not uttered a word in this chapter devoted to
making a clear distinction between the fields of action granted the underlying agents of textual narrative and stage narrative? Does this
filmic monstrator have the same narrative powers, or, if you like, the
same 'demonstrative' powers, as the theatrical monstrator? The following chapter is devoted to this very question.

8 Narration and Monstration in the Cinema

Who speaks in a film? Who tells the story? In the cinema, this problem, however little it has been closely examined, soon opened up a whole new set of questions.

François Jost, '*Où en est la narratologie cinématographique?*' 115

The film medium, of course, is quite different from the media used to convey textual and staged narratives. But this does not prevent us from identifying some common bonds among these narrative media. It is common for authors to resort to comparisons with plays and novels when trying to determine cinema's narrative status, as this comment by Christian Metz illustrates:

Béla Balázs demonstrated early on that the cinema, apparently the stage play's twin sibling (because its events are acted out and mimed, in a sense, by the protagonists themselves), is really closer to the novel. In film, an invisible narrator, one very similar to the narrator of the novel and like it outside the events it relates, causes the image-strip to unfold under the viewer's eyes in the same way that the narrative of the novel lays out sentences that go directly from the author to the reader.[1]

From Balázs to Metz by way of Albert Laffay,[2] Jean Mitry,[3] and many others, this sort of reasoning and these sorts of questions often appear in the work of film theorists. Despite a few more or less fundamental distinctions, nearly all of these theorists end up by concluding that, in the final analysis, film is closer to novels than to plays, precisely because of the existence and presence throughout the narrative of an underlying agent that presides over the narrative's organization and structure. Generally speaking, there is also agreement that this agent is an approximate equivalent of the narrator of textual narrative. As early as 1948 a literary theorist, Claude-Edmonde Magny, devoted four chapters of a book on the twentieth-century novel in the United States to this question of the 'equivalence' of cinematic and literary narra- tors.[4] Magny compared the inter-war novel in the United States and its 'aesthetic of transcribing events'[5] to the narrative techniques found in cinema, which tells stories *by means of the camera lens*. In the first part of her book, Magny discusses both the influence of cinematic techniques on the new form of literary narrative in the U.S. novel and the influ- ence of literary techniques on film narrative. For her, the *camera lens* is a true *narrator*:

> The most common technique used by the novel (until the end of the nine- teenth century, for example) to ensure the indispensable continuity of the narrative was to have recourse to a narrator … In short, to impose an or- ganizing consciousness between the narrative and the auditor, whose responsibility was to 'report' the story. The cinema does the same thing with the lens of its camera, a veritable retina upon which the entire story will be painted.[6]

As we can see, Magny is not particularly exacting. Should we, like her, view the camera as a narrator? Should we promote it to this rank for the sole reason that it is able to replicate events? Is merely engrav- ing the characters in action onto film enough to go beyond mimetic di- egesis? These are some of the questions we must answer if we are to identify the various parameters of narrative activity in the cinema.

We could take any number of paths to get to that point. In the case of staged narrative, I thought it best to proceed, first of all, by identify- ing (and naming) the theoretical underlying agent responsible for communicating the narrative: the monstrator. This path was necessary for the good and simple reason that there is some hesitation, in theo- ries of the theatre, to acknowledge the existence of such an agent. The problem is different in the case of the cinema, as we have seen above, since the existence of an underlying agent, whether we call it a 'film narrator' or a 'great image-maker,' is generally accepted. We can iden- tify and recognize this agent all the more easily because, much more so than in the theatre, it leaves quite evident traces of its passage. We can therefore take this to be an uncontested element of film theory, as these comments by Jacques Aumont et al. in their book *Aesthetics of Film* make clear:

> For our purposes, the narrator will be the director, in that he or she chooses a certain sort of narrative sequencing or construction, a certain type of découpage, and an editing style, in opposition to other options offered by film language. The concept of narrator, thus understood, does not, however, exclude the idea of narrative and invention: the narrator certainly produces both a narrative and a story and may invent certain narrative strategies or plot constructions.[7]

This is an unequivocal statement: an underlying agent responsible for communicating film narrative exists, and we are able to identify it by its role and functions. The originality of the proposal of the authors of *Aesthetics of Film* lies precisely in the way they set out these functions. For once, they do not all converge on editing alone, as is usually the case in studies that attempt to identify the activities of cinema's narrative agent. While editing is in fact this agent's privileged field of action,[8] it is important to identify the other places where its narrative 'voice' is moored.

We have seen in the preceding chapters, moreover, that the underlying agent responsible for film narrative, the 'great image-maker' if you will, is, at the very least, a 'double agent.' For in film there is both a monstrator and a narrator. In this sense, cinema 'monstrates' and 'narrates' at one and the same time. But where does film narration begin and film monstration end? I have developed a hypothesis on this question,[9] which has generated some interest and a few critiques. I have been reproached on several occasions (and justly so, moreover) for not taking sufficient account of the essential difference between what I have called *theatrical monstration* and *filmic monstration*. On this point, I hope to make amends in the remaining chapters of this book. I have also had the rather frequent impression that there is a certain amount of resistance to my desire to make editing the *sine qua non* of admitting the film agent to the realm of *narration*. I have two comments to make on this point.

First of all, I presume that the new distinctions I will make here between filmic and theatrical monstration will finally do justice to the former. Second, I presume that this 'restoration of privileges' will attenuate the need many people have felt to view as 'narratorial faculties' some of the techniques used during the shooting of a film, such as camera movements. These are the principal factors that contribute to the distance – an important distance, it's true – between filmic and theatrical monstration. We must realize, moreover, that the limits I have imposed here on filmic monstration and narration are as much the result, if not more, of what I described earlier as 'theoretical decrees' as they are of an inherent division within the object of study. Filmic narration and monstration – and this is unavoidable – are mental 'views.' They are (most definitely!) 'projections' of a system of thought seeking conceptual tools to better understand a reality that, in the first place, comes before the 'mental view' it inspires and that, furthermore, is not obliged to conform to that view.

If, for me, (specifically) *film narrative*[10] originates with editing, it is because this appears to me to be the best theoretical solution to the narratological problems we encounter when examining the case of cinema. There are several reasons for this. First of all, on the level of *temporality*, that essential parameter of narrativity, editing allows film images to accede to heretofore unseen dimensions of monstrational discourse – a discourse that, at this level, is constrained. Second, editing constitutes a different 'moment,' a different instance than that of the film shoot. This is true as much on the phylogenetic and linguistic levels as it is on the level of film production in general. And finally, in light of these two reasons, it seems useful to me to be able to establish a boundary between the two *distinct* levels of narrativity, narration and monstration, if only to avoid leaving narratologists and scholars the burden of having constantly to trace the boundaries between the two on a case-by-case basis, using criteria necessarily at the limit of objectivity. We will now attempt, therefore, to distinguish the narrative responsibilities of film narration and monstration.[11]

One of the reasons for thinking that the underlying agent in staged narrative remains riveted to monstration alone has to do with the fact that it is limited to a single time: the present. In this sense, Ivo Osolsobé remarks, 'we can say that the "grammar" of [what I call] the exposition knows only the present tense.'[12] Monstration takes place in the present; it is impossible to have shown by showing. In the cinema, however, the situation is completely different from that in the theatre, because of the 'simple' fact of editing, an activity that makes it possible to link different spatio-temporal segments to each other. Indeed, in the theatre, as Anne Ubersfeld remarks, there is no 'going backwards, nor is there the sort of dissection of the image perceived by a single glance, the sort of framing and cutting up into shots that, in cinema, lead the viewer by the hand.'[13] This possibility that the agent responsible for film narrative will take the viewer in hand is precisely what is most often invoked to distinguish cinema from the theatre on a narrative level. Before even thinking about the temporal manipulations made possible by editing, we can agree that editing is the privileged means by which the film narrator is manifested. As all film theorists have shown, it is because of editing that the viewer has the sensation of not being alone in watching the story unfold before his or her eyes. Through camera movement, primarily, the viewer perceives the role of that assistant the film narrator (which can also be an opponent!). Because, like the textual narrator, the film narrator imposes (can impose) a gaze upon the viewer – unlike the theatre, where, as Ubersfeld remarks, 'the viewer must frame and organize his or her perception, must remember; it won't happen very often that the task is made lighter by little visual reminders.'[14]

In textual and film narrative, the story told, in other words, is the work of an *intermediary gaze*. The necessary presupposition of this intermediary gaze is, precisely, that the narrative agent engages in a 'moment of reflection,'[15] a moment necessarily situated between the moment when the events took place (or are supposed to have taken place) and the moment when they are perceived by the narratee. And this is not the case with the 'scenes' produced by the monstrator, whether in the theatre or the cinema.[16] The film monstrator, whose activity is essentially identified with the activity of shooting the film, is not able to open a temporal breach within which it would be possible, as the agent responsible for communicating the narrative, to inscribe a moment for reflecting upon the story told and then restore its substance through the filter of its gaze. But the reason for this, unlike in the theatre, is not because of the here and now of spectatorial vision. Put another way, it is not because of the viewer's *vision* and the *action* represented, because in cinema the monstrator always shows something that, in one sense or another, *has already taken place*. Rather, it is because the *action* represented coincides with the *vision* of the monstrator – the vision of the camera, in effect, which we might view, in some sense, as having been delegated by the monstrator to take the viewer's place in the present tense of the action being filmed.

The reason for this is that the monstrator, any monstrator, has its nose glued to the here and now of 'representation' and is incapable of opening a breach in temporal continuity. Although what it shows me in the present may well have taken place before it shows it to me,[17] the process of monstration is still a strictly synchronic simultaneous 'narration,' to use Gérard Genette's term.[18] Only the narrator is able to take us with it on its magic carpet ride through time. The intersection, the encounter, of two gazes – that of the narrator and that of the narratee – opens the breach wherein it is possible to inscribe temporal '*difference*': I see *now* (indirectly, in the case of textual narrative; 'directly,'[19] in the case of film narrative), *extra muros*, what the narrator-assistant *saw* before me, *intra muros*. The narrator *re*-places, before my eyes, and in an order that suits it, events that have *already* taken place.

As far as cinema is concerned, the conclusion we must draw from this is that the 'editing' activity of the film narrator makes it possible to inscribe a true narrative past tense on the story.[20] We must agree then that while the shot is in the present, while it is in fact a past made present, this mastery of time, one of any narrator's possible activities, is made possible by a number of editing practices (but not all editing practices, of course). Hence the importance of this comment by Metz, in response to the claim that 'the tense of the diegesis [is] the present':

> Isn't it the film image, rather, that is always in the present? And the film, for its part, is it not always in the past, just like the novel? Because, like it, the film is a narrative. It is not a special feature of the novel to transport everything it names to the realm of the already-occurred. This, rather, is a feature of all narrative, of all closed sequences of unrealized events, whether these events are expressed by speech, writing, or images.[21]

This comment needs to be enlarged upon and made more precise. The image, on the level of the shot (that is, an uninterrupted series of photograms), is in the present tense. But editing makes it possible for a narrative agent to intrude and take the viewer 'by the hand' and submit him or her to different temporal experiences. Here lies the importance of making a clear distinction between the time of the action and the time of the viewing, as Jean-Paul Simon has suggested:

> We shouldn't confuse the story as a whole – the film's telling of such-and-such a story – which was placed in the can before the viewer consumes it (like a book awaiting a reader in order to re-produce itself) with the temporal markers that make possible the direction of the narrative and the resituating of the viewer and his or her awareness of the narrative's temporality. This is the difference between the time of the action and the time of the viewing.[22]

Through editing, the narrator is able to exercise its power on the story told. And if we can state that editing makes it possible for the narrator to absent itself from the present (from the present of the story told), this is because the situation is analogous to the one that prevails in the production of a film, beyond any narratological considerations. Thus, the editor (who corresponds, in the real world, to the narrator) takes the material (the shots) that have been put 'in the can' by the monstrator (the camera) and structures it, after the 'shown' has already decidedly taken place. And, like the narrator of textual narrative, the film narrator can be, to return to the comment by Otto Ludwig I quoted earlier, 'the absolute master of time and space ... It can think, it represents without being limited by any aspect of reality, it stages unhindered by physical impossibility; it has all the powers of nature and all the faculties of the mind.'[23]

The film monstrator, on the contrary, is shackled to reality, to *its* reality: the camera. This is a twenty-four-frames-per-second reality.[24] The camera-monstrator's work is necessarily continuous in nature (at least under the normal conditions in which films are shot and projected). And this is true even though this work is founded upon discontinuity: for the linking of photograms produces an impression of continuity out of fundamentally discontinuous material. What could be more discontinuous than a series of photograms breaking movement up into segments? Between each pair of images there is, of necessity, a missing interval, a gap, which even slow-motion photography cannot avoid. But when the images are projected – a procedure that synthesizes the images and 'brings them to life' – this discontinuity evaporates (recall that Metz said of the camera that it is a machine for leaving out photograms, not for accumulating them). And this 'life' given to the images is (necessarily) in the present tense: here the past is quite simply made present.

If we now refer to Émile Benveniste, who commented that the present is 'the coincidence of the event described with the agent of discourse that describes it,'[25] it becomes apparent that what the monstrator produces, the shot, is extremely ambiguous on a temporal level. What, in fact, is the event this discursive agent, our monstrator, is describing? Is it the event produced in front of the camera during the process of putting the film 'in the can' – the film shoot? Or is it the event produced during the process of reconstituting the film – its projection? It should be apparent that the monstrator's 'expression' takes place at the time of projection and that the 'event described' took place at an earlier time, when the film was shot. The illusion of the present tense produced by our viewing of the shot is thus, decidedly, a mere simula-crum of the present. But it remains the case that whether in the past (as it is in reality) or in the present (as it is projected) the *shot* 'reveals tem-poral planes without distinguishing between them,' as Francis Vanoye remarks.[26] Vanoye understands quite well that the film image 'is not in the present tense, even if, for the viewer, it unfolds in the present.'[27] How then are we to resolve this temporal ambiguity? What we need to do is simply to view the film monstrator's monstration as a kind of *quoting*, in both its narration of events and its narration through speech. Literally, the film monstrator quotes its characters when they speak: it extracts a segment of linguistic reality and reconstitutes it lin-guistically (through the sound track). Metaphorically, it carries out a kind of *quoting* as well when it presents us, visually (through the film image), with a segment of the actions and gestures it has extracted from the reality present when the film was shot. In a novel, the line 'Then Peter replied, "I'm quite sick"' is viewed as a past event, even if the sentence Peter utters is in the present. The film monstrator does the same thing when it *quotes* (when it reconstitutes in the present what had taken place in the past), on the sound track, the phrase Peter pro-nounced. And it does the same thing again when it *quotes* in the pres-ent Peter's past actions.[28]

The fact remains, however, that the single shot to which the monstra-tor is constrained prevents it in no uncertain terms from modifying the tense of the narrative *énoncé*. This tense is an eternal past that, even though it moves forward, can never become another tense. Only the nar-rator can inscribe, between two shots (by means of cuts and matches), the marks of its gaze. Only the narrator can order the viewer's reading[29] and transcend the temporal singularity that ineluctably constrains the monstrator's discourse. Through matches, the film narrator, just like its textual counterpart, is able, in Jaap Lintvelt's words, to 'make the tempo-ral distance between the present tense of the narration and the past tense of the story stand out.'[30] It is through these matches, no more and no less, that the narrator 'speaks.' And, as a 'sovereign speaker,'[31] the narra-tor can choose, through its speech, to what extent it will display the power it has over the temporality of the story told. It is no less true that the film narrator has at its disposal almost all the same possibilities for modulating time as those available to the textual narrator.

Film narrative is thus, overall, the product of the overlapping of two distinct layers of narrativity. These derive from the two linkages that take place within cinema's dual changeability:[32] the linking of photo-grams and the linking of shots. But what our discussion in this chapter

Figure 8.1

Mega-narrator
(Great Image-maker)

Film monstrator:
film shoot
{ linking of photograms
punctiliarity

Film narrator:
editing
{ linking of shots
pluri-punctiliarity

should have demonstrated is that these two narrative layers do not derive from the same kind of semio-narrative operations and that, in the end, they presuppose the existence of (at least) two different and distinct agents, each responsible for communicating one of these two layers. In order to create a pluri-punctiliar or multiple-shot film narrative, there must be, first of all, a monstrator that, at the time of shooting the film, places a multitude of micro-narratives (shots) 'in the can.' Without a doubt, each and every one of these shots has a degree of narrative autonomy.[33] They are produced through monstration and are incapable of narration, in the sense that I use the term. Next, there must be another narrative agent, the narrator, which is able, if it is narratively assured and seizes hold of these micro-narratives, to work on their narrative substance and to quash the autonomy of the shots produced by the monstrator and inscribe upon them the trajectory of a continuous and consecutive reading through the gaze it casts upon this substance and its transformation of it.

The underlying agent responsible for communicating film narrative is thus a 'double agent.' Here lies the originality and specificity of film narrative. The film *narrator-monstrator*, a true *mega-narrator* (and this is how I propose from here on to call this agent responsible, in the end, for the veritable mega-narratives found in cinema), thus carries out a process of joining or fusing the two fundamental modes of narrative communication: monstration and narration. Figure 8.1 maps this out.

But a question arises when we analyse this figure. How can we accept that the first sub-agent, the film *monstrator*, has the same name, 'monstrator,' as the agent responsible at bottom for staged narrative when the activity we associate with the former, the *film shoot*, is not, at least at first glance, of the same order as the staging of a play? Are there grounds, once again, for making a distinction between them? This is the question the following chapter will attempt to answer.

9 The Film Narrative System

Camera movement throws the monstration/narration dichotomy into crisis. And, in a larger sense, it throws into crisis any exclusive correlation of
framing to a (spectatorial or narrative) point of view.

Jacques Aumont, 'L'image filmique de film?' 7: 139

If we are to grasp fully the phenomena at work in any narrative communication in the cinema, we must at all costs measure the distance
separating staged and film monstration. One of the hypotheses that led
me to make an initial division of the film mega-narrator into the monstrator and the narrator had to do with what we might call the different
'fields' of 'cineastic' activity. It occurred to me that, in the production of
a film, there is a *manipulation*, on the one hand, of those elements we
now, following Étienne Souriau, generally refer to as the *profilmic* ('everything found in front of the camera and registered on the film') and,
on the other, of the elements of what I have called the *filmographic*
(modifying slightly the meaning of this term as proposed, also, by
Souriau). Thus, for me what pertains to the filmographic is any effect,
any effect whatsoever, that derives from the cinematic apparatus and
that, without affecting in any concrete way the profilmic during the
film's shooting, transforms the viewer's perception of this profilmic
material when the film is screened. Thus, on the one hand, we have the
profilmic, or everything that is manipulated by the filmmaker when
placing it before the camera, and on the other there is the *filmographic*,
or all those activities involving the cinematic apparatus and which the
filmmaker is also called upon to manipulate. These activities include,
on the one hand, all the practices related to the overall procedure of

shooting a film: camera movements, framing, filming, etc., and on the other, all the practices that form part of the overall procedure of *editing*: matching shots, creating syntagmas, synchronization, trick effects, etc. For me, the monstrator's activity is related to *all* aspects of the pro-filmic and to *a part* of the filmographic – that part, precisely, where the profilmic and the filmographic meet: the shooting of the film. After the film shoot, the work of structuring the narrative, in which editing of course occupies centre stage, devolves to the film narrator. After I had made this initial division of the activities of the agent I now call the film mega-narrator, Tom Gunning proposed a new distinction in order to highlight the network of properly filmographic activities carried out by the film monstrator, which are denied to the theatrical monstrator. He thus proposed to view film discourse as being the product of an in-teraction between the following three levels: the profilmic, the en-framed image, and editing.[1] He thus left my first field (the profilmic) intact, but made an important distinction at the level of the second field, the filmographic. Hence, we must view the process of creating film discourse as involving three levels of cineastic activity. These lev-els, we might note in passing, ensure that the film is 'three removes from nature,' to borrow Plato's judgment of all works of art.[2] Indeed, each field of activity makes possible the manipulation of *filmed reality*, distancing it a notch at each stage from referential reality. These three fields of activity, which I call the profilmic, the filmographic: shooting, and the filmographic: post-shooting, correspond to three categories of manipulation, which I have labelled as follows:

1. The profilmic system
2. The shooting system
3. The manipulation of recorded images system

Each of these three levels corresponds to a field of activity involved in making a film. I thus propose, in order to distinguish between them quickly and to highlight their respective qualities, to identify the first with *putting in place* (or *mise en scène*, in the literal and almost theatrical sense of the term), the second with *putting in frame*, and the third with *putting in sequence*. Hence table 9.1.

Activity number 2, in the centre of the table, which I call the *putting in frame*, truly lies midway between the other two. As we shall see, this activity even has an intermediary and truly *mediating* role between the other two. Indeed, this activity comes into play differently than the

Table 9.1
Film discourse operations

1. the profilmic	the profilmic	the profilmic system	putting in place
2. the enframed image	the filmographic: shooting	the shooting system	putting in frame
3. editing	the filmographic: editing	the manipulation of recorded images system	putting in sequence

other two, depending on whether we view it from the perspective of the point of departure (*the field of cineastic activity*) or the point of arrival (*the mode of narrative communication*). When it comes down to it, this is not surprising, if we consider the fact that the activity involved here (the film shoot, or, in other words, *putting into film*) is truly situated within the bounds of two 'worlds.' It is in fact during the film shoot that *putting in place* and *putting in frame* meet and collide. From a narrative point of view (from the point of view of communicating a narrative), there is *nothing particularly cinematic* about putting in place (about the manipulation of the profilmic). Putting in frame, on the contrary, gives rise to the mega-narrator's first steps in the specifically cinematic field of narrative. And yet, despite this difference, both of these activities, putting in place and putting in frame, belong to the same realm, in terms of their mode of communicating the narrative: that of monstration. Figure 9.1 is an attempt to chart this ambivalence.

In addition, each of these three activities might justifiably be considered, each in its own way, as a form of rewriting. Indeed we might, following David Bordwell, see film as a palimpsest[3] and view film production as an act of writing containing (at least)[4] three moments. A film is in fact a palimpsest, one that bears the successive marks of these three levels, whether their trace is visible or simply implicit. These levels are lodged within three distinct fields of activity, fields that deserve to remain distinct for the purposes of our discussion, despite their eventual coexistence in the finished work, if only because they involve *distinct* domains, *distinct* 'abilities,' and, in the end, *distinct* (narrative) agents. We must therefore return to the film monstrator and carry out one more 'schism' within that veritable 'conglomerate,' the filmic mega-narrator. Let's return, then, to the previous figure, 9.1. The first two activities described there pertain to the *film monstrator* and form a part of monstration. The third activity pertains, however, to the film

Figure 9.1

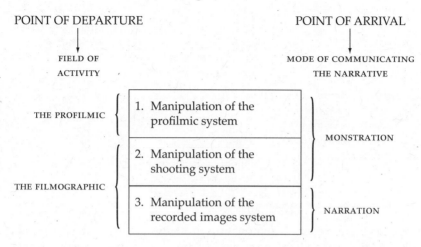

narrator. We must henceforth take the view that each of these discursive activities is the product of an agent[5] that is fully constituted as such. This leads us to divide our film monstrator in two and to identify the initial activity, the cinematic equivalent of the theatrical monstrator's role in the theatre, as the result of the contribution of a specific agent, one that enjoys relative autonomy and that I propose to call from now on the *profilmic monstrator*. Likewise, the second activity, which brings into play the entire realm of recording the image, will be seen as the product of the agent I will call the *filmographic monstrator*. We should agree that the 'voice' of these two monstrators, which are true sub-agents, is modulated and controlled by another agent, one operating at a higher level, that unites these two. This agent I will call, by analogy with the mega-narrator, the *mega-monstrator*.[6] This makes possible the next figure, 9.2, which follows from the previous one but also takes into account the developments it has helped bring about.

This way we can really take into account the truly cinematic specificity of film monstration in comparison with its equivalent in the theatre, theatrical monstration. Film monstration is not restricted to the kind of monstration found in the theatre. This fact makes it possible to reconcile the theoretical schema I am proposing here with certain requirements formulated by Gunning: 'The frame and point of view of the single shot are for me the first act of the filmic narrator, and his

Figure 9.2 Film narrative's enunciative system

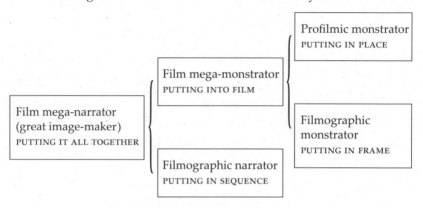

first separation from the monstration of the theater.'[7] It is true that *filmographic monstration*, and this is self-evident, overdetermines *profilmic monstration*, which is the cinematic equivalent of *theatrical monstration*. It overdetermines profilmic monstration, and even causes it to change its register: hence my use of the superlative 'mega.' By pushing the staged (the profilmic) into the arms of the filmographic, cinema elevates monstration to a higher level: it transforms it into *mega-monstration*. This mode of narrative communication combines both levels of monstration. And this second-level form of monstration, filmographic monstration, is distinct from the first level, that of simple profilmic monstration, in that it too, in a sense, is able to inscribe the *viewer's reading*; it too is the work of an *intermediary gaze*. These are two faculties that, in the end, cannot be attributed to the *filmographic* narrator alone. But we must be careful not to delude ourselves: while *filmographic monstration* may very well be able to disassociate itself from *profilmic monstration*, and while it may be able to render itself autonomous in relation to it and to take on another linguistic layer, it remains just the same riveted to the here and now of the *énoncé*, just like profilmic monstration. The *viewer's reading* set out by the filmographic monstrator and the *intermediary gaze* it offers us cannot overcome the contingencies of the immediacy and simultaneity inherent in the always-and-already-in-the-process-of-unfolding scene in front of it. The only 'analysis' of the profilmic it can offer us is one made on the spot, by providing to the viewer only what *presents* itself to the camera's gaze or, in any event, what is accessible, at *present*, to this gaze. Like any good monstrator, it does not have the right to modify time. Like all common monstrators (and even like all common mortals), if it wants to go to the other side of the window it must *take the time* to go outside the house. It is impossible for it to perform what, for every *narrator* worthy of the name, is child's play: to resituate itself instantaneously (time) from one place (space) to another. Because the monstrator does not have the power of *ubiquity*.

This does not prevent the filmographic monstrator from playing an important role in transforming referential reality. It is quite true that the filmographic monstrator inscribes a *point of view* (and, generally speaking, only one)[8] upon the material. It frames the profilmic objects in a way that can privilege one object over others. It has a choice of *focal lengths* (and can thus distance itself from the norms of realist representation), of *aperture size* (and can thus control the degree of the image's clarity), of camera *mobility* (and can thus link, for example, different profilmic objects), etc.[9] And, ultimately, it transforms *profilmic volume* into a *two-dimensional image on the screen*, which is no small feat.

The filmographic monstrator, however, like the profilmic monstrator,[10] has a rather transparent discourse, despite all the opportunities offered to it to make its mark on the very material at its disposal. In any event, one thing is certain: the filmographic monstrator, *from the outset*, is better able to render its presence invisible than the filmographic narrator. This is all the more true, and evident, when we consider the relationship of each of these agents to the 'cinematographic' process at the root of their respective existences. Indeed the narrator, at this level, is absolutely incapable of rendering its presence completely invisible, of effacing all trace of its narrative (editing) activity, of effacing the marks of its enunciation (or, to be more precise, of its narration).[11] A shot change, no matter the precautions taken, will always be visible, even if some matching techniques make it possible to render these less noticeable. At this level, any juxtaposition of two shots is located irredeemably on the side of 'discourse' rather than on the side of 'story.' The filmographic monstrator, on the contrary, although it may be able to indicate its presence (and this on a very large scale), is able, on this level, to remain completely invisible. Indeed, while the linking of any two shots is necessarily a little bit 'boisterous,' the linking of photograms is almost always silent[12] and not remarked upon.

And yet the filmographic narrator and monstrator can reject these intrinsic conditions imposed on them by their status. This explains why, throughout film history, we see filmographic narrators we might describe as being 'monstratively inclined' and filmographic monstrators we might describe as being 'narratively inclined.' We might even say that the filmographic narrator of the institution that cinema became has principally been (and remains today) a *monstratively inclined narrator*. The narrator that takes every possible precaution to render invisible the matches it effects is nothing other than a narrator that wants to give itself the airs of a monstrator. In this way, the narrator has recourse to a series of techniques that are capable of transforming its discursive *énoncés* into (the appearance of) story *énoncés*.[13] We say no less when we observe, as Michel Colin has done, that 'film sees itself primarily as narrative – in other words, it tends to suppress every mark of discourse.'[14] But this *presentation* as narrative (narrative as a story *énoncé*, in Émile Benveniste's terms) is, more or less, a 'false' *representation*.[15] Because, as Alain Bergala remarks, 'the most narrative form of editing is still discourse, is still an act of enunciation, even when it is placed in the service of the most transparent narrative.'[16]

So too the narrator that acts in this way conforms to the principles that regulate (constrain) the monstrator's activities (this is why we call it a 'monstratively inclined narrator'): it tries to make us believe that, like the monstrator's camera (in those – frequent – cases where the camera accepts its status and professes to be objective), it is only a 'powerless' witness to the 'drama' that, 'by chance,' is taking place before it. In Michel Marie's words, 'the specificity [of the] classical text [is] to obscure completely the discursive agent that produces it, by proceeding as if it was only a simple transcription of a prior and homogeneous continuity.'[17]

Similarly, the filmographic monstrator tends, to the extent this is possible, to wear the glad rags of a narrator – by employing camera movement, for example. This makes it possible to link various filmed motifs, thanks to skilful trajectories that are often calculated in advance. Despite these narrative pretensions, however, we should agree, as I remarked earlier, that the filmographic monstrator remains at the level of monstration. These camera movements are carried out within the continuity of the shot, and the linking of photograms prevents any temporal interval. Despite the camera's comings and goings, what is shown in the shot is only a piece of 'reality.' The camera's domain is the isochronous. Whatever it does, at its monstrative level, the time of the 'shown' will always be isochronous with the time of the 'showing.'[18] This is the 'yoke' to which the Lumière operators were attached, along with anyone else, during cinema's early years, when shots were not assembled in any way.[19] It is thus not at the level of modifying time that the filmographic monstrator can truly manage to demonstrate its presence in the course of the narrative.

The mega-monstrator, meanwhile, that veritable 'two-headed monster' that fuses the two levels of monstration made possible in the cinema, has at its disposal a true repertoire of resources it can draw upon, indiscriminately, from within the profilmic or the filmographic. At a time when the filmographic monstrator was still most often found *in the wings*, when it had not yet taken *centre stage* – that is, during the period of early cinema[20] – the mega-narrator developed a number of 'abilities' that were virtually 'narratorial,' probably as a form of compensation. The filmmakers of the day felt 'narratorial' urges, which they initially attempted to palm off on the monstrator. This, moreover, is probably why camera movement, contrary to what was long believed (see any book of film history), was not only frequent in the first decade of the past century but also quite advanced.[21] At a time when editing had not yet entered into spectatorial mores, following the action by means of a (usually horizontal) pan was greatly preferred, whenever possible, to making a cut.[22] Photogrammic continuity was probably seen as the guarantee of a greater (and easier) comprehension on the part of the audience. A film by Edwin S. Porter, *Stolen by Gypsies* (Edison, 1905), demonstrates this well by adopting both strategies at once. In this film we see two very early examples of techniques that privilege the *filmographic* monstrator and the filmographic narrator – all at the expense of the *profilmic* monstrator. First, let's describe the segment in question (a description I've borrowed from Jon Gartenberg):[23]

Shot 3 shows us a nanny with a baby in a yard outside a house. The mother asks the nanny to come indoors and she leaves the baby alone. A gypsy enters the frame from the left and makes off with the baby. The camera pans to the left to follow him to a carriage waiting in the street in front of the house. The carriage then departs, travelling towards the back of the frame.

Shot 4 shows us the carriage as it continues its course a little further away.

Shot 5 returns us to the yard and we see the nanny discover the child's disappearance. When the nanny raises her arms to the sky in despair, the camera pans to the right, towards the back of the house, in the opposite direction to that taken by the kidnappers. The mother and nanny then see burglars fleeing the scene with a sack and, believing them to be the kidnappers, begin to chase them, with the other domestics in tow.

We can see that the mega-narrator has chosen on two occasions to show a complex action in *a single shot* (shots 3 and 5), thereby opting to let the *filmographic monstrator* perform the work – rather than the *profilmic monstrator* (which could have manipulated the profilmic objects – the film's characters – so that the three sites of the action in shot 5, for example, were closer to each other, thereby making it possible for the entire action to be shown in a single, fixed composition); or, yet again, rather than the *filmographic narrator* (here, a cut could have been made in shot 3 and a 45° matching shot inserted to show the gypsy fleeing with the child). Instead, monstration has been privileged in these shots – and filmographic monstration at that. But in shot 4, a completely different attitude is assumed. There, the filmographic narrator, freeing itself from the bonds that ineluctably constrain monstrative discourse,[24] crosses space with *a single bound*, catches up with the horse-drawn coach, and assures the viewer that the kidnappers have indeed quit the scene. The proof of this is that in shot 4 the carriage continues along the path it had begun at the end of shot 3.[25]

A few years earlier, Porter had produced a film with different monstrative strategies. *The Life of an American Fireman* (Edison, 1903) reveals the extent to which it was possible to privilege the profilmic monstrator in an era when editing had only begun to be used.[26] Thus, ellipses were created, as I have remarked elsewhere, 'through the manipulation of the unfolding action rather than the manipulation of the images by editing.'[27] In shot 8 of this film the mega-narrator poses as a monstrator rather than as a narrator in order to remove a temporal segment it had perhaps deemed unnecessary. This is in the shot we see, from inside a bedroom of a house in flames, of a firefighter entering the room through the window from a ladder. The firefighter seizes the woman he has come to save, hoists her onto his shoulders, and takes her back through the window to the ground. He then reappears at the window and re-enters the room in order to save a child. Now, the time that elapses while the firefighter has disappeared from sight, when he had to descend with the woman, deposit her on the ground, and climb back up the ladder,[28] is clearly insufficient: he is only absent, in fact, for two or three seconds. There can be no doubt that here the profilmic monstrator[29] has intervened. Rather than cutting the film (which would produce a true temporal ellipsis), this monstrator manipulates the profilmic action, in order to shorten its duration, when this action occurs outside the range of the spectator's immediate field of vision.[30]

Figure 9.3 *Life of an American Fireman*, Edison, 1903 (Cinémathèque québé-coise/British Film Institute)

There is another means the profilmic monstrator (just like the theat-rical monstrator) can use to 'artificially' compress the duration of the narrative. This technique results in a sort of condensing, a kind of sum-mary. The profilmic monstrator is able to compress the action being shown without, however, segmenting it. An example of this is the Georges Méliès film *Le Sacre d'Édouard VII* (*The Coronation of Edward VII*, Star Films, 1902), which shows a reconstitution (actually, an antici-pation) of the crowning of the new king of England. This film, which is composed of just one shot, is only about five minutes long (there is, however, at least one edit, but this was done in such a way as to be im-perceptible, because the framing and the position of the characters were identical,[31] as in the stop-camera technique). And yet it has the 'pretension' of showing the 'entire' referential action: it opens as the ceremony begins and ends with its completion. Here the monstrator fashioned its profilmic material in such a way as to ensure that each segment of the action followed immediately upon the previous, with-out any 'ceremonial' pause between them. Moreover, the monstrator was obliged to give only the highlights of this action and to 'sum up' the rest. The film, then, truly does contain temporal 'vanishing acts' (Méliès's specialty!), but the 'reality' shown remains in the form of a single, unsegmented block.[32]

At this stage of our discussion, we can easily identify the means at the disposal of the profilmic and theatrical monstrators. And we can also see quite well the importance of the *filmographic* monstrator, which alone is capable of elevating monstration in the cinema to a level specific to it. But, at the same time, we can't help but see, with even more evidence at our disposal, the intermediary role played by *filmographic monstration*, divided as it is between the collateral relationship it maintains, at the level of its mode of action, with profilmic *monstration* (both pertain to *monstration*) and, at the level of 'agency,' with *filmographic* narration (both operate within the same field of action). Narration and monstration: a potential dialectic between two modes we have identified in the hope of proposing a new reading of film narrative; a new reading whose tenets derive from a belated awareness of films at the root of a new 'language,' an awareness that also helps us better understand films closer to us in time, which chapter 13 will address. But first, we must refine our understanding of the narrator. To do this, we will have to 'camp out' once again in the midst of early cinema in order to set out, initially, in search of the film narrator's origins. Or, more precisely, to enquire into some of the conditions that led to this narrator's emergence early last century.

10 The Origins of the Film Narrator

Some even wanted the novel to be a sort of cinematic stream of things. This was an absurd idea. Nothing sets us further apart from what we have already perceived than that sort of cinematic approach.

Marcel Proust, *In Search of Lost Time: Finding Time Again*, 1911[1]

We saw in the Introduction how Albert Laffay might be viewed, metaphorically, as the 'father' of film narratology. If he can be seen in this light, it is because of the influence his work has had on an entire generation, despite the fact that this work was never formalized. His influence has been more indirect than direct, in particular through the writings and narratological concepts of Christian Metz, who himself has declared that he attended the Laffay school of narratology.[2]

Nevertheless, we must look to another body of work for the first examples of *theoretical reflection* on film narrative, even though this work has had no influence whatsoever, as it has only recently been discovered.[3] These writings are more proto-theoretical than truly theoretical in nature, and yet we must acknowledge their great subtlety and relative soundness. I refer here to the great number of legal documents (depositions, testimony, summations, verdicts, etc.) that history has bequeathed us as a result of the frequent recourse to the courts by the principal film companies in the United States at the turn of the past century. These court cases forced many players in the film industry to give their opinion[4] of their 'film practice' and led the courts to render verdicts that, at the very least, are well documented. What's more, we might even read these declarations in the light of the dialectic that opposes the two narratological concepts of monstration and narration.

The debates these battles gave rise to, which took place throughout the entire period of the 'gestation' of the film narrator, deal specifically with issues around the close relationship between the film *monstrator* and the film *narrator* and the respective limits of each – and thus their relative degree of 'power.' Naturally, however, these debates took a form more legalistic than narratological.

A widespread practice at the turn of the century was to dupe a competitor's films in order to market them yourself, an improper but not necessarily illegal practice.[5] Every leading U.S. company did it: Edison, Biograph, and especially Lubin, which made this practice their 'house specialty.' Many successful films were brazenly duped in this way, making it possible to make money from the work of your competitors. One of the most famous cases was that of the Georges Méliès film *Voyage dans la lune* (*A Trip to the Moon*, Star Films, 1902), which was widely distributed in the United States, where it was a huge success, without Méliès ever seeing a penny of the receipts. A series of incidents around the distribution and exhibition of this film led Méliès to dispatch his brother Gaston to look after his affairs in the States and, among other things, to see to the copyrighting of his films there.

Incidentally, it was shortly before the illegal exhibition of the Méliès film in the United States that the first interesting legal battle around duping took place. In May 1902 the Edison company took Lubin to court in order to prevent it from continuing to sell copies of *Christening and Launching Kaiser Wilhelm's Yacht 'Meteor,'* which was shot in February of that year. This legal battle saw many ups and downs, which we won't dwell on here.[6] We can say, however, that it was very important because of the jurisprudence it established for most of the cases that followed, in particular for the case I will discuss below, which, from 1904 on, pitted the American Mutoscope and Biograph Company against the Edison Manufacturing Company. The court documents from these two legal battles are of immense importance to anyone who wishes to understand the way film narrative was conceived of in those days: here is practically the only contemporary testimony in a period that had not yet produced any important writing on this new art form. Indeed, these legal battles over copyright obliged all parties to articulate their conception of the 'aggregate' of film images that is any film narrative. They did so in thorough and detailed declarations that address the principles of continuity and discontinuity from every angle, in keeping with what we here have called, following Román Gubern, the linking of photograms and the linking of shots.

In most cases, the defendants fell back on the issue of how films were copyrighted in an attempt to have the plaintiff's case dismissed. Between 1895 and 1915, the way in which copyright was registered was modified several times. At a time when most films were still made up of one shot, the Lubin company attempted to capitalize on the uncertainty and ambiguity of the rules around copyrighting a film in an effort to convince the judge that the film it had duped couldn't be protected because of a technicality. The uncertainty and ambiguity at work here were inevitable, because there were still no specific rules in place for copyrighting a film. Indeed, the first reaction of many parties, faced with this new object the film strip, which linked a consecutive sequence of photograms to render a scene, was to register their films as still photographs. Films made before 1900, which usually consisted of a single shot, were thus registered as a single photograph (even if, of course, the multiple nature of these photographs was recognized). A company wanting to protect its rights thus sent two paper copies of the film to the Library of Congress in Washington, DC, and paid the fee required to register a *single* still photograph (50 cents). This was the generally accepted procedure, and it would be hard to imagine a producer contesting it and demanding to pay 50 cents for each photogram in order to protect them all and thereby conform to the spirit of the law. This, however, was what would come to pass!

The problems this issue raised are important for us because they emphasize the 'artistic' specificity of each level of a film's production. The process of creating a film's discourse operates on each of these levels: the profilmic, the filmographic at the shooting stage, and the filmographic at the editing stage. These newly discovered legal documents thus constitute, at least to the best of our knowledge, the first coherent attempt to think about the filmmaking process and to assign to it a place within a larger portrait of human activity. They also set out one of the first approaches on record to the cinema *as an art form*. In this way, some of the participants in these debates wondered about the 'nature' of the sequence of photograms that make up a film. They discuss, for example, the possible artistic quality *in itself* of the uninterrupted film shoot of the *natural* behaviour of people participating in the *real* launching of a boat. It is thus possible to take the view, as the Lubin company's representative argued, that the mere shooting of a scene does not, in itself, have any artistic value. Here are the remarks of the 'interested party,'[7] one John J. Frawley:

There is no particular skill or intellectual conception or original effect embodied in the photographs representing the launching of the 'Meteor.'
These photographs are purely the results of the functions of cameras, and
a dozen different photographs with a dozen different cameras from the
same general location would necessarily have obtained the same results.
The cameras were placed in a convenient and obvious positions [sic] and
represents [sic] the objects as they subsequently arranged themselves.[8]

In the end, it matters little whether Lubin or its representatives truly
believed such hypotheses. What matters is whether or not the courts
agreed, for they were establishing jurisprudence that could play a crucial role both in the recognition of cinema as an art form within society
as a whole and, of course, in its economic development. We can well
imagine the consequences of a verdict to the effect that documentary
films, as opposed to 'staged' (fiction) films, were not protected by copyright. Frawley's argument, which in the end did not carry the day (although initially Lubin won its case in the lower courts), prompts a
number of remarks concerning the various agents of film discourse as
they have been conceived of in this book. First of all, we should agree
that his argument concerns only what we have called film monstration.
There is no concern here with that higher layer[9] of narrativity produced
by the manipulation of the images once they are shot. Rather, what is at
issue here are the 'qualities' of the mega-monstrator's intervention. First,
Frawley settles the score with the film monstrator, whose passivity is
complete and whose 'personality' is non-existent. Whoever the camera
operator may be, as long as the camera is positioned in 'the same general
location' the same shot will be obtained. The profilmic monstrator fares
no better and is judged just as severely. The profilmic monstrator has not
moulded profilmic reality – profilmic reality has appeared before the
camera through its own vital force. True enough, in the case of 'actuality
films,' the manipulation of the profilmic realm appears to be resolutely
refused to the monstrative agent. This argument, however, did not prevent the opposing party from taking the opportunity presented by this
court case to set out a counter-argument to Frawley's view of what we
have called the artistic qualities of monstration. For the head of production at Edison, the film monstrator has an important role to play in the
cinematic rendering of an event, even if it has no real control over it:

In taking moving pictures photographically, great artistic skill may be
used. As a rule the nature of the subject taken prevents the artist from

grouping or draping the objects photographed. But on the other hand, artistic skill is required in placing the camera in such a position that the lights and shades of the picture when taken shall have proper values, and the groupings of the figures and the background shall constitute a harmonious whole and have a graceful composition.[10]

The film monstrator's 'framing' activity must be seen as distinct from the profilmic monstrator's 'staging.' Each of these agents enjoys a degree of autonomy and each can contribute in its own way to making the work 'more artistic.'

The lower court, however, ruled in Lubin's favour and dismissed the case for entirely different reasons. Lubin had adroitly won the battle on two fronts. Not only could the film he had duped not legitimately be considered a work of art, but it was not even protected by copyright law. In his verdict, the judge ruled that 'every photograph [read: photogram], no matter how or for what purpose it may be conjoined with others, shall be separately registered.[11] In a sense, this decision denied the *apparent continuity* of the *linking* of the photograms that make possible the mega-monstrator's 'expression.' It also cast doubt upon the consistency of the work of monstration and the nearly-identical quality of each pair of sequential photograms within a shot. The judge who heard the appeal of this decision understood this well and, in the language of the day, employed an argument we might describe as proto-theoretical in reversing the lower court's decision:

i) since the series had been taken from one camera at one operation;
ii) since there was no distinguishable difference detectable by the naked eye between the separate pictures; and
iii) since the economic or commodity value of the footage depended on its status as a single entity, the series was practically one picture.[12]

While the first two points are based more upon the intrinsic qualities of the object at issue, the shot, and upon the operations required for its production, the third moves in a radically different direction. Here the film's commercial use and, ultimately, its social recognition were in a sense called to the witness stand in order to guarantee the *unity* of the work of monstration.

Nevertheless, this was just the beginning. A later case, brought about by the unbridled competition between U.S. companies at the turn of the century, saw 'legal-narratological' thought, in response to the question of editing, taken to the even more thorny level of film narration. The film at the root of this dispute is interesting in many respects. *Personal* (Biograph, 1904) was one of the first accomplished *chase films*, which would soon become very popular. Not only is this film fairly well known even today, but in many respects it represents the prototype of a genre of great importance, as we have already remarked, to the development of editing itself. Indeed, the progression inherent in the theme of the chase film helped alter prevailing views towards the *shot*. The dominant conception of the shot had led filmmakers to view it not only as an autonomous tableau but also – one thing implies the other – as a properly centripetal unit. This view was increasingly shaken by the breakdown of profilmic space, which had begun to 'fall to pieces,' a breakdown that was repeated each time a chase film was shot. Off-screen space seemed to call out to the camera, and the camera soon began to respond to this call with increasing frequency, thereby forcing a more systematic recourse to the 'organic' juxtaposition of different shots. This had an effect not only on the work of the profilmic monstrator (it was no longer necessary, for example, to keep the actors in a confined space) or on that of the film monstrator (here, for example, camera movement was no longer the only possible option for connecting two elements of the profilmic space). The obligatory matching of different shots of a continuous activity that could not easily be depicted in a confined space also led filmmakers to revise their perception of the film as a mere 'aggregate' of shots, to use an expression of the day. It also led them to help bring about the emergence of the film narrator, the agent responsible for connecting shots. This agent would take film narrative to hitherto unseen heights, as we have seen.

This second court case is particularly important in that the views expressed there on linking shots take as their starting point earlier opinions, from the court case discussed above, on linking photograms. We are thus forced to consider both what is similar and what is different about these two forms of linkage. As we remarked above, the first case 'settled' the issue of monstration's punctiliar or single-shot quality: a series of photographic negative impressions of 'one act or event' portrayed 'on single negative film, by one operator and a camera operated from a single point' was one negative.[13]

The second case takes the opposite view, even as it bases itself upon the jurisprudence established in the case dealing with punctiliarity. In the *Personal* case, what is at issue above all is pluri-punctiliarity – that other dimension so important to the development of the cinema and

film narration. As we have seen, pluri-punctiliarity, a product of editing, made it possible for films to go beyond monstration alone and to
enter into the realm of narration. The issues at stake in this second case
are thus entirely different, especially since Edison was not taken to
court for having *duped* the Biograph film but for having '*stolen*' the
idea, the 'script' – for having made a pastiche, a *remake* of a work held
to be original – and for subsequently marketing it under a different title: *How a French Nobleman Got a Wife through the 'New York Herald' Personal Columns* (Edison, 1904).[14] When we compare the two films, the
reason for the litigation jumps off the screen at us. It's obvious: the latter film, shot for Edison by Edwin S. Porter, repeats the Biograph film's
storyline in every detail.[15] What's more, Porter used virtually the same
locations as the Biograph film, and the settings are virtually identical
(Grant's Tomb, among other places). The crowning fact, at least from
our point of view, is that it seems as if the film narrator responsible for
linking the shots in Porter's film went to the same school as the film
narrator in the Biograph film! The two films are cut and joined in a
similar way; on every count, the Porter film is an imitation.

Edison's lawyers, this time acting on its behalf as the defendant, developed a two-pronged strategy, just as Lubin did in its battle with
Edison a couple of years earlier. Once again, the main thing at stake
was the validity of the copyright. Edison's first argument was that the
copyright protected only the strictly photographic aspect of the work
and that, as a result, the case was groundless – for Porter had not in the
least duped the work, he had only reproduced, in his own manner, the
story told. We can see quite easily how this case was distinct from
the first, even though we sense the earlier case's constant presence
throughout the deliberations, whether in the shadows or in the full
light of day. For what was being claimed here was the filmmaker's
rights, no longer to the images produced, but to the ideas behind the
construction of a narrative told in images.

The Lubin case came into play, for the most part, with respect to the
defendant's second argument: Biograph's copyright could not be valid
because it had only paid to copyright a single 'photograph' (read: shot)
within a film clearly made up of eight 'photographs' (read: shots).
Edison's lawyers maintained that complete protection could only be
obtained by 'filing eight distinct titles, making eight distinct deposits
of copies, [and] paying eight distinct fees.'[16]

In other words, the Edison company, basing itself upon the recognition of the *unity* of the product of monstration (the *punctiliar* single

Figure 10.1 *How a French Nobleman Got a Wife through the 'New York Herald' Personal Columns*, Edison, 1904 (GRAFICS)

shot), sought to play the card of the *disparity* of the product of narration, the film's *pluri-punctiliarity*. The whole trial came down to a long and interminable (but so very interesting) dispute between, on the one hand, the plaintiff (the Biograph company), which was trying to prove that a film, despite its multiplicity of shots (its *pluri-punctiliarity*), is a single and unique entity and that it could be copyrighted as a *single* photograph, and, on the other hand, the defendant (the Edison company), with Edwin S. Porter himself in the starring role (despite the fact that he is praised by many film historians as *the* continuity filmmaker in early cinema), which moved heaven and earth to demonstrate to the judge that a film such as *Personal*, despite being the product of a kind of linearity, is merely a *disjointed* assemblage of *discontinuous* scenes.[17] The Biograph film could not be viewed as a single photograph because, to quote the Edison lawyers writing a year later, using here an expression of Porter's, in reality it was only an '*aggregation* of photographs and as such cannot, in our opinion, be covered by

Figure 10.2 *Meet Me at the Fountain*, Lubin, 1904 (GRAFICS)

a single copyright.[18] Unlike *Christening and Launching*, *Personal* is not a 'connected series of "undistinguishable pictures."'[19] Rather, it is made up of 'eight distinct acts or events,' which were not filmed with a camera 'operated from a single point.'[20] The essential distinction between a punctiliar or single-shot film and a pluri-punctiliar or multiple-shot film and, in the end, between monstration and narration in the cinema, is summed up here at an astonishingly early date in the following declaration:

> Another fact noted ... in the Lubin case was that the negative simply photographically reproduced 'in *continuous* form the view which would be represented to the eye of an onlooker *on the spot* occupied by the camera.' Complainant's so-called negative reproduces in *discontinuous* form *several* views ... which could not possibly be presented to the eye of an onlooker, unless he traveled with the photographer and his pantomimic troupe from Grant's tomb through and around the surrounding country.[21]

Figure 10.3 *Dix femmes pour un mari*, Pathé, 1905 (GRAFICS)

What is being said here, as early as 1905, is that the punctiliar or single-shot film ('the view') is essentially based upon continuity – that the linking of photograms, the work of the mega-monstrator, is 'continuous' in nature. And that this mega-monstrator is a little bit like a viewer (the 'onlooker') who is a constituent element of the here-and-now ('at the spot') of the filmed event. What is also being said is that a pluri-punctiliar or multiple-shot film ('*several* views') cannot be viewed as a *single* object: it is not a single strip of film (the 'so-called negative') but a composite series. The film narrator's product is, instead, 'discontinuous,' and cannot be the work of the monstrator alone ('which could not possibly be presented to the eye of an onlooker'). The pluri-punctiliar or multiple-shot film is thus the work of a narrator that, in the gap[22] produced by the juxtaposition of two shots, makes us travel in the time and space of the monstrator's successive shots ('unless he traveled with the photographer and his pantomimic troupe from Grant's tomb through and around the surrounding country').

But what the defenders of this position do not see is that it is possible to imagine the pluri-punctiliar work of the film narrator as being just as unified, in the end, as the punctiliar work of the mega-monstrator. By insisting upon the distinction between punctiliarity ('the view') and pluri-punctiliarity ('*several* views'), Edison and its lawyers take up the cause of a cinema of discontinuity in the form of tableaux: a cinema more monstrative than narrative, and one definitely closer to the by-gone cinema of the Lumière brothers than to the cinema yet to come of someone like David Wark Griffith. Is it entirely without relevance that those who rose to the challenge posed by the Edison clan's argument and who responded in such resolute fashion to the claim that 'the negative alone requires the work of authorship,'[23] and who thus countered this thinly veiled attack on the film narrator, were the representatives of the very company that would soon hire the same D.W. Griffith to direct its films?

Is Edison's attachment to the monstrator – which alone is worthy of being called an author – the result only of a momentary legal strategy, or does it represent a steadfast statement on the proper form of film entertainment and, in the end, a very precise conception of what film 'narration' should be?[24] It seems that as early as 1904 Edison did not believe in longer films. In a sense, it rejected the 'progressive' views of the Biograph company that, already in those years, opposed the reign of monstration and clearly favoured narration, as the following declaration makes clear in an almost manifesto-like fashion:

> The photographic art has advanced beyond the point of a single view of a single object ... in *showing* not only scenes of objects and persons in motion, but also the *continuous action* of objects and persons in the portrayal of episodes, public functions and events ... The composite photographs, showing *continuous and progressive* action of objects and persons, practically constitute books written in the primitive characters of the race, as illustrated in the picture-writing of the Indians and other early peoples, and in the picture-written books for children of today.[25]

All this, of course, is pure rhetoric: Biograph wants to win its case and is trying to demonstrate by any means possible that the film *Personal*, like other pluri-punctiliar or multiple-shot films, is a single photographic entity ('a single photograph of the whole').[26] But where it counts is when this same kind of statement, only clearer and going much farther, is found coming from the mouth of the judge and serves as jurisprudence. Thus on 6 May 1905 Judge Lanning ruled that, although they might be shot from different points, 'a series of pictures that may be thrown in rapid succession upon a screen *telling a single connected story*'[27] could be copyrighted as a *single and unique* photograph; in other words, copyrighted purely and simply as if it were (or in the same manner as) a still photograph. This recognition of the *film narrator*, which now has a right to exist, also legitimated ('legalized') that agent which, as Judge Lanning himself explained in a purple passage that merits quoting here, is the *film* equivalent of the *textual* narrator:

> I am unable to see why, if a series of pictures of a moving object taken by a pivoted camera may be copyrighted as a photograph, a series of pictures telling a single story like that of the complainant in this case, even though the camera be placed at different points, may not also be copyrighted as a photograph ... In that story, it is true, there are different scenes. But no one has ever suggested that a story told in written words may not be copyrighted merely because, in unfolding its incidents, the reader is carried from one scene to another.[28]

What Judge Lanning is saying here is that the film narrator, whose pluri-punctiliar or multiple-shot linkages are just as legitimate as the punctiliar or single-shot linkages carried out by the film monstrator ('a pivoted camera,' giving rise to a pan)[29] is entitled to use a multiplicity of viewpoints ('even though the camera be placed at different points') in the same way as the textual narrator (whose 'reader is carried from one scene to another'). We should probably view this text, which records the birth of the film *narrator*, as the starting point of narratological theory of the cinema.

But this figure whose birth I have discussed here, this film *narrator* whose existence I have tried to legitimize – does it really deserve its name? Aren't we playing a dangerous game, and don't we run the risk of spreading confusion by employing, without apparent verification, concepts and terms derived from other practices and fields of study? Now that we have identified this new figure and detailed the conditions under which it exists and the context in which it emerged, it may perhaps be time to look at the concept underlying the name we have given it.

11 Narrator(s)

And I would be living with the anxiety of not knowing whether the Master of my destiny, less indulgent than the Sultan Shahriyar, when I broke off my story each morning, would stay my death sentence and permit me to take up the continuation the following evening.

Marcel Proust, *In Search of Lost Time: Finding Time Again*, 191

One of the problems in narratology (and the same is true for several other fields of study in the humanities) is the sometimes misplaced, or at any rate often sloppy, use of certain terminology. This, as we have seen, is true of the word 'narrative.' And, as we shall see, it is also true of the word 'narrator.' These terms are so loaded that a whole range of concepts can be found in them. This is normal and there is nothing to be appalled at, but, at a certain point, some fine tuning is required. Such is the case with the word 'narrator,' which has become so commonly bandied about that we might wonder if we shouldn't simply try to avoid it altogether. This term is a hundred times more polysemic than is generally believed.[1] It didn't need the arrival of narratologists to gain admittance to dictionaries that, frankly, don't have a heck of a lot to say about it. In any event, they have much less to say, as a rule, than the most laconic narrator. Thus, the *Oxford English Dictionary* gives only two very brief definitions: 'a. One who narrates. b. One who speaks a commentary in a broadcast or a film; hence also, a character who relates part of the plot of a play to the audience.'[2] The French *Robert* gives two equally brief definitions: '1. Someone who narrates, recounts, who creates a narration, a narrative. 2. In novels, the protagonist of the narrative process (on the same level as a character), whether depicted or not, and distinct (or distinguishable) from the author.'[3] And that's it! Brief but sound definitions. It is up to the speaker to make clear to which kind of narrator he or she is referring. This is why, throughout this book, I have always *qualified* the 'narrator' in question: the *underlying* narrator, the *textual* narrator, the *film* narrator, the *filmographic* narrator, the *mega*-narrator, etc.

The problems caused by the use of a word that, at bottom, is simple enough arise above all from the fact that each time narratology advances a notch the 'narrator' in question becomes less 'worldly' and increasingly de-humanized and de-anthropomorphized. The narrator *transmutes* both to the extent to which the narrative within which it functions is subjected to a process of *trans-semiotization* and to the degree to which the narrator itself is *fictionalized*. Here I refer especially to those cases in which the entire story a film 'tells' is supposedly told by a character in the film. This character, who calls him- or herself the 'narrator,' appears to be the agent responsible in the end for all the narrative utterances projected onto the screen. There are many such films, and some of them intertwine several narrative 'threads' that, as we shall see, are quite easy to untangle in the end. At the outset, the word 'narrator' designates a human being, a flesh-and-blood person (the *OED* refers to 'one') who tells a story, *verbally, in front of* you. The *bard* and the Ancient Greek *rhapsodist* are the earliest examples. The *storyteller*, who comes out of what is known, where I come from at least, as 'traditional oral culture,' is another example, closer to us in time. But there are also *Mom* and *Dad*, who serve as narrators when they tell a child a bedtime story. In fact, in modern life we are all called upon at various times to be true narrators.

The first essential quality of a narrative configuration such as those presupposed by the examples I have just given is that this configuration implies, at its source, an agent that always operates *'in praesentia.'* This kind of narrator is always located in close proximity to the people to whom they are telling their story, so much so that the latter are always able to 'touch' them.[4] Moreover, this agent always tells its story *orally*. Imagine a flesh-and-blood Shahrazad who, in 'real' life, 'really' told her husband a story every night. The *underlying narrator* would be Shahrazad and *none other*. The bard, the rhapsodist, the storyteller, Mom and Dad, a real-life Shahrazad – all these narrators have one thing in common: they are *human* beings (or at least I imagine them as such), *autonomous* beings who, as *storytellers*, exist only through their own actions. Even when their story is borrowed from another human being – even when, to put it another way, they are not the *authors* of the story they are telling – they remain the *underlying* and *primary narrators* of that story. The simple reason for this is that, as narrators, they are not the 'creatures' of anyone.

The second narratological problem we encounter because of the concept of the 'narrator' derives from the practice of what, above, I have called quoting. These narrators often relate the speech of others in their narration – speech that can be just as narrative as their own. A verbal narrator may thus 'yield' (at least in appearance, for it is always the narrator speaking, even when speaking for someone else) to another character in his or her story. This character is entrusted, for example, with the narration of his or her own story. One such case, in which the verbal narrator yields to another character only occasionally and for a very brief period each time, is that of the ancient bard who recites the *Odyssey*. This narrator, at various times, 'yields' to Telemachus or Athena or Penelope – characters who are 'present' in the scene being described by the narrator and who, on occasion, profit from this 'presence' by *narrating* what *happened* before.[5] The verbal narrator, the bard, can also, and this is a second case, 'yield' for a very long time, for a much longer section of the narrative. This is the case of the narrator – the 'living' narrator – who, during the narration of the *Odyssey*, arrives at books 9 to 12, where it is Odysseus who 'speaks' and narrates without interruption.[6] What is going on here? Who is speaking at this moment? When Odysseus 'speaks' and narrates, is it still the bard who is speaking and narrating? The answer is plain: in a narrative that presupposes a *verbal* narrator, a flesh-and-blood presence, at bottom it is always this *narrator* who is speaking. Of course, on a certain level Odysseus can be seen as a 'narrator,' one called upon to intervene momentarily; but the sole 'true' narrator, the underlying and primary narrator, is, in this case, the bard.[7]

A third problem the narrator presents narratology lies in the fact that the situation I have just described can be multiplied endlessly, something Gérard Genette saw well enough. Shahrazad showed the way by opening up several successive narrative levels in the *Arabian Nights*. For while it is always possible for a narrator (whom we'll call X), who may be the underlying narrator, to *narrate* what one of his or her characters (whom we'll call Y) *narrates*, it remains entirely imaginable and possible that one of the characters of Y's narrative (whom we'll call Z) will *narrate*, in his or her turn, a story or part of a story. And, in English, we have no other choice than to call a 'person' who is narrating, even if that person is fictive, a *narrator*. But *one* (X with respect to Y and Y with respect to Z) is not the *other* (Y in one case, Z in the other), because *one* (X or Y) has produced the *other* (Y and Z respectively). Or, better yet, because *one* (X) has created *another* (Y) who has created *another* (Z). The empirical speaker, in the case of verbal narratives *only*, remains the *primary* narrator, the *underlying* narrator, a true *supra-diegetic agent* (who is always and already *extra-diegetic*). Because, as a 'performer,' this narrator is responsible for every narrative disengagement or change of gears (in other words, for every change in the narrative level, for every shift to the – narrative – speech of another). And, we must repeat because it is not a mere detail, this is true even if the narrator is not the true *author* of the narration[8] that he or she weaves before us.[9] This underlying narrator quotes whomever he or she feels like and makes that character relate, however the *narrator* pleases, some story or another in one (narrative) form or another. This narrator can thus turn, at will, *his or her* characters, those necessarily *intra-diegetic 'beings of sounds and intonations,'*[10] into *storytellers*, into necessarily *supporting* narrators, to whom the narrator has *delegated* the task of revealing, through the narrator's voice alone, some of the vicissitudes that that character has (supposedly) experienced. Hence the very useful concept of the *delegated narrator*: every delegated narrator (Y and Z, for example) is the *product*[11] of the narrative agent immediately above it (thus Z is a narrator delegated by Y, which is itself delegated by X). Any narrator who delegates is *responsible for the voice* of his or her delegated narrator, and every delegated narrator is the product of a delegating narrator. And a *delegated* narrator – Y, for example – can also be a *delegating narrator*. However, in the case of a verbal narrative, which is told *in praesentia*, only the first of the delegating narrators, the one at the top of the pile, the one who performs, can be called the *'underlying narrator,'* the only narrator of the bunch who is not both producer *and* product.

I said above that because of a process of trans-semiotization, the concept of the narrator is called upon to become less 'worldly,' to lose its 'humanity,' and that this process causes the narrator to 'wither away.' In fact, this 'de-anthropomorphization' varies according to the difference between the level of abstraction present in the initial semiotic vehicle and the final semiotic vehicle. The 'concreteness' of *in praesentia* verbal narration is, we can readily agree, a thousand miles from textual narration, which is carried out *in absentia*, and this is one of the reasons for the difference between them. The 'live,' *real-time* narration of the former is replaced, through words on a printed page, by a *delayed-time* indirect narration. At random (do you believe me, dear reader?) I open a book entitled the *Arabian Nights* and see there, on page 27, a series of graphic signs telling me that a paper 'being,' a being without a body, is speaking to me (?), is telling me (?) a story: 'So I took me a concubine, who brought to me the boon of a male child fair as the full moon, with eyes of lovely shine and eyebrows which formed one line, and limbs of perfect design.'[12] I'm well and truly being told a story, and the person speaking, there is no other possibility, is a *narrator*. I continue reading and I realize that the person speaking is, in addition, a *diegetic* character in *another* narrative. This character-narrator is, in fact, a sheik who, having unexpectedly encountered a merchant condemned to death by a genie, attempts to buy the merchant's life by telling the genie his story. Hence the attribution that precedes the above quote in the text: 'Thereupon the old man began to tell / *THE FIRST SHAYKH'S STORY*' is immediately followed by the speech of another agent ('Know O Jinni! That this gazelle is the daughter of my paternal uncle').[13] This is an indisputable indication that it is not me, the reader, to whom the sheik is speaking, but a genie, an internal agent of the diegesis – not of the diegesis produced by the sheik, but of the diegesis the sheik is also a part of and which is produced by another, superior agent. I thus easily figure out, by reading this short and simple passage ('Thereupon the old man began to tell / *THE FIRST SHAYKH'S STORY* / Know O Jinni! That this gazelle is the daughter of my paternal uncle') that there are two voices here, the voice of the *delegated narrator* (the sheik) and that of the *delegating narrator*, who has yet to be identified.

If this delegated narrator, the sheik, is addressing not me but the genie when he tells his story, then, for its part, is the delegating narrator, the voice that says, 'Thereupon the old man began to tell ...,' addressing me, the reader? I investigate and discover, to my great surprise, that the agent speaking here is a woman, that her name is Shahrazad,[14] and that she is no more speaking to me than the sheik. She is *telling* this story of the merchant to her husband, King Shahryár,[15] another diegetic character. It is a story within which the sheik *tells* another story. Her husband intends to cut off her head when the night is out, but she uses her talent for telling stories, night after night, each story more captivating than the last. This narrator of a thousand and one nights, is she the *underlying narrator*? Certainly this woman, the heroine of the framing story, as it is known, narrates most of the time. Her voice appears to modulate this 'story of the merchant and the genie.' However, although she may be a narrator, she can't claim to have the same status as a 'living Shahrazad' like the one we discussed above. Not only is she only a paper being, like any textual narrator, but she is the *heroine* (and thus a character) of a *narrative* (the framing story). This narrative is that of another agent, one that is superior to her.[16] And this agent's voice, the *primary* voice, modulates, controls, and above all *produces* all the others. This voice is that of the *underlying narrator* – the 'great writer,' to use an expression equivalent to the 'great image-maker' in film. This voice speaks of Shahrazad in the third person and, addressing no diegetic agent, opens the book with these words describing the family of Shahrazad's husband:

> Therein it is related … that … there was a King of the Kings of the Banu Sásán in the Islands of India and China, a Lord of armies and guards and servants and dependents. He left only two sons, one in the prime of manhood and the other yet a youth … So [the elder] succeeded to the empire; when he ruled the land and lorded it over his lieges with justice so exemplary that he was beloved by all the people of his capital and of his kingdom. His name was King Shahryár.[17]

This underlying narrator is also responsible for the thousand and one attributions that introduce Shahrazad's speech night after night: 'And Shahrazad perceived the dawn of day and ceased to say her permitted say. Now when it was the fifty-seventh Night, She said …'[18] Naturally, if I open the book here and there at random I'll be more likely to find her speaking than I am to find the underlying narrator speaking.[19] But we must be clear, as Gerald Prince remarked about attributions, that 'whatever the diversity of voices at work, in the end (inevitably!) it is the same voice narrating.'[20] This voice is that of the *underlying narrator,* the 'great writer,' the equivalent of the flesh-and-blood narrator's 'great speaker' of verbal narrative – the image *in* the text (and thus intratextual) of that extra-textual being, the flesh-and-blood author. And narratologists *must not* identify this agent with the author, even timidly.[21] In the case of textual narrative, there is no need for narratologists to work back to the living source, because textual narratives are not performed '*in situ.*' The creative act *has taken place* (after which the author is no more and no less than a 'has been'). The only *in situ* agent *present*, the only agent from whom some sort of performance is required, is the *reader.* It is the reader who must reconstruct the narrative, *now.*

Hence the need to 'boot' the author out of narratology, which is essentially a science of narrative and narrators, not of those who create these![22] And it is not because the author is 'human' that we kick him or her out, because the equally human storyteller of traditional oral culture has a place in narratology. It is simply because, as I have tried to demonstrate, the author is not a narrator. Or, if you prefer, a narrating agent. While we might view the author as *already* having been involved in the task of narrating, he or she is no longer narrating for me, the reader of this *recorded account* that is any textual narrative. This textual narrative is distilled in the *present* by the author's intratextual image, the underlying narrator, which is not a human being but a construct. Oswald Ducrot summed this up when he remarked, 'While you have to be alive to write, this isn't necessary in order to tell.'[23] This, however, does not mean that all authors, as such, are ejected beyond the bounds of narratology. Some of them, having chosen the path of the here-and-now, do not record their event. They can thereby transform themselves, by popular demand, into narrating beings, into narrators. This is the case with those storytellers who recite a story of their own invention, which nothing prevents them from doing. I repeat, however, that they thereby enter narratology as narrators, not as authors.[24]

To put the whole matter a different way: the semiotic vehicle of *verbal narrative* is, despite appearances, quite different than the semiotic vehicle of *textual narrative*. While both derive from one and the same 'dialect,' and while textual narrative may thus appear to be only the transcription of verbal narrative, we must not forget that they presuppose two completely different *narrative and declaratory systems*. Verbal narrative features a narrator who is *present* and quite real. Even if this narrator tells a story that he or she has not *really* authored, he or she *really* does tell it, in person. Whether this narrator is the author of the original narrative or not, the facts of the matter are altered by his or her status as the author-of-the-narrative-such-as-it-is-performed, the author of the narrative performance, of the performance of a narrative that may exist prior to this performance. Indeed, this status turns the storyteller, that agent who tells stories using his or her own voice (in the literal sense), into one of the rare examples of an organic cohesion between the extra-textual agent (the author) and the intra-textual agent (the underlying narrator). Narratology must be careful to distinguish between these two agents; but here they are superimposed – a case of the return of Plato's *haplē diēgēsis*, because Plato's simple narrative is a form in which the *underlying narrator* is a 'living being.' In circumstances such as these, narratologists must agree to create room for the author, which the narrator may also be, contrary to the case of textual narratives. For while the narrator may be particularly visible in verbal narrative, on the 'stage' where the narrative unfolds (or is delivered), in textual narrative the narrator can only be the *source* of a text. This text is then 'narrativized' through the obligingness of an all-powerful reader. The author lies at the *source* of textual narrative, and thus *before* it and *beyond* it.

Herein lies the need to put the author back outside the text by means of this cornerstone of the *narrative system* I'm proposing here, the *underlying narrator*. This narrator is a paper being even less corporeal than the characters of the narrative, because it is not acted out. It is an agent with no name, with no personal name, because it is not a person but, precisely, an agent, one that arranges and puts things in place. This prevents it, irreducibly, from saying '*I.*' We should assume that such an agent exists in *every* narrative, even one that begins deictically, with 'For a long time, I went to bed early'[25] or 'Mother died today.'[26] This *im*personal (or rather, *a*personal) agent cannot, because it is not acted out, introduce itself. It can, therefore, only introduce others – those acted-out agents that move about in a diegetic universe from which this primary agent is definitively excluded. This agent's invisibility is easily achieved because its textual nature, its 'pencilistic' essence, if you'll permit, makes it easy to *obliterate* it, to *rub it out*. As easy as it was for one of the 'presenters' of the *Arabian Nights*, for example, to rub Shahrazad-the-narrator and the framing story that gave her 'life' out of this version of the book:

> The stories that make up this volume have been chosen with great care from among the 180 stories in the *Arabian Nights* ... Since the framing story to the *Arabian Nights* is only completely intelligible within the entire collection of stories, it was not possible to include it here.[27]

The late Shahrazad! The ineffable but not ineffaceable Shahrazad ... a being more of ink or lead than of paper. And thus delible. And I can imagine Camus, too, rubbing out, in a stroke of genius, all the attributions throughout his famous novel, beginning with the inelegant (and apocryphal) sentence 'And Meursault, despite being so indifferent to everything around him, sat down and wrote: "Mother died today..."' I can imagine Proust, too, the night before delivering his manuscript to the printer, 'suddenly' deciding to remove every 'he' from his saga and replacing them with 'I,'[28] a more truthful 'he' than this sham 'I,' this necessarily sham 'I.' Because if Proust, as a writer of fiction, allowed himself to fabulize to the first degree by textually describing the fictive activities of his Marcel, he carried out a second degree of fabulation by bringing his book to the world with the pretence, achieved by interpolating 'I' here and there throughout the text, that Marcel was Marcel Proust.[29]

The underlying narrator is the agent that speaks of others by saying 'he' or 'she,' but that never agrees to talk about itself, that never proffers an 'I.' It is the agent we must suppose exists and whose image, lying beneath the surface throughout the work, we must therefore find, from the moment the agent we have identified as the primary agent lets slip a self-incriminating 'I' – which, in the final analysis, automatically condemns it to being only a secondary agent.

This intra-textual image of the author, which corresponds more or less to the *implicit author*, whose traces Wayne Booth was right in seeking out,[30] will thus never be clothed in the cheap finery of anthropomorphism.[31] Because in the end, this agent is nothing more than a 'wordmill,' a 'telling machine,' to use a term of Stendhal's.[32] Delegated narrators alone present human characteristics (even though they are only fictive beings). This is because they are *fictionalized* – the work, precisely, of the *underlying narrator*. This underlying narrator cannot be fictionalized in this way because of its primary role, its place at the source of all things, which prevents it from being 'fictionalized' in any way whatsoever. This underlying narrator is without a doubt the only 'onlooker' not, at the same time, being 'looked at' – the only *teller* not to be *told*.

By touching things up a little, we will see that film narrative works in just the same way. It is equally possible in film narrative to resort to any number of *delegated narrators*, who share the same features as their counterparts in textual narrative. By this I mean that, like Marcel or Meursault, they give the impression of distilling the narrative as a whole – like textual delegated narrators, delegated narrators in film give themselves (false) airs of being mega-narrators. This is true, for example, of Walter Neff, the hero of *Double Indemnity* (Billy Wilder, U.S., 1944), of Von Stratten in *Mr. Arkadin* (a.k.a. *Confidential Report*, Orson Welles, U.S., 1955), and, more recently, of Romano in *Oci Ciornie* (*Dark Eyes*, Nikita Mikhalkov, Italy, 1987). These characters are all narrators who present themselves as underlying but whom narratology should have less trouble 'unmasking,' because we are dealing here with films and not texts. For it is eminently more difficult to drive the underlying narrator out into the open in a semiotic vehicle that, because of the 'unbearable lightness' of the abstract words it expresses, has greater powers for rendering the underlying narrator invisible. Because, despite their 'impalpability,' the cinema's so very concrete images show Neff, Von Stratten, and Romano to the viewer 'life size' and reveal these characters' very nature as *shown*. They demonstrate that they are 'iconic attributions,' the necessary product of another's gaze, of the gaze of another agent. This gaze is that of an organizing agent which, precisely, shows us this acted-out agent. It is the gaze of a 'shower,' of a monstrator that, because of its 'speaking part,' is the representative, while these films are running, of the mega-narrator our enquiries above brought to light. How indeed could Neff, Von Stratten, Romano, and their ilk, despite their role as narrators, be anything but the product of the gaze (and the writing) of another agent, the underlying narrator? Aren't they, at bottom – and this is not negligible – mere *sub*-narrators: *identified as such, explicit, acted-out,* and *delegated?*

Herein lies the desire, more on the part of narratologists who work with film than of those who work with texts, to locate and identify the decidedly non-anthropomorphic agent responsible for the work's narrative utterances. As André Gardies has remarked, 'In the case of cinema, it would be well to identify the agent making this utterance, beyond its diegetic manifestations in the form of characters and steering well clear of any sort of anthropomorphism.'[33] For it is true that it is easier to convince ourselves of the 'machine-like' – and thus resolutely non-anthropomorphic – nature of an agent that is ultimately responsible for a product that is only partially but truly the product of the machines used to record the sound and image, the sound recorder and camera.

Paradoxically, however, cinema has on occasion created a special place for a completely anthropomorphic narrator – even a truly 'anthropic' one. Indeed, there was once a time, at the turn of the twentieth century, when two concurrent and simultaneous narrative performances took place whenever a film was shown. These two performances were relatively independent of each other and did not use the same semiotic vehicle or the same means of expression. On the one hand, there were the images used in the visual narrative. This

Figure 11.1 *Double Indemnity*, Billy Wilder, 1944 [Still] (Cinémathèque québécoise)

was seen at the time as somewhat lacunary, to the degree that it was accompanied, on the other hand, by a lecturer, a true storyteller who, as an assistant to the narrative, propped up the visual monstration with his own verbal narration. This made it possible for the cinema to achieve veritable narrative 'feats' that it would achieve using solely cinematic means only some years later, with the arrival of the 'talkies.' This quite original combination of an iconic mega-monstrator and a verbal narrator (who sometimes competed with the film narrator, who spoke as yet only 'baby talk') was inherited from magic lantern shows and created a narrative complex of great interest to anyone wishing to understand the variety of narrative possibilities available to film's mega-narrator and the later role of the 'voice-off' narrator's narrative 'voice,' which would take flight with the talkies. The final two chapters of this book will deal precisely with these two kinds of narrative systems, each of which presupposes the use of the human voice.

Figure 11.2 *Dark Eyes*, Nikita Mikhalkov, 1987 [Still] (Cinémathèque québé-coise)

12 A Monstrative Entertainment, Assisted by Narration

Descended from the fairground barker, and more specifically from the magic lantern lecturer, the film lecturer had, it seems, particular importance during the first decade of film exhibition. He furnished audiences with an oral commentary accompanying the projection of the film ... and influenced in a crucial manner the way films were experienced during the earliest period of film history.

Tom Gunning, David Wark Griffith, 84

We know that so-called silent cinema was a time of numerous and diverse experiments in the three kinds of cinematic sound, as Christian Metz understood them: sounds, speech, and music. What is less well known, and what we too often neglect to take into account, is the absolutely primordial importance of this fact. It was exceedingly rare for a film screening in the silent era to take place in complete silence.[1] One of the fundamental, but too often overlooked, aspects of early cinema is that even then film shows were almost always as much an *audio*-visual entertainment as were the theatre or the circus, for example. Of course, it is difficult today to study this aspect of film shows with as much confidence as we could wish, because only faint traces of them remain, traces for the most part rare and incomplete. Nevertheless, sound was a fundamental element of silent cinema, one we should take into account if we are to have a complete understanding of film during this period. This is especially true given that one of the forms this sound took, the lecturer's narrative speech, is of primordial importance to anyone who wants to understand the diverse forms of film narrative.

The essential difference between the sound of silent films and that of talkies is, obviously, that with a few exceptions the former was not recorded but was a unique performance limited to a single screening. This had a profound impact on the viewer's experience, which was stamped with the live and haphazard nature of the performance, the complete opposite of the system under which recorded sounds and images were consumed after the 'talkie revolution.' Viewers today, despite their superficial and momentary belief in the present-tense quality of the film's sound and images, know that the performance they are witnessing is, in principle, unalterable from one screening to the next. We know that the next person to sit in our seat, at the next screening, will have the same experience we did. Only some technical mishap in the projection booth or some unusual event in the cinema beneath it is capable of disrupting the unfolding of events just as we are seeing them. Everything (or almost everything) has been foreseen, from an 'elsewhere' that is, above all, a 'before.' At the cinema, we are thus always conscious that we are not actors in some sort of 'happening,' unless the film is called *The Rocky Horror Picture Show* (Jim Sharman, U.S., 1975). We are certainly asked to participate actively, but this participation is above all psychic in nature. The sound in a 'silent' film, on the other hand, as we will now discuss, was a unique performance, given anew at each show. It thus operated entirely differently than sound in film today. As Norman King has so aptly described, sound performances during this era produced effects in the cinema that recorded sound could not, a sense of immediacy and participation. Live sound actualized the image and, merging with it, emphasized the presentness of the performance and of the audience.[2]

Under conditions such as these, a film's 'performance,' contrary to the way films came to be viewed after the arrival of the talkies, was not the mere reprise of a show that had been 'canned' beforehand and elsewhere. And this is probably true of the great majority of public film screenings between 1895 and 1927, accompanied as they were by live music, by sound effects, or in some cases by dialogue acted out behind the screen by flesh-and-blood actors. Or, finally, as was frequently the case before 1910, by the commentary of a 'lecturer,' who would explain a film's narrative development or patter away as the film unfolded in order to highlight what viewers saw – and heard. The sounds of so-called silent cinema were present to such a degree that viewers were undoubtedly familiar with this aspect of a film's exhibition. Film history books are full of examples showing beyond any doubt that the film-going experience in those years was also an auditory one. And within that experience, speech, even recorded speech, was often privileged over other sounds. Already, even before the invention of the Lumière cinematograph, Edison and Dickson had made a few attempts to synchronize (recorded) sound and images for the kinetoscope. And Chronophone Gaumont's 'Phonoscènes' enjoyed a relatively long life in Paris between 1906 and 1912.

But we mustn't forget that beyond these examples the Lumière cinematograph had piano accompaniment right from the start. The screen's uneasy silence was probably seen as a defect even in these first days of film exhibition.

The cinema was thus an audio-visual entertainment right from the start. But instrumental music played live by a pianist or, quite often, an entire orchestra, was only a tiny part of the various ways in which sound was explored during this period. At the turn of the century it was not uncommon, for example, for singers to perform, particularly whenever song slides were shown. This form of entertainment is of special interest because of the way it juxtaposed the live voice with pre-recorded images.[3] We might also mention the fairly frequent phenomenon of flesh-and-blood actors hiding behind the screen in order to deliver their lines in sync with the actors on the screen; Edison's *College Chums* (1907), for example, was made expressly for this purpose.

For us, however, the most important of these numerous examples of how sound was used remains the lecturer. The lecturer was, until recently, largely neglected in studies of the period and little was known about him. As I remarked in the previous chapter, this figure – part acousmatic, part visualized, to use Michel Chion's terms[4] – came straight out of the magic lantern show. Indeed, the cinema extended the tradition of using screens for mostly narrative purposes.[5] The narrative quality of the stories told by magic lanternists owed much more to the commentator-lanternist himself, who functioned as a narrator and a storyteller, than it did to the sequence of slides, which were few in number and immobile. Given their relatively sparse number (often no more than a dozen) and especially their absence of movement, the narrativity of these slides, which simply followed on one after the other, was relatively weak and undoubtedly quite indecipherable. The inevitably numerous and abrupt ellipses could only produce an extremely perturbing effect of discontinuity. This is why I believe it is more correct to see magic lantern projections as verbal narratives embellished by on-screen illustrations. There the lanternist's text took

Figure 12.1 *College Chums,* Edison, 1907 (GRAFICS)

precedence over that of the slides, despite the latter's 'spectacular' quality (in the sense of appealing to the eye). This paradox, however, is easily understood. Because if we wish to tell a story, we must make use of one of the two fundamental means of communicating a narrative: narration or what I have called monstration. To tell a story, you must either narrate the various events it is made up of (narration), which is what the lanternist does, or show them (monstration), which is what his glass slides do. The relative narrative 'deficiency' of the fixed images probably made the characters appear not to be autonomous, and this explains the recourse to verbal narration. In the case of the magic lantern show, monstration was not enough to communicate a narrative project of any complexity, because of the immobility of the images and the muteness of the 'actors.' Monstration functions perfectly well, on the contrary, in the theatre, for example, where there is no need to resort to a superimposed narration: the characters both move about and speak. The actors, through their performance (their acting), tell the story and act it out, right before our eyes. There is no need for the intervention of a lecturer such as the lanternist.

The cinematograph, whose models were both the magic lantern show and the theatre, is situated mid-way between these two spectacles: early cinema went beyond the magic lantern show (film characters, like those of the theatre, are more 'real' and 'move about') and yet fell short of the theatre (film characters, like those of magic lantern shows, are less 'real' and less 'talkative'). This lack of speech in early cinema meant that its monstrative quality was, there too, felt to be a relative shortcoming. This is probably why, in part,[6] film shows took a truly hybrid form in these early years: by virtue of the movement inherent in their images, they borrowed characters who 'move about' from the theatre while retaining the commentator from the magic lantern show, who compensated for the void left by the impossibility of hearing these characters speak.

It appears that the cinema had intermittent recourse to the film lecturer between 1895 and 1910. He was certainly never a necessary presence everywhere films were shown, even when he was most in fashion. This gave rise to a fair number of problems, because some films were expressly produced with the idea that they could only be understood with the help of the lecturer's mega-diegetic speech.[7] But what was this lecturer's real role? Why were his services necessary?

In the first place, the lecturer's explanations served to resolve a number of problems around the film's intelligibility. Until about 1901, there was no great need to resort to the lecturer in order for audiences to understand the story being told, because most films were relatively simple and quite easily understood. For the most part, they were made up of a single shot, and they most often sought to provide nothing more than visual pleasure. The narrative was not prominent and audiences 'read' it in a manner that was as much topological as it was chronological. It was simply a question of viewers seeing and looking, and for this there was no need for a lecturer-assistant. This is not to say that there was no lecturer present in those years, far from it. Because we mustn't forget that back then exhibitors were solely responsible for the shows they *produced*: they decided in which order to show the films, they chose the music played, and they introduced other media to the show. In some cases their work consisted in part in enticing passers-by to enter the show by acting as a 'barker.' This was particularly important in these early years, when there were very few fixed and permanent venues in which films were shown and thus little in the way of established film-going habits. The barker could also continue his commentary beyond the beginning of the film and become, presto, the film lecturer, whose aim in those years was to entertain the audience and hold their interest.

Around 1902, however, films began to get longer, stories became more complex, and, above all, shots became more numerous. Indeed with the arrival of pluri-punctiliar or multiple-shot films (which were very few in number before this date), narrative continuity, which hitherto had been fairly easily procured by the film mega-monstrator, the agent responsible for the punctiliar or single-shot narrative, found itself under threat. Each break in the narrative gave rise to spatial or temporal ellipses, created holes in the narrative, and left the door open to interpretation, if not outright incomprehension. Herein lay the difficulty of producing a clear and intelligible narrative, at a time when editing was only at a rudimentary stage of its development and the agent responsible for ordering shots, the film narrator, had not yet arrived on the scene. In the words of Tom Gunning, before about 1910 'the narrator ... is sporadic, an occasional specter rather than a unified presence.'[8]

In the meantime, there were only two ways to provide a degree of continuity between shots and to make it possible for viewers to grasp the meaning that was being produced in fits and starts on the screen as the camera stopped and started. One way was to turn the management of the narrative over to the *narrative voice of the lecturer*, and the other was to resort to *intertitles*, which, incidentally, began to appear around 1903. Since the film's characters had no voice (dialogue would have helped viewers more easily grasp the meaning being produced diegetically), and since films were becoming longer and more complex, it came to be seen as necessary to resort to a *narrator*. And this narrator, at a time when the narrative faculties of *editing* had not yet been developed, carried out its task of narrating through speech, whether this language was in the form of text (intertitles) or spoken words (the lecturer).

This need to resort to a narrative voice beyond the film's images appears to have been felt at two distinct moments before 1910, at least in the United States. The first was between 1902 and 1904, for reasons I have just explained. The second was from 1908 onwards, when the film industry was undergoing a number of major changes. Between these two dates the need for a narrator was much less urgently felt, although without ever disappearing entirely.[9] For it was in 1904 that a very simple kind of editing, the syntagmatic juxtaposition of shots through the use of spatial and temporal matching shots, began to appear. This made possible the rise of a narrative form that would soon see its glory days: the chase film. Because its subject matter supposed a relatively linear movement of two types of characters (the pursuers and the pursued), this very popular genre not only facilitated the development of an 'editing frame of mind,' it also made it possible for filmmakers to practise using the mental matches required to link two distinct shots separated by a spatio-temporal gap. In any event, most chase films shot between 1904 and 1907 were very easy to understand and could easily forgo an outside narrative voice, whether in the form of intertitles or a lecturer. We can assume that the growing popularity of this genre between 1904 and 1907 contributed at the same time to the apparent decline of the lecturer.

Beginning in 1908, however, the film industry underwent a profound transformation. One of the principal manifestations of this transformation was the appeal to a middle-class audience, which until then had remained more or less aloof from the dark places in which, in some people's view, debauched entertainments were shown. This avowed desire to increase the audience for film had a number of consequences I cannot discuss in detail here. It is clear, however, that such an attempt to 'elevate' the audience could only work if the subject matter of films was also 'elevated.' This explains the systematic recourse, beginning in those years, to tried-and-true literary and theatrical works. One of the first such movements was the *film d'art* in France. The task of systematically adapting great literary works, however, was not without its problems, because, as Tom Gunning explains, 'this ambition was the cause, at the same time, of a crisis in film narrative; faced with the adaptation of *verbal* works, presented *without sound*, audiences found them incomprehensible.'[10] To this we must add that film narratives, whether adaptations or not, started to become somewhat longer and increasingly complex. Filmmakers began to take certain liberties and produce narratives much more difficult to understand. It was frequent, between 1908 and 1909, to see letters to the editor or articles by critics in trade journals complaining about the complete incomprehensibility of certain films and the difficulty in understanding many others. As early as September 1906 *Views and Film Index* had taken a very clear stance on the matter in a veritable indictment entitled 'Moving Pictures – for Audiences, Not for Makers': 'Manufacturers should produce films which can be understood easily by the public. It is not sufficient that the makers understand the plot – the pictures are made for the public.'[11]

Later, in February 1908, an article appeared in *Moving Picture World*[12] in which the author stated, in all seriousness, that only one film in fifty was adequately understood by viewers unless it benefited from commentary by a lecturer before or during the screening. We can thus easily imagine that one of the principal concerns of producers of the day was to encourage filmmakers to find a way to create ambitious narratives that could dispense with the services of the lecturer – a useful assistant, certainly, but an oh-so-cumbersome one. In fact, there was a solution that did not rely on the lecturer's voice: this was to transfer any comments he might make, and if possible to summarize them in the process, into intertitles, which would then be sprinkled liberally throughout the narrative. While this solution had the advantage of rendering the narration external to the images uniform and, especially, of giving complete control over the work back to the producer (control that had for too long been left in the hands of the exhibitor), it had its own drawbacks, drawbacks that were significant enough to make it inadequate. In order to be truly effective, this method required that the intertitles be employed frequently ('at every place on film wherein an explanation is necessary,' an Iowa exhibitor remarked in an appeal to producers).[13] And there were two major objections to this solution: intertitles increased the cost of a film significantly (at the time, films were sold by the foot or metre), and they interrupted the flow of images.

In the end, the solution that won out over all others, as film history has shown, was to incorporate the film narrator into the film itself. And it was in 1908 that one David Wark Griffith began to make films – films that would end up establishing a narrator that no longer had need of the *human voice* to convey its own *narrative voice* and succeed, by means of editing, in insinuating itself *among the images* in order to present and order them, and even to comment on them. As Tom Gunning remarks:

> The *narrator-system* could be described as an interiorized film lecturer ... However, this narrator was not located off-screen, but was absorbed into the images themselves and the way they are joined. The *narrator-system* seems to 'read' the images to the audience in the very act of presenting them. The narrator is invisible, revealing his presence only in the way he reveals the images on the screen.[14]

As cinema developed it thus gave rise, for the numerous reasons I have just outlined as well as others besides, to the emergence of the *film narrator*. As I have remarked, the film narrator was responsible for a film's editing or, more precisely, for all those operations involved in the manipulation of already-filmed images (the work of the mega-monstrator) at the production level. This collusion between the *film narrator* and the *film mega-monstrator* (the latter being the result itself of a collusion between the *profilmic monstrator* and the *film monstrator*) gave birth to the agent I have named the *film mega-narrator,* the agent ultimately responsible for communicating a film's mega-narrative. And just as the lecturer, that flesh-and-blood oral narrator, had been 'breathed into life' by the very phenomenon he commented on from outside it, so now the viewer could also aspire to enter the fiction in turn.[15]

We have thus passed from one mode of consuming film to another, from a cinema (early cinema) that supposed a relationship of *exhibitionist encounter* between the viewer and the screen, to a cinema that remains dominant to this day and that supposes instead a form of *narrative absorption* on the part of the viewer; an absorption into a world that reveals to the viewer a series of moving pictures that, having found a degree of equilibrium and autonomy, are able to dispense with that cumbersome figure the lecturer, a veritable 'explainer of films.'[16] The human voice was thus evacuated from cinemas for a good number of years, leaving it a place on the film strip that was only textual, in the form of intertitles. At times these conveyed the voices of actors, at others the voice of the mega-narrator. Finally, it was only when intertitles fell into disuse, with the appearance of recorded and synchronized sound tracks during the 'talkie revolution,' that a commentator's voice-off (or rather voice-over) resurfaced: a true lecturer's voice, but now it was embedded in a parallel track on the film strip. The added difference being that viewers were now dealing with an acted-out voice that had been recorded and, in order to be heard, had had to irrupt into the profilmic 'world' (if only on the level of the sound track) as an agent that, unlike the lecturer, had had to push its way into the film.

Such an intrusion into the realm of the diegesis by this seemingly more legitimate narrator, or at any rate by this narrator better integrated into the film than the early cinema lecturer's unique performance, served to muddy the waters considerably. I mean narratologically speaking, of course, because film narrative, despite its apparent similarity to staged narrative, became able to imitate, in an even more euphoric manner, textual narrative. Or rather, a certain kind of textual narrative: that textual narrative which *pretends* to be distilled, word by word and sentence by sentence, by an explicit and acted-out narrator (who is thus a delegated and secondary narrator). This narrator's power lies precisely in making the textual narratologist believe that he or she is the *underlying narrator*. It is thus not surprising, especially since film narratology is itself modelled, inevitably, on textual narratology, that such a narrator, who seems to be completely extra-diegetic, has pulled the wool over the eyes of film narratologists in the same way it has pulled the wool over the eyes of 'indigenous' narratologists and has contributed to balling up the skein of narrative threads, the yarn that makes up even the least complex of film narratives. The following and final chapter of this book will be devoted to these questions, which are of primordial importance given that one of my objectives is precisely to provide the reader with tools for understanding how film narrative works, whatever the era. Many films blithely mix narrative levels (*Dark Eyes*, for example), and the ground we have covered so far should make it possible for us to evaluate the role in the narrative fabric of the human voice that narrates, sometimes throughout the entire film, the vicissitudes of its characters, and that often seems to give impetus to the advancement of the narrative – the voice that 'tricks' us, viewers and narratologists alike, into thinking that it alone distils the vivid 'story'[17] it presents us in images and sounds.

13 Delegated Film Narrators

When we turn to sound film, it is difficult to grant that the film is only transmitting a story... There still exist, at least by rights, two levels: one ... is to be found in the image, while the other ... is transmitted by the dialogue.

François Jost, *Cinémas de la modernité: Films, théories*, 26

The arrival of sound recording considerably altered the narrative economy of film. After the frenzy of the century's early years, 'silent' cinema had become increasingly ... silent. Although there were many examples of live 'sound tracks' throughout the 1920s, films were now usually accompanied only by a piano or orchestra. Dialogue was now normally found only on intertitles, the lecturer having fallen silent long before.[1] The 'talkie revolution' put the human voice back on the agenda, allowing cinema to explore new narrative avenues, particularly by resorting to that assistant known as the voice-off narrator, a worthy successor to the early cinema lecturer. Unlike its turn-of-the-century ancestor, this acted-out narrator, because it was incorporated into the film itself, could, moreover, attempt to 'suggest that anyone other than himself is speaking' (Plato 393a), could attempt to convince everyone, from the mere filmgoer to the narratologist, that *it* was always the one speaking and telling, *throughout* the film's chain of events, whatever the means of expression used in any given moment of the discourse. We must, therefore, attempt to grasp this syncretic[2] phenomenon of the 'sound and dialogue film narrative' in its entirety if we are properly to appraise the specificity of each of the various narrative levels upon which and with which the film narrator can act. The film narrator: that 'great image-maker,' or what we have termed the film mega-narrator.

While we might view the discourse of the film mega-monstrator (responsible for staging events on film) and of the filmographic narrator (responsible for linking them to each other) as being located on a distinct (and subordinate) level from that of the mega-narrator (responsible for their specifically filmic expression), we must ask ourselves how the reappearance of the lecturer in the form of the verbal narrator fits into this system. The verbal narrator, who is more or less (but always to some extent) acted out, offers commentary – conveyed from a greater or lesser distance (the character he or she represents may or may not be a protagonist in the story) and from a more or less fixed point of view (remaining invisible or not) – on the sounds and images telling a story for which this agent itself appears responsible on a narratological level. The first thing we must remark upon is that an agent of this kind can take the form, on both a narratological and a diegetic level, of different narrative systems. It can be involved in the narrative to varying degrees. It seems to me that this agent's most radical and important distinguishing features, in this respect, concern the use it may make of the language's deictics (thus establishing the degree to which it is a speaking agent) and, especially, its propensity to use, in reference to itself, the word 'I.' Because while it is true, as Émile Benveniste claims, that the moment speech is anchored by an 'I' 'a human experience takes form anew and reveals the linguistic instrument behind it,'[3] the status of any film narrator that manifests itself verbally must be seen to change entirely according to whether this agent permits itself to proffer one or more 'I's to designate itself.[4]

Let's take an example: Nikita Mikhalkov's *Dark Eyes* (1987), which had just been released at the time of this book's first edition. This film is quite typical of a narrative with an acted-out narrator (Romano, played by Marcello Mastroianni) whose task is to recount some of his past adventures. On a certain level, the film is quite easy to summarize: a waiter getting on in years who works in the dining room of a cruise ship tells a passenger about his meeting a young Russian woman, with whom he fell in love. That's all. The framework of this narrative, which we would have to describe as 'primary,' has a disarming simplicity, and its diegesis is of very short duration: only a few hours at most pass between the time of the obliging passenger's arrival in the dining room and the moment when Romano's boss calls him to order, thereby putting a definitive end to the narrative. At a stretch, the camera might

Figure 13.1 *Dark Eyes*, Nikita Mikhalkov, 1987 [Still] (Cinémathèque québécoise)

very well have restricted itself to this setting and remained focused on this somewhat 'over the hill' waiter and his diegetic listener for the entire 114 minutes of the film. Happily, the story Romano recounts verbally contains episodes juicy enough to be of interest to the viewer. Even more happily, 'someone' had the bright idea of erasing the image of this waiter and the sound of his voice here and there throughout the film and of replacing these with the sounds and images of the *very story* he is telling – to the great delight of the film's viewers, for this means that we have something to look at other than these two men, of whom we soon see all we need to see. And to the great detriment of narratologists, who must deal with a relatively complex film narrative within which a verbal narrator, one acted-out and on-screen, transforms the task of attributing narrative responsibilities into a narratological nightmare.

This way of telling stories through the medium of film (or rather, of telling through the medium of film a story that someone is 'filmico-verbally' telling) adds a new layer in which a narrative voice can manifest itself – in a medium whose narrative possibilities (or rather its mega-narrative possibilities) are, as we have demonstrated, already rather polyphonic. Such an inopportune intrusion into the filmic mega-narration by a narrative agent proffering 'I's to all and sundry made it possible for cinema to accede to a kind of narrative that, structurally speaking, had usually been the preserve of textual narrative: personal narration. These 'I's that soon came to be sprinkled throughout the text of the film narrative thus created a filmic being who, in the manner of textual narration, could pose as the apparent illocutionary source of narrative utterances and thus add new weight to the already heavy task that befalls the film narratologist. This is even more true given that this intrusion of the 'I' is made through non-visual means, as this remark by François Jost describes quite well:

> In cases where narrators designate themselves as such (as storytelling agents) by means only of an intertitle or a voice-off, we can assume that every image in which they appear as a character is a part of their narrative and that they are thus playing the role of the 'great image-maker.' Narratological analysis becomes more complex when a character places him- or herself in the position of a *storyteller* within an image.[5]

A procedure such as this (putting a character in the role of a storyteller) made possible the appearance in film of the delegated narrator, that traditional kind of secondary narrator who is also a storyteller (telling a story) and a story told ('someone' tells what this agent tells): a worthy successor to Shahrazad, Jacques le Fataliste, des Grieux, and their ilk. It is a model to which we owe this re-assertion of the narratorial 'I' in the foreground of a medium to which it was not particularly well suited, because, structurally speaking, specifically 'cinematic' language is not equipped with this strictly linguistic sememe, with this seemingly so simple pronoun to express the first person.

Of course techniques exist for expressing a degree of subjectivity, without using 'I,' techniques within the reach of both the most everyday filmographic narrators (the act of sequencing) and the most everyday film mega-monstrators (the act of filming). As Jost explains so well:

> The narrative act is really only perceptible when the image is disassociated from mimetic illusion (through mis-framing, bizarre camera movements, matching shots, etc.). In other words, when, by means of visual *énoncés*, the signs of enunciation are perceived. It is because I suddenly have the conviction that 'the film is speaking cinema' that I also become aware of the fact that someone is in the process of telling me a story. To the extent that everything takes place as if someone suddenly asserted his or her 'subjectivity' in film language, I can view this mode of narration as identical to linguistic *discourse* and thus speak metaphorically of a *first-person visual narrative*.[6]

Metaphorically? Yes, prudence dictates this. For this avowed presence of a strictly cinematic narrative 'subjectivity' (mis-framing, bizarre camera movements, etc.) has equivalents *on the same level* in any kind of narration: textual narrators can also reveal their subjectivity in a non-linguistic manner by introducing abrupt ellipses at any moment in the sequence of narrative events they are presenting, and verbal narrators can do the same by replacing, for example, the inaudible period at the end of each sentence with a resounding sneeze ... In short any narrative that we can *metaphorically* see as being delivered, by virtue of this very fact, in the 'first person.' But a single non-metaphoric way of telling a story in the *first person* exists. And this way consists, precisely, in using *wherever possible* the *first person*, for which the sememe par excellence is the simple 'I' we discussed above. And in order to say 'I,' or its equivalent in other natural languages, such a signifier must be a part of the vocabulary of the person using it. Now, while it is possible for the apparently primary agent[7] of textual narrative and for the agent

fundamentally responsible for verbal narrative to designate themselves by using this deictic par excellence, this is ontologically impossible for the agent fundamentally responsible for film narrative. This
agent cannot say 'I' (or its equivalents in French, Spanish, etc.) because
it does not speak English (or French, or Spanish). It 'speaks' the language Jost described: 'cinema.' So, at most, this agent can *have another
agent say* 'I.' This agent will be subordinate to it at the same time as it
must necessarily, in order to enunciate this 'I,' be *embodied*, be *acted out*.

This agent that says 'I' in the cinema must be acted out and thus 'an-
thropomorphize itself' because English is a *language* (in the proper
sense of the term), while what we call, perhaps somewhat improperly,
film 'language' is the result of a series of strictly 'mechanical' operations whose human origins, which of course are not in doubt, are not
immediately apparent.

It is thus through a *verbal* narrator, delegated by it, that the film
mega-narrator succeeds, if not in saying 'I,' at least in making us believe more or less that it has said it. And it is through this narrative dislocation, which can take such a highly developed form in literature
(see the *Arabian Nights*), that the film mega-narrator makes room in its
discourse for the verbal narrative of a delegated narrator. It thereby be-
haves in the same way as some textual narrators sometimes do. In the
same way? Yes, but with greatly different implications, because of the
kind of semiotic equivalence established in each case between the underlying narrator and its delegated narrator. This immeasurably and
irrevocably distinguishes textual narrative from film narrative. For textual narrative delegates in a manner we might call 'homogeneously intradiegetic' (which, moreover, is complete, a point we will discuss
below), while film narrative delegates in a 'symmetrically intradiegetic' manner in which the relationship between the two agents is the
opposite of homogeneous. This relationship is heterogeneous (and, as
we shall see, remains incomplete). It is homogeneously intradiegetic in
the first case because it is by means of the *same* semiotic vehicle, the
same dialect as it uses, spoken language, that the textual underlying
narrator makes its delegated narrator recount events (sub-recount
them, in fact). The underlying film narrator, meanwhile, literally be-
stows *only* speech on the agent to which it has thereby confided the recounting of events (or rather their sub-recounting). This process is thus
heterogeneously intradiegetic. On the one hand, we have a *monodic*
'sovereign speaker' that speaks and, in *speaking*, grants *speech* to another speaker, which is just as monodic as it is, which uses the same

means of expression, and which will in turn appear to be a 'sovereign speaker.' On the other hand, we have a 'great "image-maker"' (but also, so as not to leave the other elements of film expression in the lurch, a great 'speech-maker,' a great 'noise-maker,' a great 'writer,' and a great 'musician') – a great polyphonic image-maker that grants its delegate a sole means of expression, speech, while it remains the illocutionary source, without any delegate, of the images, sounds, music, and possibly even the text surrounding the second-level narrative discourse that is offered to us by all the Romanos of this world. Even so, their verbal discourse will soon be obscured, as is the case with the hero of *Dark Eyes*, and replaced with a visualization of the events being recounted – events that we cannot, as we shall see below, attribute to the delegated narrator, given its slim degree of responsibility.

This disparity between the two kinds of narrative dislocation brought on by the intercession of 'subaltern' agents is not without consequence – the most important probably being that such a dislocation has a more obvious effect on textual narrative than it does on film narrative, because the underlying narrator of textual narrative, by virtue of its monodic nature, *disappears completely* between two forms of attribution. Take the *Odyssey*, from book 9 to book 12, and try to find there a single trace of the underlying narrator – which, nevertheless, is the agent that speaks of Odysseus and so kindly opens up his quotation marks: 'Lordly Alkinoos ... I'll tell you my long way home with all of its troubles. Zeus weighed me with hardship after I left Troy.'[8] In textual narrative, to invite someone else to recount events is to agree to keep quiet, to accept that the *delegated narrator* take the place, the entire place, that the underlying narrator occupies as *delegator*. This is not the case in film narrative. Thus, while the primary narrator in the *Odyssey* must keep quiet if I am to hear Ulysses speak, this is not the lot of the underlying narrator in film narrative. When Romano starts telling his story in *Dark Eyes*, and while he remains there, in full view, talking to his companion of Russian origin, the film narrator – the mega-narrator – does not by any means keep quiet. On the contrary, this narrator keeps speaking – speaking cinema I mean – and gives us no end of narrative information – as much if not more information (because it informs us of the fact that this man has a story to tell) than it gave us at the beginning of the film barely five minutes earlier. Because in reality, if the delegated narrator of textual narrative (think of Odysseus, but also Shahrazad) *completely* occupies the narrative perspective, it is because this delegated narrator takes over *completely* from the delegator.

The delegated narrator in film, meanwhile, by virtue of its heteroge-neous (and *incomplete*) intradiegeticity, far from taking over completely for the mega-narrator, is itself only a *part* of the underlying agent's dis-course. This agent merely agrees to grant the delegated narrator the foreground of the image – just like the theatrical monstrator, moreover, which, in a similar situation, merely allows any verbal 'narrator' pres-ent to occupy the front of the stage.

Although they may occupy the foreground of the image (in the cin-ema) or the front of the stage (in the theatre), delegated narrators who have been invited to verbally tell a story (or part of a story) in a me-dium based on monstration are incapable, unlike their textual homo-logues, of occupying the entire narrative perspective. The work of the film mega-narrator and the theatrical monstrator, even if it is rendered invisible to the highest degree, remains perceptible. These primary agents *show* us those secondary agents. This is part of their narrative activity, which must be in harmony with the other parts of the story being told. Here the cinematograph, 'the most precious and most amazing of all magic devices' (Ingmar Bergman),[9] nevertheless came to use its narrative abilities to the fullest possible extent by replacing the delegated narrator's verbal narration with an 'illustration' of that narrative. This technique allows the cinema to set one within the other and to set the various levels of narrative one within the other in a man-ner just as organic as that found in textual narrative. This was to be-come the privileged means whereby the film mega-narrator 'does not attempt to direct our imagination towards anyone else, or suggest that someone other than himself is speaking.'[10] Thus, in *Dark Eyes* the mega-narrator, after having allowed its delegated narrator to speak for a few moments, suddenly decides – because of course it is this agent that decides – to replace the *verbal* discourse of its delegate with a *visu-alization* of the events this delegate is verbally narrating and to trans-port the viewer to another time and place. This visualization, and here my hypothesis contradicts what is generally believed on this topic, is the work of the mega-narrator and not the delegated narrator, as I will attempt to demonstrate. And this is true no matter how commensurate the delegate's verbal narrative may be with the audio-visual narrative used to 'illustrate' it.[11]

Just as delegated narrators in textual narrative are seen as responsi-ble, on their own level, for their own narrative (even if in the final analysis the *underlying narrator* is responsible), so too in film narra-tive delegated narrators are seen as responsible for the narratives they create (even if, obviously, the film mega-narrator, the film narrator, is responsible). But for which narrative exactly is the delegated film narrator responsible? We should agree from the start that the narrative layer this agent is responsible for is composed *only* of the words this agent enunciates.[12] No such sub-agent can be held responsible for the visualization of the story he or she is telling. Moreover, nothing leads us to believe so, even though this is generally what is thought. Jost, for example, remarks that 'in cases where the narrator's voice gives way to visual narrative, it is generally assumed that the narrator is the agent responsible for this visual narrative [= the "great image-maker"].'[13] Nothing leads us to believe so because, in the end, delegated narrators such as Romano are not well known within their diegetic world for being adept at using film language.[14] Romano, like the common run of delegated narrators – such as textual narrators, for example – is adept only at using a natural language (Italian, Russian, French, etc.), the only effective means available to him for telling his story about his meeting a young Russian woman to his diegetic auditor and, indirectly, to the film viewer; unless, and this is not the case, he was diegetically deprived of speech and thereby reduced to laboriously miming his story with the necessary gestures, or to communicating it with sign language. In any event, because he is not a filmmaker but was originally an architect and is now a waiter, such a character-narrator cannot have recourse to the sounds and images of cinema to tell his story. A narrator such as this, let's agree, cannot narrate 'filmically.'

It is thus possible in film narrative to have two narratives, one subordinate to the other, while at the same time both are under the direct responsibility of a *single agent*, the mega-narrator. The narrative dislocation produced by the visualization of a secondary narrative (we should perhaps say 'audio-visualization') is thus completely different in nature from the dislocation produced in textual narrative, which, and herein lies the difference, normally interposes an intermediary agent (a sub-agent) between the agent responsible for the dislocation and the narratee. Given the polyphonic nature of its discourse, the film mega-narrator can thus maintain the intermittent presence of a verbal narrator whose only function is to authenticate the mega-narrator's own visualization of the events that make up the thread of the (secondary) story being told. Thus, the complete and homogeneous nature of film narrative does not, unlike the nature of textual narrative, necessitate recourse to a secondary agent, to a delegated narrator. The film narrator remains the sole agent responsible for the visualized 'version' of the secondary narrative, unlike the underlying narrator in textual narrative. In the latter, the underlying narrator (such as the primary agent in the *Odyssey*) or, when this agent has been effaced (as in *The Stranger*), its delegated narrator (Meurseault) – indeed all textual narrators, at any level – must call upon a secondary narrator (such as Odysseus in books 9 to 12) in order to effect its narrative dislocation. Even though it is always the underlying narrator that, *in the final analysis*, is the agent speaking through an interposed delegated narrator, the textual narrative system reduces this primary voice (the voice recounting the primary narrative) to a momentary but quite apparent silence.

Although the delegated narrator in film cannot narrate 'filmically,' cannot be the narrator of the secondary narrative in its audio-visual version, neither can we view this agent as the one that focalizes this audio-visual narrative, a narrative not the product of its own efforts but rather of this agent's 'creator,' the film mega-narrator. This mega-narrator is the ultimate agent that, in its telling of the story (the substory) by audio-visual means, is at leisure to appear to be telling the story as if its focal point were the delegated narrator. This has the effect of heightening the viewer's pleasure and reinforcing the ritual of identification between the viewer and the narrative agents responsible for each layer of the narrative. The filmic mega-narrator profits from the scopic drive that consumes every film viewer in order to take its place as the 'all-narrating' one. It is thus the only agent to which we can impute responsibility for the *gaze* that gave birth to the secondary narrative as it has been visualized. This gaze cannot be attributed to the delegated narrator. And this is true even when the film mega-narrator chooses to imitate the narrative attitude this same delegated narrator may have displayed towards the events that make up the story in question. It is true even when the visualized narrative's 'focalization' (Gérard Genette) or 'ocularization' (Jost) seems to have been modelled on the delegated narrator's point of view, which of course is only an illusion.

There is, however, one place where the textual and filmic systems meet, and the illusion created by this isomorphism is probably what has sometimes led narratologists and film theorists astray and caused them too often to attribute responsibility for the visualized secondary narrative to the delegated narrator. Like secondary textual narrative, which momentarily blocks out any other narrative perspective, secondary narrative in film, once it is visualized, *conceals* the primary narrative and alone occupies the entire range of signifying elements (film's five means of expression). Narratologists of cinema, seeing that in textual narrative the delegated narrator, even though it is only a sub-agent, can thoroughly and rather easily replace the primary narrative of the underlying narrator with its own secondary narrative, quickly endowed the secondary narrator in film narrative with the same powers and attributes. But we should examine this situation more closely and acknowledge that the homogeneous and complete intradiegeticity we discussed above is more easily obtained in textual narrative, where it is impossible for two agents to speak at the same time. This is because of the medium's monodic nature (its quality as a single means of expression). Hence the complete evacuation of the primary narrative the moment the secondary narrator begins to speak. In a completely contrary manner, the primary narrative is completely evacuated in film only once the delegated narrator has disappeared completely (from the image track) and fallen completely silent (on the sound track). This is what happens in *Dark Eyes*, when Romano-the-storyteller[15] (the Romano who is a waiter on a boat) is banished from the image and sound tracks and replaced by the (younger and more handsome) Romano-in-the-story-told, acting out the story. Every means of expression (moving images, sounds, speech, written matter, music) are put at the exclusive disposition of the secondary narrative. This secondary narrative of Romano's adventures – I refer here to the *visual* narrative of these adventures – banishes the primary narrative (the framing narrative that tells the story of Romano-the-storyteller) in the same way as Odysseus's secondary narrative in books 9 to 12 banished for its duration the primary (framing) narrative by covering over and replacing one monody (that of the underlying narrator) with another (that of Odysseus-the-story-teller). In film, however, this banishment occurs not because one *monody* has been covered over and replaced by another, but rather because one *polyphony* (made up of the five means of expression found in the cinema) has been covered over and replaced by another.

This is how I propose to resolve, theoretically and practically, the numerous paradoxes that film narratology, which in my view is based too much on existing literary models, has been unable to avoid. These paradoxes arise in film narratology whenever it is held, contrary to the theses I have outlined in this chapter, that the secondary narrative, when it is visualized, remains the responsibility of the delegated narrator, just like that narrator's verbal narrative or the secondary narrative of a delegated narrator in textual narrative. For how can a narrative that, in a sense, is the reconstitution of a given agent's gaze see that same agent in all its exteriority?[16] How can we explain the fact that narrators of Romano's ilk show[17] situations and events that they themselves have not personally experienced and that they have been informed of only in a quite summary manner? (This is something they all do at one moment or another of 'their' narration.) Let's take this to its logical conclusion: how are narrators such as these, and examples are a dime a dozen, able to reconstitute scenes in the story they are telling with which they are not even familiar?

A narratological theory of cinema, like theories of other semiotic vehicles, must, above all, be narrato*logical*.

Conclusion

A word beats on the page.

Danielle Gaudreault, 1987

Here we are at the end of our story, a story with words and ideas that, because they are the work of a living person, also have a kind of life, will live on beyond the book in which they are imprisoned. It is up to the reader to free them and to give them this life in his or her turn. This Conclusion marks the end of a book in which many doors are left open and many questions unanswered. But nothing is achieved by going too far too fast. My hypotheses here are merely premises that, if they are worthy, must be put to the test before taking them to their final battle positions. They must be tested theoretically but also, and I believe especially, analytically. Because while the sum total of the hypotheses formulated here seek to contribute to improving our understanding of the narrativity of the work of novelists, playwrights, and filmmakers, it is no less true that they have an avowed practical goal: to allow us better to grasp and distinguish among the various narrative 'voices' that band together to furnish us with the narratives we so avidly consume. This may also, or at least this is my hope, facilitate the task of those who analyse these narratives. Being perhaps in a better position to arrange them hierarchically, the readers may be better able to understand the various narrative strata and agents and the relationships among them.

In the case of cinema, these questions have been (and remain) of great relevance, because the study of cinema as a narrative and enunciative phenomenon is on the upswing again today, even as it has always played a major part in thinking about the medium over the past several decades. This is all the more true when we consider that film narratology has become an autonomous field of study and that film analysis, or so it would seem, will always be in need of new conceptual categories in order to remain fresh.

In any event, I hope the path I have taken has been beneficial to the reader, if only in that this path has made it possible, at the very least, to identify clearly the attributes by which textual, staged, and film narratives are distinguishable from each other – or which they share. We have seen, among other things, that the respective semiotic media underlying each of these narrative expressions are not, in actual fact, what they appear to be. Thus, while the cinema, like the theatre, is forged from concrete materials (sets, actors, etc.), its own discursive process renders it irredeemably 'unconcrete' at each of its stages of production. In this way, and despite its homology with the theatre, film narrative lies on the side of textual narrative. This latter, despite its continuum of indisputably abstract *words*, is perhaps not as far removed from referential reality as is generally believed. Is there not indeed a single step from the referent to the textual sign – a radical step, we must admit, but a single step just the same? This step transcodes reality into words, which are no doubt abstract and which seem, to those of us who use them all day long, to have so little mystery about them. A single step and, at bottom, a single intermediary, the textual narrator, which is as concrete and seemingly alive as the words it uses are abstract. Is it not, in fact, the simplest and most natural thing to believe in the humanity of a 'being,' the textual narrator, which, although it is only made of paper, like the reader often bears a name and carries out a primary activity, storytelling, that leads it to manipulate language, an anthropomorphic activity of the highest degree? Doesn't the film narrator, on the contrary, appear to be a kind of demi-god capable of synchronizing, modulating, masterminding, and even producing a multimedia performance in which the various elements – images, sounds, speech, text, music – are thrown together and intermingled? A narrator that, in order to do this, uses machinery of all kinds: cameras, microphones, sound recorders, editing tables, mixing boards, projectors, etc.? How removed all that can seem from the expressive spontaneity of the seemingly quite simple narrative system that brings textual narrative into being: a narrator who whispers into my ear, almost privately; and a story, many of whose features I myself am left to imagine, because this story is not delivered to me, as it is in the cinema, in all its signifying depth. This medium's story comes to me by means of a slighter system – a system as light as a feather, a feather we pick up to write with, I'm tempted to say. A system so slight, in the end, that it seems almost out of place to describe it as a system, for while its signs are no doubt abstract, one of its intermediaries, the textual narrator, is as concrete as its human appearance would suggest. Indeed, Meurseault may very well have existed in reality, and couldn't this character very well have written *The Stranger*?

And are the images the cinematograph presents me with as concrete as people would sometimes have me believe? Isn't film's *impression* of reality, as this word indicates so well, and as has often been demonstrated, merely an illusion? Aren't the 'pieces of reality' that make up a film, despite their appearance of concreteness, just as far removed from reality, if not more, as the words that convey textual narrative? When all is said and done, yes they are. Because, to the slightness of the enunciative system of the latter corresponds the 'unbearable heaviness' of the enunciative system of film narrative. This narrative is distilled by the underlying film narrator, a mechanical mega-narrator I know more or less consciously to be, despite and above all else, non-individual. So much so that, in order to convey its narrative message to me, it has to delegate its acolyte and assistant, which is just as mechanical as it is: the 'projector.' A system so heavy, finally, that its theoretical counterpart cannot be light. Hence our use of apparently incongruous expressions to explain, despite their apparent cumbersomeness, film's *narrative system*: the mega-narrator, the filmographic narrator, the film mega-monstrator, the filmographic monstrator, and the profilmic monstrator. This system is based upon a series of manipulations and interventions that – as we discussed in chapter 9, using a judgment of Plato's that he considered applicable to every work of art[1] – make the cinema 'three removes from nature,' if not more.

The first level of manipulation is the profilmic monstrator's act of staging. It is extremely rare for the camera to record, for example, the image of a real member of the working class. Instead, as we all know, it shows us a simulacrum of a worker – Jean Gabin, for example. This is one remove from reality but also 'one degree of art more,' as Marcel remarked about his grandmother, who, in an attempt to 'introduce … several "layers" of art,' preferred to send her grandson reproductions (in time, photographic reproductions) of Corot's painting of the Chartres cathedral rather than photographs of the cathedral itself.[2]

Next come two series of cinematic operations that distance film from reality, one remove each. The first is the filmographic monstrator's act of framing. I needn't point out that today the myth of the camera as a 'window on the world,' as a camera lucida, has very few followers. Instead we have, literally, the myth of the 'cavern,' with all its connotations. The film image is a simulacrum of a simulacrum and the lens of the camera, the 'camera obscura,' is the passage into the cavern, in which we see a 'doctored' image of an already 'doctored' reality, as Jean-Claude Dumoncel remarks: 'The myth of the cavern must thus be deciphered from top to bottom as a meditation on *art*: the shadows on the rear wall of the cavern are not shadows of a tree or a bull but rather shadows of *statuettes*: they are copies of copies.'[3]

Finally, there is the filmographic narrator's act of sequencing. This agent is responsible for the editing or, more generally, for the manipulation of the recorded images and sounds. This is the final stage of cineastic intervention, but by no means the least important. André Bazin, as early as the 1950s, saw it as a radical agent of abstraction. Despite its apparent transitiveness, it is possible to be shrewd ·in dealing with it: 'When you're filming people, you capture the reality. In the process of editing, the reality disappears and you have a film reality,' the filmmaker Holly Dale once remarked.[4] Let's take this observation one step further and agree that captured reality, due to the simple fact that it has been captured by a camera and recorded on film, is *already* a *filmic reality* that; once it has been re-formed (put into form a second time) at the editing stage, becomes an *undisguised filmic reality*. And if we now take into account the transformation of the profilmic reality itself in those cases (fiction films) where this is a given (Gabin dressed up as a worker), we see that cinema unfurls before our eyes a filmic 'reality' to the power of three: one power for each of the three phases of film discourse necessary to the final act of creating the narratives offered to us by the cinema.

I hope that the approach I propose here, which supposes the coexistence within the same medium of those two modes of communicating a narrative, narration and monstration, will make it possible to better grasp the narrative mechanisms at work in the cinema and, indirectly, to shine light on the narrative workings of textual and staged narratives. I also hope that the narration/monstration dialectic, which enables *narrative* to become a *system* in the movement from the *literary* to the *filmic*, makes possible a better understanding of the various tensions that lead narrative, there and elsewhere, to its

END(S) ...

Afterword (1998):
Cinema, Between Literariness
and Intermediality[1]

When this book was first published, narrative questions had grown in importance in cinema studies. Film narratology had been well established for some years and many specialists in the field published studies addressing this issue, sometimes exclusively.[2] Numerous students were attracted to the field and wrote dissertations on the problems associated with defining film as narrative, not without many anguished nights on their part ... Indeed even if we see film narratology as a perfectly legitimate and fully fledged discipline, at the time a consensus was sorely lacking on such fundamental concepts as 'narrative' and 'narrator.' Paradoxically, despite this somewhat uncertain state of affairs, film narratology made progress in the study of one concept, focalization, which, while of great importance, was still subordinate to the fundamental issues of narrative and narrator. On this question, which interested narratologists of all kinds, we might even say that the most interesting and stimulating ideas came out of film narratology. Moreover, the problems related to focalization have traditionally occupied a greater place, in this particular field, than those directly related to narration proper. We see here a hypertrophy that is not at all accidental. In fact it may be normal that the question focalization attempts, at bottom, to answer ('Who sees?'), because of its immediate reference to the visual, has attracted the attention of specialists of the visual such as cinema scholars.

However, this great question, 'Who sees?', is incapable of subsuming all the other questions film narratologists should ask themselves. With respect to my method, it seemed clear to me that it was preferable to attempt to provide a satisfactory answer to the question 'Who is speaking?' This question precedes that of 'Who sees?' and is not an easy one to answer, if only because of the multiplicity of the means of expression cinema employs in order to produce meaning.

Who is speaking in a film? This is the ultimate question, to which I attempted a response in this book, one entirely devoted to questions of narrative communication. This question leads us to pass incessantly from the filmic to the literary and from the literary to the filmic, with the precise goal of unpacking some of the component parts of the narrative system.

Since this book was written (between July 1987 and February 1988, from a doctoral dissertation written between 1979 and 1983), I have continued to think about the principal questions I raised in it.[3] Since that time I have, in particular, tried to refine some of my hypotheses on the various questions around narrative, as well as those concerning their applicability to early cinema. I was drawn to the concept of *narrativity* in order to attempt, first of all, to trace its origins. I then proposed that we introduce into the field of early cinema studies the concept of *intermediality*,[4] with the goal of shedding new light on the relationship between the cinematograph and the other media that welcomed it at the turn of the last century. This led me once again to the great contrast traditionally made (in film theory at least) between *narrativity* on the one hand and *theatricality* on the other. I contest the validity of this opposition. Here, I would like to extend the ideas found in this book using the following three more recent paths of research, whose most important elements I will now sketch out.[5]

1. The Origins of a Concept: Narrativity

The reader will no doubt have remarked the tribute I pay in this book to Albert Laffay. As early as 1947, in what, before the innovations introduced by Christian Metz, was the backward field of cinema studies, Laffay was already speaking of *point of view* and *narration*, using expressions as precise and precocious as 'narrativizing operation,' 'centre of perspective,' 'permanent centre of vision,' and 'ocular perspective.'[6] However, I may not have sufficiently acknowledged the important role Christian Metz's early work had on the development of a specifically cinematic narratological theory and even on narratological theory in general. Research I carried out a few years ago, with a view to presenting a paper at a conference on Metz's work, made it possible for me to see to what extent the earliest semiotic discussions of cinema had literally been 'contaminated' by narratological concerns.

This research also allowed me to realize that Laffay's theories had something to do with this 'contamination,' in that they seem to have literally struck the young Metz's imagination, thereby influencing his part of the semiotic project, at least with respect to narratology.[7] However, Metz did not wait to read Laffay before becoming interested in problems around narratology in the cinema. In his very first article, 'The Cinema: Language or Language System?' he revealed an overriding interest in the cinema's ability to tell stories, an interest so great that in 1964 he became the first scholar to use the term 'narrativity,'[8] despite what you read in the leading language dictionaries, which date its first appearance to an article by Algirdas-Julien Greimas published five years later, in 1969.[9]

When we examine the various occurrences of the term in Metz's inaugural article, we can see that the way film semiology conceived of narrativity is unequivocally connected to 'intrinsic narrativity' as I define it in chapter 3 of this book. This intrinsic narrativity is directly connected to different means of expression, some of which can be seen as intrinsically narrative. Metz's position was distinct from the prevailing view, which privileges what I have suggested we call 'extrinsic narrativity.' This latter meaning, which is the one found in dictionaries, is concerned only with narrative content, independent of the means of expression by which it is communicated. With time, this initial meaning, which Metz implicitly attributed to the concept of 'narrativity' and which is concerned with the intrinsic narrative potential of the medium itself, receded and became lost to view in the work of Metz himself. For Metz came surreptitiously to adopt a new meaning for 'narrativity,' one that would soon prevail in those fields more concerned with narrative content (and the forms of this content) than with its expression (and the different kinds of media used).

This sense of the word, which is of particular interest to the issue at hand here, was well set out in Metz's work right from the beginning, even if it was not distinguished from the other possible meaning. It was from this starting point that Metz proposed the remarkable formula whereby the cinema, which had so quickly set out on the path of 'novelistic fiction,' had narrative 'built right into it.'[10] This intrinsic ability is so important that Metz emphasized it in one of the headings of his article 'A Non-System Language: Film Narrativity.'

In another article Metz set out his true narratological beliefs, and once again emphasized narrativity by titling the first subsection 'Cinema and Narrativity.' Here Metz revealed quite well how the very question of narrative can only involve a semiology of the cinema. For Metz, narrativization poses questions of central importance to film semiology: How does the cinema indicate succession, consequence, spatial proximity, or distance, etc.? These are central questions to the semiotics of the cinema.[11] Isn't it remarkable that the first thing Metz thinks of when asked to address the readers of the journal *La Linguistique*, which commissioned this article, is precisely the question of narrativity? Isn't it in fact remarkable, from our perspective, that the first thing Metz concerns himself with, in an article nevertheless entitled 'Some Points in the Semiotics of the Cinema,' should be, once again, narrativity? In the end, this isn't surprising, if we agree with the following observation: given the intrinsically narrative nature of the medium under study, Metzian semiology is in fact, more often than not, a narratology.

Then, in 1966, in his famous article 'Notes toward a Phenomenology of the Narrative,'[12] Metz reversed the term's meaning, thereby giving precedence to extrinsic narrativity. In this article, which was concerned more with the problems of narrative content than with the forms of expression communicating that content, Metz addressed the 'diversity of semiological vehicles that can carry the narrative.'[13] Here he revealed himself to be concerned with the same issues as, for example, Claude Bremond, who devotes himself entirely to problems of narrative content and who was at the time building his career on it.

As for film theoreticians, Metz passed the baton to Jean Mitry as early as 1967. Mitry, in his *Histoire du cinéma*, used narrativity, in the implicitly intrinsic sense, as a linchpin for one of his most important hypotheses on early cinema's development in the early 1910s:

> In 1909 ... the only two tendencies we can identify with any validity are *theatricality*, or dramatic constructions that imitate theatre and were produced by *applying* theatrical staging to the cinema (the film *Assassinat du duc de Guise* was the first accomplished example of this tendency), and *narrativity*, or the descriptive continuity of an action freed from the shackles of the stage. This tendency rests completely upon the dynamic use of editing. This conception of a *narrative* in moving pictures was first outlined in a significant manner in *The Great Train Robbery* and in Jasset's serial films.[14]

This important and fundamental hypothesis has virtually dominated early cinema studies for the past twenty or thirty years. In my view, however, it suffers from a shortcoming that renders it practically useless today. This is why we will encounter it again in the third section of this Afterword, where my task will be to reformulate its tenets and conclusions. In the meantime, however, we must take a detour through the cultural and media context in which the cinematograph came into the world at the beginning of the last century.

2. Early Cinema's Intermedial Meshing

The cinema's privileged relationship with narrativity, as well as the special role film theory has always accorded narratological concerns, may well be, in a fitting return to its origins, the repercussion or echo several decades later of cinema's alignment with literary 'cultural series'[15] in the 1910s. This alignment won out over the great many other cultural series that early cinema, or, to be more precise, 'animated views,' had attempted to model itself on: fairy plays, wax museums, stage or circus acts, plays, etc. My present research focuses precisely on this question and suggests that it was apparently this alignment with the literary model, which may have been both conscious and unconscious, that governed the process of cinema's institutionalization in the 1910s. This is the view of the literary sociologist Denis Saint-Jacques, who has recently arrived at conclusions similar to my own, while starting from completely different premises:

> Before the emergence of cinema there was a revolution in collective historical structures of the imagination that was absolutely decisive for the entire history of modern media: that of the popular novel ... This mutation marked the entry of the working classes into a culture that gradually became common to society as a whole and ... this convergence was the product of the establishment of a cognitive model in which both the imaginary and the real were perceived in similar ways. This model is the novel ... When U.S. cinema moved towards narrative fiction, it is easy to see in which direction it was led: towards this novelistic cognitive model, if not towards literary genres ...[16]

This privileging of what I call here the *literary cultural series* is a generally acknowledged fact (the very fact that Metz points out when he informs us that cinema very quickly adopted, and then kept to, the path of 'novelistic fiction').[17] We must acknowledge, however, that this path does not impose itself distinctly, as a discrete phenomenon. Rather, this tendency takes various forms and is part of a broad and relatively complex socio-cultural context, one made up of clusters of the cultural, artistic, and linguistic determinants at work in the principal industrialized countries at the turn of the last century.

However, the 'literary model,' we should agree, was just one of many paths open to the cinema, one that was offered to it only at a relatively late date. Early cinema, in fact, is a privileged site for understanding and thinking about the phenomenon of intermediality, with which it is increasingly associated. A minimal definition of intermediality would be the process whereby form and content are transferred and migrate among media, a process that worked surreptitiously for some time but that, in the wake of the relatively recent proliferation of media, has today become a norm to which every medium is likely to owe a part of its configuration. A film that takes its inspiration from literature or theatre, for example, is intermedial, as is any film influenced by these other media. But, in the very first years of its existence, film was especially intermedial in a way it may never be again (unless the multimedia era we are on the brink of ends up truly redefining each medium, giving rise to a wholesale decompartmentalization).

Intermediality is, I believe, an indispensable concept for studying and understanding early cinema, a concept that allows us to formulate propositions that provide new insight into the place of early cinema in film history, for early cinema was, in fact, the product of what we might call an intermedial meshing. It is in the light of this question of the necessary intermediality of the culture of animated views that we should enquire into the 'meshing' of which early cinema is the product, and in this light we must try to untie the knot of the principal 'intermedial' connections that gave rise to pre-institutional cinematic practices.

In the beginning, in fact, cinema was so intermedial that it was *not even* cinema.[18] Part of this 'cinema' was entirely theatrical, or at least 'stagey,' while another part was photographic and yet another part belonged to the travelling fair and its attractions. So-called early 'cinema' – which we'll call instead animated views – was not really cinema, because when we speak of 'cinema' today, we're thinking not only of the technological or mechanical projection of moving photographic pictures on a screen, whether accompanied by recorded sound or not. What we are clearly referring to when we speak of cinema today, if only implicitly, is the 'institution' that cinema has become – with, like any institution, its rules, constraints, exclusions, and procedures.

In traditional film history, the important date – the date when it be-comes possible to establish a 'before' and an 'after' – is 1895, the year the 'basic apparatus,' that universal subject of fantasy, was invented: the Lumière cinematograph. There was thus a sort of continuity break caused by the mere arrival on the market of a motion picture camera. My position, however, is that there was no continuity break with the invention of the cinematograph, but rather a break when the institu-tion 'cinema' began to take form, sometime in the early 1910s, possibly the emergence of what we call 'film language.' The existence of a 'be-fore' and an 'after' in film history thus derives from the phenomenon of cinema's institutionalization. In other words, early 'cinema,' or rather the period of animated views, is not a part of the same cultural paradigm as institutional cinema. Pre-institutional practices – pre-institutional in relation to the institution 'cinema' – in place during the period of animated views were thus bound by the rules, constraints, exclusions, and procedures of institutions other than cinema, an insti-tution that did not yet exist.

The cinematograph's lack of institutionalization was thus the lack of a *specific* institutionalization. Just because there was not yet a specif-ically *cinematic* institution does not mean, of course, that there were no other institutions with whose norms and rules the cinematograph complied within the socio-cultural sphere in which the first camera operators worked. Thus, to take only the example of France, which is especially representative, the Lumière brothers' film practices fol-lowed in the path of the institution of photography, while Georges Méliès followed in the path of the institution we could call stage en-tertainment. Each of these institutions has its own rules and conven-tions, and the Lumière brothers on the one hand and Méliès on the other submitted to these, to a certain extent, even though the tool of their trade, the motion picture camera, had not initially been foreseen by the institution concerned.

Nevertheless, a threshold was crossed, a paradigm changed, the mo-ment the film world no longer operated fully within an alien cultural series and attempted instead to develop discourses and practices out of the very newborn world of the cinematograph; the moment film people tried to leave off practising, with the help of the motion picture camera, this or that kind of cultural series and decided, rather, to *import* into cin-ema the practices, methods, and procedures of a cultural practice alien to the cinema. And, clearly, the first such model for the cinema was the theatre: at first, at the turn of the century, melodrama, and then, around 1908, 'legitimate' theatre, bourgeois theatre, with the notable example being the *film d'art* in France.

As far as melodrama is concerned, a relatively early declaration in a Pathé catalogue of 1902 might be described – though I'm not entirely sure – as a moment of rupture, as the crossing of a threshold. Here is the notice accompanying the film *L'histoire d'un crime* ('The Story of a Crime'): 'By now nearly every subject matter has been used ... And yet a genre remains that no producer has dared attempt: the Drama. Why? Does this mean that, unlike the others, it will not be successful? We believe otherwise.'[19]

With this turn to the cultural series 'melodrama,' and the attempt to import its principles into the cultural series 'animated views,' the various levels of production in the Pathé workshop were subjected to the influence of extra-cinematic cultural series in fashion at the time of early cinema (*L'histoire d'un crime* was similarly inspired by a series of wax-museum tableaux). But it is one thing to make films in the manner of another, extra-cinematic cultural series, which is what Lumière and Méliès seem to me to have done, and quite another to import such-and-such an element of an extra-cinematic cultural series into cinema, as Pathé did.[20] Pathé's cinema was a cinema in the process of institutionalization, within its own sphere and according to its own rules (even if these are only partially sketched out). This was 'cinema' itself, in the process of formation as a distinct cultural series, one that integrated on its own terms a cultural series alien to it: theatrical melodrama. And this is what Pathé and other producers involved in this vast project of valorizing the cinema continued to do, around 1907-8, with the *film d'art* and the SCAGL (Société Cinématographique des Auteurs et Gens de Lettres). Not with melodrama, this time, but with theatre.

After 1908, with the *film d'art*, theatre thus became the focal point for filmmakers in search of a model; the 'theatuh,' we should specify, that was to remain the *nec plus ultra* of cinematic representation until such time as it became clear that the theatrical model presented a number of problems on the level, precisely, of representation. In the end, and without leaving behind those aspects of theatricality that are essential to cinema, other models were sought out.

On this question, the testimony of one of the most important directors of the day, Louis Feuillade, seems to me of capital importance, as he reveals the importance – the supremacy – of the theatrical model in cinema. In 1910 Feuillade wrote an article in which he really gives the impression of struggling like the devil in a bath of holy water against the prejudice in favour of theatre in film circles that was already-always in force at the time:

> I don't believe that the cinematograph will be condemned to remain dependent on theatre alone. Whether in historical reconstructions or mythological films, in joyous, sad or spectacular films, film authors are confined to theatrical genres, and these films are called comedies, dramas, or fairy plays.
>
> In reality, however, cinema derives as much if not more from painting as it does from drama, because it addresses our vision through the play of light and perspective, through the qualities of composition.[21]

We can see here quite clearly how the question of models was in the air in cinema in the early 1910s. Here, Feuillade looks to painting as a model, without displaying much fervour. Nevertheless, the claim he makes is interesting. He seems to be saying that, yes, the theatre is unquestionably the model for cinema, but that it is not enough, given what we today would call film's pictorial specificity, which theatre is cruelly lacking.

Throughout the 1910s the cinema thus continued on its merry way, searching for a model, and ended up encountering en route another cultural series, literature. It began to leave behind the model of theatricality in favour, not of what Jean Mitry calls narrativity, but rather of textual literariness.

It isn't that the novel had not already worked well with the cinema. Many films had been inspired by tales, short stories and novels. But what is at issue here is not the question of a film's source, but rather the question of the mode of representing narrative information. It would not be out of line, moreover, to maintain that the various literary 'adaptations' in the cinema before, say, 1910, were *cinematic* adaptations of *literary* works using a *theatrical* model.

As I mentioned above, by contrasting theatricality with literariness rather than with narrativity I am contravening a 'tradition' inaugurated by Mitry. In doing so, I have come to understand better one of the most important transitional periods that historical chance has bequeathed the cinema.

3. Giving Wings to Film Narrative: Literariness

To speak, like Mitry, of cinema passing from theatricality to narrativity in the 1910s, we neglect the very materiality of the media in question.

This, in my view, is something we should avoid. In addition, by proceeding in this way we are emphasizing secondary matters: 'theatrical'
acting styles, 'theatrical' sets, etc. We also introduce an annoying contradiction between theatricality and narrativity, one that is difficult to
shake off afterwards. What is to be gained from such an opposition
when we can all agree that the 'theatrical' *Assassinat du Duc de Guise*
(1908) is in the end just as narrative as a film that is as important to the
development of a 'seemingly' distinct cinematic language, say, *The
Cheat* (1915)? True, a film such as *The Cheat* contains procedures and elements of great importance on the filmographic level, but it is not really narrativity that is furthered by the emergence and growth of such
procedures and elements.

In order to resolve this problem, it would be useful to bring the very
materiality of the medium in question into play. One of the criteria for
the specificity of a medium is precisely the distance established, within
the medium itself, between the signs it employs and the reality it depicts; in other words, the difference between the signifier and the
referent. The extent of this distance enables us to rank media among
themselves and to measure the extent of their intersemiotic compatibil-
ity. On this question, the traditional view has always favoured a 'me-
dial' arrangement, which I believe to be an incorrect approach. I refer
here to that great trilogy that, in the study of the narrative properties of
film narrative, with respect to textual narrative and staged narrative,
sees narrativity, on the one hand, and theatricality, on the other, as ten-
dencies that have influenced the course of film history. Thus, it has become pretty well generally accepted, since Mitry, that early cinema was
constantly being torn between these two models: that of narrativity
(supposedly a feature of textual narrative) and that of theatricality
(supposedly a feature of staged narrative). It seems to me, however,
that this opposition between narrativity and theatricality is lame, because it poorly identifies the formal and expressive elements that must
be brought out if we are to have a clear understanding of the phenomena at work in the cinema's development in the early 1910s.

Literariness and theatricality are thus not concepts for identifying a
'property' of the text being studied; rather, they take into account,
above all, the expressive material by which the text is conveyed, in this
case textual and theatrical language.

For narrative isn't everything, especially if we view theatre as narrative, as I have done in this book. What, then, was specific about the
way that what we call film 'language' was constituted in the 1910s,

when film ceased to be 'animated views' and became institutional narrative cinema?

Narrativity is one quality of 'texts,' whether textual or staged. It matters little what means of expression is used; both 'staging' and 'verbifying' share this quality. Hence the need to employ this other concept, literariness, to attempt to describe cinema's language-like ability to produce different *énoncés* at a higher level of abstraction than the mere monstration of events, whether physically on stage or virtually on screen. The effectiveness of this approach is something filmmakers began to sense, and to carry out, some time in the 1910s, thus making it possible for this literariness to position itself as the foremost aspect of the 'linguistic' (I should say language-like) specificity of cinema, which, as we know, was in the process of becoming institutionalized.

In light of the principles I have laid out in this book (particularly in chapter 5), I think it would be useful to shift our thinking in a way that would take into account a definition of narrativity that allows us to see it as being present as much in the theatre as it is in literature. What would then distinguish the staged from the textual would not be narrativity but rather literariness.

Literariness has to do with the literary, a quality we can agree is found only in written texts (or verbal texts) presenting a number of features agreed upon in the 'literary institution,' or at least at a certain synchronic moment in the history of this institution. Literariness is a particularly loaded concept, if only historically, because it comes to us straight from the Russian formalists. Here I will privilege a somewhat instrumental definition of literariness (which, as Gérard Genette remarks, is, 'according to Roman Jakobson's widely accepted definition ... the aesthetic aspect of literature')[22] and restrict its application to a strict linguistic sense (as opposed to a specifically theatrical language). Literariness would thus refer to the distance between referent and signifier at the level of those great sets of signifiers it is composed of (actions, scenes, spatial or temporal segments, etc.) whenever language, which is highly abstract and conceptual, comes into play. To communicate to the reader the great number of signifiers, made up of gestures, emotions, attitudes, and relationships at work in the vigil beside a recently deceased mother, for example, Albert Camus arranges nothing but words in *The Stranger*. In addition, he has us believe that the person using these words is the principal protagonist of the story he is telling. These words recall, suggest, or describe the various components of the action – the gestures, emotions, attitudes, and relationships that constitute the story – while keeping a relative but clear distance, as the arbitrariness of the linguistic sign obliges them. Literariness is no more and no less than the 'non-mimetic diegesis' whose outlines I attempted to sketch earlier in this book. In the sense in which I understand the term, literariness and theatricality form a system.

On a semantic level, the term theatricality is more or less the equivalent of literariness, now no longer a writing system in the narrow sense of the term but part of a system based on the theatrical representation of action with flesh-and-blood actors. From the outset, this system is more concrete than language, and it functions with less distance between the referent and signifier than does language. To communicate to the viewer the great number of signifiers, made up of gestures, emotions, attitudes, and relationships at work in the vigil beside the corpse of a recently deceased mother, for example, the playwright would be led to select, for example, a number of gestures, emotions, attitudes, and relationships to be acted out on stage by actors working at his or her behest. Actors no doubt are able – if you'll allow this digression – to use words to explain some of the gestures, emotions, attitudes, and relationships that make up the warp and woof of the story being told, but, in so doing, they would be resorting to what we would have to agree is a form of literariness, a secondary literariness that theatricality can always accommodate whenever the protagonists of its action use their ability to create dialogue to narrative ends.

Theatricality thus evokes the distance, which is lesser in theatre than it is in literature, between referent and signifier at the level of its great numbers of signifiers (actions, scenes, spatial or temporal segments, etc.). This is because of the highly concrete nature of the language that forms the very basis of theatrical representation. We can see in theatricality the principal features of the 'mimetic diegesis' whose outline I have also attempted to sketch in this book.

But what exactly is a filmic literariness, the ability of film language to produce different *énoncés* at a higher level of abstraction than mere monstration? This literariness is located at various levels of filmmaking activity, but is at work principally on two levels: in the intertitles and in editing.

The reader will hardly be surprised, I suppose, that literariness can be found in film in the form of the film's intertitles, those literally textual and to a certain extent literary elements. The literariness of intertitles is seen in various ways, and it would require much more space than I have available to me here to show how they function in the theoretical framework I have developed in this book.[23] I will thus limit myself to a few comments, especially since the literariness of intertitles is almost one of their intrinsic qualities. This literariness is evident in particular in the verb tenses they employ, and also in their mood. An image preceded by an intertitle in the past tense has a quality that monstration alone could not give it. The same is true of the verb's mood. Despite the images' penchant towards the singulative, it is easy enough, as I have demonstrated elsewhere,[24] to impart an iterative quality to the images by means of intertitles. These two examples, and others could be found, help give the cinema literary wings, which allow it to detach itself and take flight from the phenomenologico-singulative attachment to which its constitutive iconicity dedicates it.

The same processes are at work in editing. I have perhaps not stated often enough how systematic alternation, for example, can be modulated in different ways. I hope some day to be able to undertake a study of all the instances of alternation in D.W. Griffith's work in order to lend weight to this assertion. Alternation is of fundamental importance, because it makes it possible to give the image a number of values that would normally be absent from iconicity. Moreover, alternation can be modulated, something that, to my mind, has not been remarked upon often enough. It can be modulated in the sense that it becomes possible, according to the way the content of a film's images is affected by the location and frequency of the cuts, to produce different kinds of *énoncés*, even if the method used appears to remain the same (an alternating succession of images coming from two different sets of actions, on the A-B-A-B-A-B model). The only different form of modulation that film theory has traditionally recognized with respect to alternation is the distinction between parallel editing (or parallel syntagm, to use Christian Metz's term) and alternating editing (or syntagm). What has perhaps not been fully commented upon is how each of these categories can include different types of *énoncés*, and that it is through them in particular that cinema is able to leave the realm of theatre and take on pretensions of literariness, or of the filmic equivalent of literariness.

While the logical basis of alternating editing's expressivity normally is that of literature's 'meanwhile,' the bases – plural – of parallel editing deserve to be spelled out, given that they are quite numerous. The traditional meaning of the parallel syntagm, the equivalent of the literary's 'over here and over there,' which compares two sets of actions without indicating their temporal relation, is, it would seem, far from being the only logical link possible in parallel editing. This is the case, for example, in the editing of a film such as Griffith's *One Touch of Nature* (1908), which shows two parallel actions whose simultaneity is not in doubt – the two actions end up crossing paths – and which could be summarized as follows: 'Once upon a time there was a little girl who lived in a happy family but who was seriously ill. *Somewhere else*, there was *also* another little girl who was mistreated by her guardians ...' 'Somewhere else ... also': a logical connection of a properly literary nature, and one the cinema adopts as its own, but not without engraving upon it a distinctive mark. Literariness, or the filmic equivalent of literariness, as I said above. Should we thus speak of *filmicality*?[25] This is a question I will attempt to answer in a later book. It is a question that is, therefore, ...

TO BE CONTINUED ...

A.G., July 1998

Notes

Acknowledgments

1 Especially between 1984 and 1991, as part of the Groupe de recherche et d'analyse filmographiques (GRAF) at Université Laval, which I led with Tom Gunning. The principal funding for GRAF's activities came from the Social Sciences and Humanities Research Council of Canada (SSHRC), the Fonds québécois pour la formation de chercheurs et l'aide à la recherche (FCAR), and the Société générale du cinéma du Québec.

2 André Gaudreault, 'Récit scriptural, récit scénique, récit filmique: Prolégomènes à une théorie narratologique du cinéma,' unpublished PhD dissertation (Université de Paris III [Sorbonne Nouvelle], 1983).

Introduction

1 I will speak of *textual narrative* rather than *written narrative* for the simple purpose of introducing the necessary coalescence of product (narrative) and vehicle (text). The phrase *written narrative* gives the impression of the complete autonomy of these two and is altogether too passive.

2 I have borrowed this last expression from Danielle Candelon, whose doctoral dissertation has only one problem – it has not yet been published. See 'L'Auteur implicite dans le discours du récit: Une analyse de l'oeuvre de Jean Simard,' Université Laval, 1977. Candelon develops certain hypotheses about the theatre and narrative that are often similar to mine, even if they are founded upon different premises.

3 For a discussion of this topic see Jean-Michel Adam, *Le texte narratif* (Paris: Nathan, 1985), 173–85.

4 Gérard Genette, *Narrative Discourse Revisited*, trans. Jane E. Lewin (New York: Cornell University Press, 1988 [1983]), 148.

5   Albert Laffay, *Logique du cinéma* (Paris: Masson, 1964).

6   Ibid., 80.

7   Ibid., 81. My emphasis.

8   Ibid., 81–2.

9   I believe the choice of 'staged narrative' over 'theatrical narrative' is important, even if it puts me out of step with work in the field, including my own previous publications. I use 'staged narrative' in a restricted sense that excludes published plays, which are, according to the argument that follows, simply another form of textual narrative. I will return to this issue below.

10   Mieke Bal, *Narratologie* (Paris: Klincksieck, 1977), 5.

11   This phrase recalls (although the meaning is a little different) the famous article by Gérard Genette, 'Frontiers of Narrative,' in *Figures of Literary Discourse,* trans. Alan Sheridan (New York: Columbia University Press, 1982), 127–44.

12   I speak here of communication because what is at issue is a message with a sender and a receiver, even if in the present case their roles are not interchangeable.

13   It is even possible to think of film narrative as a 'system of systems,' since narration and monstration are also in a way systems themselves.

14   Jeannette Laillou Savona, 'Narration et actes de parole dans le texte dramatique,' *Études littéraires* 13, no. 3 (1980): 471.

15   In the case of cinema, the *concepts* diegesis and mimesis have only rarely been employed, and yet, paradoxically, film theory is responsible for the widespread use, even in literary theory, of the word diegesis (and its derivation diegetic). See, for example, Étienne Souriau, 'La structure de l'univers filmique et le vocabulaire de la filmologie,' *Revue internationale de filmologie* 7–8 (1951): 231–40. Systematic use of this term, however, came only fifteen years later, with Gérard Genette's 'Frontiers of Narrative.' Souriau, moreover, employed the term in a way inconsistent with its meaning; he did not pair it with mimesis and has it mean story rather than narrative. Thus for him diegetic space is 'the space in which all the events presented take place,' while diegetic time is 'the time in which all the events presented take place.' The author then adds: '[Diegetic time] is indeed the "time of the story," just as diegetic space is the "space of the story"' (231).

16   The term 'silent' cinema is a misnomer, as we know. The film experience at the time was anything but silent, as we will see further on. Speech and the written word, in the form of the lecturer and intertitles, played a role, as I will discuss below.

17   Film theory has benefited greatly from approaching issues one at a time, and we should accept that a method is just that, no more and no less, and

not a profession of faith. If Metz had had to take the sound track into account, one wonders when he would have been able to publish the first version of his General Table of the large syntagmatic category the image-track. We should perhaps reflect on his comment that 'image discourse *is* a specific vehicle.' Christian Metz, *Film Language: A Semiotics of the Cinema*, trans. Michael Taylor (New York: Oxford University Press, 1974 [1971]), 58.

18 As it was for many other narratologists, my discovery of Genette's book *Figures III* (Paris: Seuil, 1972) was of capital importance. This book has not been translated in its entirety, but sections of it can be found in Genette's *Narrative Discourse: An Essay in Method*, trans. Jane E. Lewin (New York: Cornell University Press, 1980 [1972]).

Chapter 1. Early Cinema and Narrativity

1 Which some cannot resist calling, wrongly in my opinion, 'primitive cinema.'

2 For a discussion of these ideas, refer to my article 'L'histoire du cinéma revisitée: Le cinéma des premiers temps,' *CinémAction* 47 (1988): 102–8.

3 This concern is particularly evident in the article written by Noël Burch in anticipation of the Brighton Conference of May 1978 (where over 500 films made between 1900 and 1906 were screened), 'Porter, or Ambivalence,' *Screen* 19, no. 4 (1978–9): 91–105 (reprinted in the conference proceedings: Roger Holman, ed., *Cinema 1900–1906: An Analytical Study*, vol. 1 [Brussels: International Federation of Film Archives, 1982], 101–13).

4 See the articles by Tom Gunning and André Gaudreault published in the conference proceedings cited in note 3 above: Gunning, 'The Non-Continuous Style of Early Film 1900–1906' (216–29) and Gaudreault, 'Detours in Film Narrative: The Development of Cross-Cutting' (181–200).

5 Inexplicably, Metz's translator has rendered this description ('la narrativité bien chevillée au corps' in the original) as '[cinema's] narrativity [has] not been endowed with the nine lives of a cat.' I have altered this faulty translation here, as I have been obliged to do at other times with this and other authors in the following pages as well. See Metz, *Film Language*, 45.

6 David Bordwell, 'Textual Analysis,' *Enclitic*, Fall 1981 / Spring 1982: 129.

7 By photogram I mean a single film frame or image.

8 Writing about these topics initially in French, I coined the nouns 'uniponctualité' and 'pluriponctualité,' based on the adjectives 'uniponctuel' and 'pluriponctuel' once suggested by a French translation of Eisenstein but apparently never adopted, except by the translator of the passage in Russian

by Yuri Lotman that follows: 'Pour le cinéma uniponctuel [point de vue unique avec la caméra fixe – translator's note], c'est la composition plastique. Pour le cinéma pluriponctuel [avec changements de point de vue – translator's note], c'est la composition par montage.' Sergei Eisenstein, quoted by Yuri Lotman in *Esthétique et sémiotique du cinéma* (Paris: Éditions sociales, 1977), 83–4. In English, these concepts have been translated as 'single set-up cinema' and 'multiple set-up cinema' by the translators of Eisenstein for the 1990s editions of his 'Selected Works' and as 'single point of view cinema' and 'multiple point of view cinema' in the English translation of Jacques Aumont's study of Eisensteinian montage. (See Sergei Eisenstein, *Towards a Theory of Montage*, in *Selected Works*, vol. 2, trans. Michael Glenny, ed. Michael Glenny and Richard Taylor [London: British Film Institute, 1991], passim; and Jacques Aumont, *Montage Eisenstein*, trans. Lee Hildreth, Constance Penley, and Andrew Ross [London/Bloomington: British Film Institute and Indiana University Press, 1987 (1979)], 174ff. and 180ff.) For my purposes here, each of these solutions is rather too cumbersome for the frequent use to which I will put these concepts. I have therefore adapted the terms I use in my French publications to English. Although in previous English translations of my work on this subject these terms have been rendered as 'unipunctuality' (adjectival form 'unipunctual') and 'pluripunctuality' (adjectival form 'pluripunctual'), I recognize that these have no immediately apparent meaning to the English reader, except perhaps a mistaken one around the most common sense of 'punctual' and 'punctuality,' which has nothing to do with the concepts under discussion here. For the present publication, therefore, I have thus changed tack slightly and now propose the following terms: punctiliar and punctiliarity on the one hand and pluri-punctiliar and pluri-punctiliarity on the other. 'Punctiliar' is a little-used and almost-forgotten English word meaning a single point in time (the *Oxford English Dictionary* gives its sole meaning as 'Of or pertaining to a point in time' – ultimately from the Latin *punctum*, point). Since there is thus little chance that its meaning will be misunderstood in a way that 'punctual' in English might, I propose to commandeer it here in my discussion of early film technique.

9 To adopt an expression proposed by Tom Gunning in the article cited in note 4. I should add that this brief outline is consciously biased in favour of the ideas I seek to advance. I do not take into account in (a) or (b) a crucial and essential editing practice with 'trick' rather than narrative purposes: the stop-camera effect. On this subject, see my article 'Theatricality, Narrativity and "Trickality": Reevaluating the Cinema of Georges Méliès,' *Journal of Popular Film and Television* 15, no. 3 (Fall 1987): 110–19. See also Tom

Gunning, '"Primitive" Cinema: A Frame-Up? Or, The Trick's on Us,' in Thomas Elsaesser and Adam Barker, eds, *Early Cinema: Space, Frame, Narrative* (London: British Film Institute, 1990), 95–103.

10 See the article by Gunning cited in note 4. See also Charles Musser, 'The Early Cinema of Edwin Porter,' *Cinema Journal* 13, no. 1 (Fall 1979): 1–38.

11 Recall that the profilmic has been defined as 'Everything that exists in the world … but especially what is intended to be filmed; in particular, anything that has been placed before a camera and been captured on film.' Étienne Souriau, *L'univers filmique* (Paris: Flammarion, 1953), 8.

12 I say 'eventually' because the filmmaker is not yet able to cut what he films (unless the 'reproduction' in question is a reconstituted set). He can only manipulate the profilmic elements and abbreviate time by condensing it. This is the tack taken by Méliès in his *Couronnement d'Édouard VII* (*Coronation of Edward VII*, Star Films, 1902), a film that reconstitutes, seemingly in a single shot of very limited duration, a ceremonial event that lasted much longer. I will return to this question in chapter 9.

13 In the early years it was the reel of film itself, rather, that 'decided' the matter: the reels for Lumière films, for example, were only about 20 metres, or some 50 seconds, long.

14 Another version of the film (a later remake), which sometimes bears the title *Arroseur et arrosé*, ends differently: the gardener, instead of spanking the boy, grabs the hose and 'waters' him; things have now come full-circle and the eponymous 'watered' waterer is now … Well, who is the watered waterer?

15 See my article 'Temporalité et narrativité: Le cinéma des premiers temps (1895–1908),' *Études littéraires* 13, no. 1 (1980): 109–37.

16 Tom Gunning suggested this idea and we eventually developed it together, presenting it in a joint paper given at the Cerisy colloquium Nouvelles approches de l'histoire du cinéma in 1985: André Gaudreault and Tom Gunning, 'Le cinéma des premiers temps: Un défi à l'histoire du cinéma?' in Jacques Aumont, André Gaudreault, and Michel Marie, eds, *Histoire du cinéma: Nouvelles approches* (Paris: Publications de la Sorbonne, 1989), 49–63. This article is now available in English translation: 'Early Cinema as a Challenge to Film History,' trans. Joyce Goggin and Wanda Strauven, in W. Strauven, ed., *The Cinema of Attractions Reloaded* (Amsterdam: Amsterdam University Press, 2006), 365–80. See also Tom Gunning, 'The Cinema of Attractions: Early Film, Its Spectator and the Avant-Garde,' in Elsaesser and Barker, eds, *Early Cinema*, 56–62; and André Gaudreault, 'L'histoire du cinéma revisitée.'

17 I am not suggesting that people necessarily came just to see the apparatus (lantern, projector, screen, etc.), although that was certainly part of the

'attraction' in the very beginning. What I want to emphasize is that spectators first came out to see the white rectangle of the screen, which functioned as a window, as an 'opening on to the infinite' (the original French
title of Noël Burch's book *Life to Those Shadows*), and it mattered little what
they actually saw on it. What mattered was that they were watching moving images, any moving images. In this sense the white rectangular screen
is part of cinema's signifier and can be considered to be the final component of cinema's 'hardware.'

18 Aumont, *Montage Eisenstein*, 57. My emphasis. (Translation modified
slightly – Trans.)

19 Ibid.

20 This shot was sold separately, leaving it up to the exhibitor whether to
place it at the beginning or the end of the film. A nice example of the autonomy of some tableaux.

21 Gunning, 'The Cinema of Attractions,' 66.

Chapter 2. Narrative Problems

1 Christian Metz, *Film Language: A Semiotics of the Cinema*, trans. Michael
Taylor (New York: Oxford University Press, 1974 [1971]), 94.

2 Ibid., 144.

3 Ibid., 94.

4 Tzvetan Todorov, *Les genres du discours* (Paris: Seuil, 1978), 76. Need we add
that this view should perhaps be tempered a little?

5 Chapter 4 of the present work is entirely devoted to this problem.

6 Todorov, *Les genres du discours*, 246–81.

7 Philippe Hamon, 'Pour un statut sémiologique du personnage,' in Roland
Barthes et al., *Poétique du récit* (Paris: Seuil, 1977), 118.

8 There is, however, one way (not much travelled) that allows for denying narrative status to cinema. Gérard Genette, who was kind enough to read part
of my doctoral dissertation, wrote in a personal letter of 22 February 1983:
'A broad definition would be to consider any kind of "representation" as
presenting a story. In this case there would certainly be theatrical narratives,
film narratives, narratives told in graphic novels and comic strips, etc.
Personally I prefer, and more so as time goes on, a narrow definition of narrative: *haplē diēgēsis*, the exposition of narrative events by a narrator who
describes these events in words (whether written or oral). In this sense there
is, for me, no such thing as theatrical or film narrative. The theatre *does not
recount*, it *reconstitutes* a narrative upon the stage, and cinema likewise *shows*
on the screen a *reconstituted* narrative, which it has created on a set. But it

seems clear to me that, in current usage, the broad definition is carrying the day and that we will have to live with this state of affairs.' A month earlier, in response to an invitation to contribute to a special issue of a film journal on narrativity in the cinema, he expressed these same sentiments in a letter addressed to the journal's editors. See *Hors Cadre* 2 (1984): 5.

9 Roland Barthes, *Critical Essays*, trans. Richard Howard (Evanston: Northwestern University Press, 1972 [1964]), 262.

10 Algirdas-Julien Greimas, *Structural Semantics: An Attempt at a Method*, trans. Daniele McDowell, Ronald Schleifer, and Alan Velie (Lincoln: University of Nebraska Press, 1983 [1966]), 201.

11 Anne Ubersfeld, *L'école du spectateur* (Paris: Éditions sociales, 1981), 241 and 331.

12 Anne Ubersfeld, *Reading Theatre*, trans. Frank Collins (Toronto: University of Toronto Press, 1999 [1996]), 52.

13 Patrice Pavis, *Problèmes de sémiologie théâtrale* (Montreal: Presses de l'Université du Québec, 1976), 72.

14 Patrice Pavis, *Dictionary of the Theatre: Terms, Concepts, and Analysis*, trans. Christine Shantz (Toronto: University of Toronto Press, 1998 [1996]), 231.

15 Roland Bourneuf and Réal Ouellet, *L'univers du roman* (Paris: Presses Universitaires de France, 1975), 24.

16 Gilles Girard, Réal Ouellet, and Claude Rigault, *L'univers du théâtre* (Paris: Presses Universitaires de France, 1978), 15.

17 Ibid., 16.

18 Claude Bremond, *Logique du récit* (Paris: Seuil, 1973), 332.

19 Girard, Ouellet, and Rigault, *L'univers du théâtre*, 125.

20 Tzvetan Todorov, 'Les catégories du récit littéraire,' *Communications* 8 (1996): 144.

21 Todorov, *Les genres du discours*, 16.

22 Laurent Jenny, in his article 'Le poétique et le narratif,' *Poétique* 28 (1976): 440–6, did try to show that poetry, or rather certain kinds of poems, are true narratives. Thus he writes in connection with Baudelaire's second *Spleen*: 'Isn't what the poem ceaselessly recounts to us precisely an "adventure of the subject"? Wouldn't it in fact be possible to devise a schema that would plot not a "logic of actions" but rather a "logic of being"? ... The poem's narrative development is undeniable. The subject attempts various similar actions; some are rejected as impossible, others are successful, and the "trajectory" of these attempts constitutes a story' (444).

23 Todorov, *Les genres du discours*, 66.

24 This was the position I took in my doctoral dissertation and in subsequent articles on film narratology. See 'Film, Narrative, Narration: The Cinema of

the Lumière Brothers,' in Thomas Elsaesser and Adam Barker, eds, *Early Cinema: Space, Frame, Narrative* (London: British Film Institute, 1990), 68–75. I continue to defend the position here, despite the criticism it has earned me. I have, however, attenuated it slightly, as will be seen in chapter 3, in order to take into account what I have found to be valid in that criticism.

25 In the sense that a segment of the *narrative* (in French, *récit*) can be categorized as *narrative* (*narratif*). We can see that this boils down to playing with words, especially in English, where 'récit' and 'narratif' are both rendered by 'narrative.' To say in English that such and such a narrative sequence (what I would call in French a *narratif*) is not a narrative (*récit*) seems incongruous.

26 See his letter of 22 February 1983, quoted in note 8 above.

27 This is a perfectly defensible position, but one I do not take, for historical and practical reasons I will discuss further on. At this point in our discussion it would be useful to agree that this area is full of possible 'theoretical decrees,' which we might view as 'necessary evils.' We should not worry about such a state of affairs, which is common in the humanities.

28 Todorov, 'Les catégories du récit littéraire,' in *Les genres du discours*, 144. My emphasis.

29 Patent held by William Paul and G. Wells, quoted by Yuri Lotman, *Semiotics of Cinema*, trans. Mark E. Suino (Ann Arbor: University of Michigan Press, 1976 [1973]), 36.

Chapter 3. In Search of the First Film Narrative

1 Christian Metz, *Film Language: A Semiotics of the Cinema*, trans. Michael Taylor (New York: Oxford University Press, 1974 [1971]), 44.

2 We should recall that all Lumière films were less than a minute in length.

3 Marshall Deutelbaum, 'Structural Patterning in the Lumière Films,' *Wide Angle* 3, no. 1 (1979): 30.

4 For example, 'it is sufficient that an *énoncé* recount an event, or a real or fictive action (and the quality of that retelling hardly matters), in order to be considered some sort of narrative.' Jacques Aumont et al., *Aesthetics of Film*, trans. Richard Neupert (Austin: University of Texas Press, 1997 [1983]), 85.

5 Tzvetan Todorov, *Les genres du discours* (Paris: Seuil, 1978), 66.

6 See my doctoral dissertation and these three articles: 'Film, Narrative, Narration: The Cinema of the Lumière Brothers,' in Thomas Elsaesser and Adam Barker, eds, *Early Cinema: Space, Frame, Narrative* (London: British Film Institute, 1990), 68–75; 'Narration and Monstration in the Cinema,' *Journal of Film and Video* 39 (1987): 29–36; and '*Mimēsis, diēgēsis* et cinéma,' *Recherches sémiotiques / Semiotic Inquiry* 5 (1985): 32–45. Note that the pres-

ent chapter takes up in part what was treated in the first of these articles, but that the conclusions reached here are significantly different.

7 We should recall its narrative 'story' (the scare quotes are a good indication of the problems raised here): a train pulls into a station from the rear of the frame and stops; its passengers, having arrived at their destination, disembark; and then those passengers waiting to leave board the train.

8 Deutelbaum, 'Structural Patterning,' 30.

9 Considered here in its true sense. For if the opening of the doors and the exiting of the workers were considered a *disturbance*, then every *modification*, even the tiniest, could also be described in this way and the term 'disturbance' would lose its meaning.

10 It should be remembered that in a letter quoted in chapter 2 (note 8), Genette referred to an entirely different case of duality in connection with other uses of the same term.

11 Claude Bremond, *Logique du récit* (Paris: Seuil, 1973), 99–100.

12 One could object that something indeed has happened: *time has passed*. But it is impossible to identify any effect of that passage of time and it thus seems preferable to think that nothing has happened. Of course, if the passage of time is perceptible or felt (because of changes that can be noted or, simply, if an external narrator informs us of changes), that is a different matter.

13 Bremond, *Logique du récit*, 325.

14 Tzvetan Todorov would probably agree: 'We may add that there are also narratives of zero-transformation: those in which the effort to modify the preceding situation fails (though its presence is necessary for us to be able to speak of a sequence, and of narrative).' *The Poetics of Prose*, trans. Richard Howard (Ithaca: Cornell University Press, 1987), 232–3.

15 Bremond, *Logique du récit*, 100.

16 Ibid., 114.

17 Todorov, *Poetics of Prose*, 233.

18 Ibid.

19 In 'Du spectateur fictionnalisant au nouveau spectateur: Approche sémio-pragmatique' (*Iris* 8 [1988]: 121–39), Roger Odin takes me to task for being 'reductive' by equating narrative with transformation alone: 'It is quite clear that there can be transformations which do not bring temporality into play: metaphor, for example.' We must not forget that I use the word 'transformation' in the sense of change or modification. But when a metaphor modifies an initial given (which is not always the case), temporality comes into play.

20 We can differentiate these two cases from each other. In the first case, the narrative blockage is because, in a manner of speaking, the narrative agent 'blocks' the film in the projector's gate. In the second case the blockage is

caused above all by the actors, by their immobility (the actors are, of course, controlled by the narrative agent).

21 Recall the usual definition of a shot: 'a sequence of cinematographic images *with no discontinuity in the taking of the image*. Or, at the editing level ... a sequence of continuous, linked images.' Michel Marie, 'Découpage,' in Jean Collet et al., *Lectures du film* (Paris: Albatros, 1976), 70. Emphasis in the original.

22 See Román Gubern, 'David Wark Griffith et l'articulation cinématographique,' *Les Cahiers de la Cinémathèque* 17 (1975): 8.

23 Christian Metz writes: 'One can always "tell a story" merely by means of iconic analogy.' Metz, *Film Language*, 118.

24 Ibid., 44.

25 Ibid., 227. (Translation modified slightly – Trans.)

26 Ibid., 226–7. (Translation modified slightly – Trans.)

27 Yuri Lotman, *Semiotics of Cinema*, trans. Mark E. Suino (Ann Arbor: University of Michigan, 1976 [1973]), 63. My emphasis.

28 I owe this idea in part to Marie-Claire Ropars-Wuilleumier, who suggested it to me during a conversation on this subject. One can establish an interesting parallel with what Christian Metz says in *Language and Cinema*, trans. Donna Jean Umiker-Seabeok, (The Hague and Paris: Mouton, 1974 [1971]), 191. Or with this comment by Metz in *Film Language*, 45: 'The sequence does not string the individual shots; it suppresses them.'

Chapter 4. Early Narratology

1 Those readers less interested in classical philosophy and the problems of philology may wish, if they are prepared to take this chapter 'on faith,' to skim through the following pages until they reach figure 4.8, which represents the culmination of my argument.

2 Tzvetan Todorov, 'Les catégories du récit littéraire,' *Communications* 8 (1966): 143.

3 Ibid.

4 Paul Mazon, *Introduction à l'Iliade* (Paris: Les Belles Lettres, 1942), 138.

5 Paul Vicaire, *Platon critique littéraire* (Paris: Klincksieck, 1960), 247.

6 In the sense in which, unlike textual narrative, which is based on *inert* words, staged narrative brings *living beings* into play.

7 Christian Metz, *Essais sur la signification au cinéma*, vol. 2 (Paris: Klincksieck, 1972), 65 (emphasis in original).

8 Ibid., 66.

9 This, we might remark in passing, would be a completely legitimate operation if it were carried out in full knowledge of the issues at stake.

10 Plato's book 3 of the *Republic* and Aristotle's *Poetics*.

11 These two kinds of mimesis are the fruit of a division that, as I have
pointed out, is not of the same order as the division underlying Paul
Ricoeur's work in his book *Time and Narrative*, in which three kinds of
mimesis are identified.

12 Quotations in this chapter from book 3 of the *Republic* are taken from two
sources: the translation by Tom Griffith (Plato, *The Republic*, ed. G.R.F.
Ferrari [Cambridge: Cambridge University Press, 2000]), a new translation
billed as being faithful to the conversational form of the text; and that by
Paul Shorey (Plato, *The Republic*, vol. 1 [Cambridge, MA/London: Harvard University Press / William Heinemann, 1963 (1930)]). The reader
may accuse me of wanting to have my cake and eat it too, but I alternate
between these two translations (with the translator's name given in parentheses in order to indicate its source) whenever I feel that one better renders than the other a shade of meaning present in the original Greek and
important to my argument. Following common practice in English, the
words mimesis and diegesis here are not italicized, except for emphasis,
but other less common words used by these authors, such as *apangellia*
and its derivatives, which sometimes replace diegesis, are italicized. In
these cases, I add the (Latinized) Greek word following, between dashes
or in parentheses.

13 Unlike many other translators and commentators, I will not render '*diēgēsis
di'amphoterōn*' as 'mixed narrative' or 'mixed style' (Griffith) because of the
confusion this has caused. For Plato, the true concept of mixing is expressed, in 397c–d, by the term *kekramenon*, which is a mixing of a different
order than the simple recourse to *haplē diēgēsis* and mimesis. I will not
discuss in detail here Socrates' comments on the 'morality' of imitation.
Chapter 2 of my doctoral dissertation, the source of this book, was largely
devoted to this question. The present chapter takes up material published
in my article '*Mimēsis* et *diēgēsis* chez Platon,' *Revue de métaphysique et de
morale* 1 (1989): 79–92. See also the extended note 18 below.

14 Gérard Genette, *Figures of Literary Discourse*, trans. Alan Sheridan (New
York: Columbia University Press, 1982 [1966]), 128. The material in
brackets has been added by me. (Translation modified slightly – Trans.)

15 Ibid. Here, the material in parentheses is in the original. (Trans. modified
slightly – Trans.)

16 In his book *The Architext: An Introduction* (trans. Jane E. Lewin [Berkeley:
University of California Press, 1992 (1979)]) Genette demonstrates a closer
understanding of Plato's text, although he repeats his omission: 'Every
poem is a narrative (*diēgēsis*) of past, present, or future events; narrative
in this broad sense can take three forms: it can be purely narrative (*haplē*

diēgēsis), it can be mimetic (*dia mimēseōs*) – in other words, as in the theatre, by way of dialogue between characters), or it can be "mixed" (in other words, in reality alternating – sometimes narrative [*simple* narrative, we must once again stipulate] and sometimes dialogue, as in Homer)' (8–9). The comments in parentheses are from Genette and those in brackets are by me.

17 Roselyne Dupont-Roc, '*Mimēsis* et énonciation,' in *Écriture et théorie poétiques* (Paris: Presses de l'École Normale Supérieure, 1976), 7. My emphasis.

18 The two major difficulties are as follows: (1) although he does oppose a certain form of imitation in book 3 (the form that leads the poet to imitate ignoble men), Plato does not conclude from this that all imitation must be rejected. This does not prevent him from stating through Socrates at the outset of book 10 of the *Republic* (595a; Griffith) that he, Socrates, was right, earlier, in his 'refusal to accept any of the imitative part of it'; (2) in 397d, Adeimantus's most important response to all these questions is at the very least difficult to resolve in a completely satisfactory manner. To a question of Socrates' that apparently asks him to choose if poets should be able to resort to imitation or not, Adeimantus replies in such an obscure fashion that the various English translations of the text are unsatisfactory – while not exactly incorrect, they do not put their finger on the issue. Thus, in the recent translation by Tom Griffith, Adeimantus replies, 'We shall allow only the pure imitator of the good man,' while in the Loeb Classical Library translation by Paul Shorey he replies 'the unmixed imitator of the good.' This is a serious dilemma, even more serious for someone relying on French translations than on English. I myself have studied this question in detail (see chapter 2 of my doctoral dissertation as well as my article '*Mimēsis* et *diēgēsis* chez Platon') and have come to the following conclusions: (1) There is no contradiction between what Plato says in books 10 and 3; (2) the best way of translating Adeimantus's reply is as follows: 'the unmixed form that conforms to what the good man does [when he has to imitate].' The chosen genre is thus a genre that resorts to both forms (*haplē diēgēsis* and mimesis), but that must be seen just the same as unmixed because it only agrees to imitate noble subjects (and rejects the imitation of ignoble subjects).

19 I must point out in all honesty that here Plato himself 'falls into the trap' that I have just identified. In 397b, he neglects to add the qualifier *haplē* to the word *diēgēsis*, although it is an essential qualifier in this passage because here there is no possibility of reference to a 'family of genres.'

20 The word *mimēsis* (as well as its derivatives, of course) was truly polysemic in ancient Greek (and this should not overly surprise us, for all

languages share this phenomenon) and Plato uses it in a very precise sense in the *Republic:* 'The word "imitation," as Plato uses it, is at no time established in a literal meaning or limited to a specific subject matter. It is sometimes used to differentiate some human activities from others …; it is sometimes used in a broader sense to include all human activities; it is sometimes applied even more broadly to all processes – human, natural, cosmic, divine.' Richard McKeon, 'The Concept of Imitation in Antiquity,' in *Critics and Criticism*, ed. R.S. Crane (Chicago: University of Chicago Press, 1952), 149.

21 This latter term is the one chosen by W. Hamilton Fyfe, unlike other English-language translators of Aristotle, who prefer 'imitation,' throughout his Loeb Classical Library translation of the *Poetics* to render the meaning of Mimesis (Cambridge, MA/London: Harvard University Press / William Heinemann, 1982 [1927]). This was probably a very wise choice, because it makes it possible to extend its use to Plato's mimesis in book 3 of the *Republic*, while nevertheless referring to another meaning the word 'representation' has in English. While Aristotelian Mimesis refers to artistic representation, Platonic mimesis refers to something more concrete, to the 'representation' on stage of a story by actors. This latter 'representation' might be seen as a sort of 'personification'; hence my earlier use of the expression 'imitation-personification' to distinguish Platonic mimesis from Aristotelian Mimesis. Fyfe's first footnote to his translation of the *Poetics* is quite relevant in this respect: 'The explanation of *mimesis* as Aristotle uses the word, demands a treatise; all that a footnote can say is this: – Life "presents" to the artist the phenomena of sense, which the artist "re-presents" in his own medium, giving coherence, designing a pattern … Since *mimesis* in this sense and *mimetes* and the verb *mimeisthai* have a wider scope than any one English word, it is necessary to use more than one word in translation, *e.g. mimetes* is what we call an "artist"; and for *mimesis* where "representation" would be clumsy we may use the word "art"; the adjective must be "imitative," since "representative" has other meanings' (4–5).

22 On this topic, see my doctoral dissertation, in which I devote an entire chapter to problems of the textual interpretation of the *Poetics*; my article '*Mimēsis* et *diēgēsis* chez Platon'; and, finally, my article '*Mimēsis* et *diēgēsis* chez Aristote,' *Cahiers des études anciennes* 24 (1990): 257–72. More specifically, the difficulty here, which is entirely linguistic, arises because Aristotle uses only one part of a two-part expression (at one time … at another time – *hote men … hote de*) and because he appears to substitute for the second part of the expression a word ('or' – *ē*) that is already present in two other places in the same phrase! All this means that we don't know which *or*

(which ē) is meant to replace the expression 'at another time' (*hote de*). If the first of these *ors* is meant to replace the latter part of the expression, 'at another time,' we are left with a three-part division of the modes of 'poetic representation' that matches completely Plato's proposals on the question. If, instead, it is the third *or*, we obtain a two-part division, one of whose parts further subdivides into two sub-genres, which also gives three divisions in total in the end (although the criteria for distinguishing among them change somewhat). These too conform, although less 'euphorically,' to Plato's theses (as for the second *or*, there is no reason to believe that it could take the place of the missing 'at another time').

23 Here I have used the translation of the *Poetics* by W. Hamilton Fyfe (see note 21), which tends towards a three-part division, to which I myself am inclined and as proposed, for example, by D.W. Lucas in *Poetics: Introduction, Commentary and Appendixes* (Oxford: Clarendon Press, 1968). Since some of the Greek words can be important to the discussion that follows, I reproduce here the original text (beginning with 'For in representing'), with the 'guilty' words in capital letters: *Kai gar en tois autois kai ta auta mimeisthai* (represent) *estin HOTE MEN* (at one time) *apangellonta Ē* (or) *eteron ti gignomenon hosper Homēros poiei ē hōs ton auton kai mē metaballonta, Ē* (or) *pantas hōs prattontas kai energountas tous mimoumenous.*

24 In chapter 19 at 1456b11; chapter 23 at 1459a17; and chapter 24 at 1459b26, 1459b33, and 1459b36.

25 This is the position adopted by Genette, in the private communication to me cited in note 8 of chapter 2, in his refusal to grant theatre and cinema the status of narrative. Each of these two positions, his and mine, has a number of points in its favour and each has its own 'spiritual father': Aristotle or Plato, let the reader choose!

Chapter 5. Textual Narrative and Staged Narrative

1 Gérard Genette, *Narrative Discourse: An Essay in Method,* trans. Jane E. Lewin (Ithaca: Cornell Univesity Press, 1980 [1972]), 164. Note however that Genette's conclusion is equally valid, in his case, for both oral and written narratives.

2 This is the position of Evelyne Ertel, for example, who comments: 'It is generally agreed today that the published and performed versions of a play are two distinct and autonomous objects (which is not to deny that they are related to each other) and that they must be studied using analytical methods proper to each.' 'Éléments pour une sémiologie du théâtre,' *Travail théâtrale* 28 (Summer–Fall 1977): 126–7.

3 This is an expression borrowed from Genette who, for his part, has used it to describe immediate discourse (the 'interior monologue'). See Genette, *Narrative Discourse*, 173.

4 Percy Lubbock, *The Craft of Fiction* (London: Jonathan Cape, 1966), 190. My emphasis.

5 Talking, Genette believes, is an extreme form of telling: 'Proust then would be ... simultaneously at the extreme of *showing* and at the extreme of *telling* (and even a little further than that, in this discourse sometimes so liberated from any concern with a story to tell that it could perhaps more fittingly be called simply *talking*).' Genette, *Narrative Discourse*, 167.

6 Otto Ludwig, quoted by William Kayser in 'Qui raconte le roman?' in Roland Barthes et al., *Poétique du récit* (Paris: Seuil, 1977), 81. It seems, however, that Ludwig described the narrator as such in this way, and not as the omniscient narrator.

7 Danièle Chatelain writes: 'Theatre requires, by definition, a narrative that will contribute to the creation of theatrical illusion: the reader must have the illusion of being present at events as they are experienced by the characters and at the same time as them, and not as a narrator would interpret them at the time of narration.' 'Itération interne et scène classique,' *Poétique* 51 (1982): 369.

8 Here I return to some of the ideas found in my article 'Histoire et discours au cinéma,' in *Le Cinéma: Théorie et discours* (Montreal: La Cinémathèque québécoise, 1984), 43–6.

9 'Deictic': 'Any term or expression which, in a utterance, refers to the context of production (ADDRESSER, ADDRESSEE, time, place) of that utterance: "Here," "now," "yesterday," "I," "you," etc., are deictics, and in a statement like "She saw him yesterday," the adverb helps to locate what is reported relative to the addresser (in terms of his or her present, what is reported occurred the day before).' Gerald Prince, *A Dictionary of Narratology* (Lincoln: University of Nebraska Press, 2003), 18. 'Shifters': 'A term or expression whose referent is determinable only with respect to the situation (ADDRESSER, ADDRESSEE, time, place) of its utterance (Jakobson): "I" and "Dad" are shifters.' Ibid., 89.

10 Catherine Kerbrat-Orecchioni, *L'énonciation: De la subjectivité dans le langage* (Paris: Armand Colin, 1980), 170.

11 Émile Benveniste, *Problèmes de linguistique générale*, vol. 2 (Paris: Gallimard, 1974), 68.

12 Émile Benveniste, *Problems in General Linguistics*, trans. M.E. Meek (Coral Gables: University of Miami Press, 1971 [1966]), 226. (Translation modified slightly – Trans.)

13 Gérard Genette, *Figures of Literary Discourse,* trans. Alan Sheridan (New York: Columbia University Press, 1982 [1966]), 127ff. In his analysis of the passage from *Gambara,* Genette demonstrates (141–2) how 'the slightest general observation, the slightest adjective that is little more than descriptive, the most discreet comparison, the most modest "perhaps," the most inoffensive of logical articulations introduces into its web [into the story] a type of speech that is alien to it, refractory as it were.'

14 Ibid., 161. To avoid confusion, here I have taken the liberty of replacing Genette's use of the word 'narrative' with the word 'story' in brackets, as I did in the previous note. The precise meaning of 'narrative,' in Genette's use of the term, is, as we know, equivalent to 'story,' and does not carry the sense of 'narrative work.'

15 Kerbrat-Orecchioni, *L'énonciation,* 68.

16 Ibid., 147.

17 Ibid., 148. In the same vein, François Récanati has convincingly argued, using the work of John R. Searle and John Langshaw Austin, that every *énoncé* is 'reflexive' because it always has a strictly illocutionary aspect, despite its locutionary façade. See *La transparence et l'énonciation* (Paris: Seuil, 1979), 118–19.

18 Tzvetan Todorov, 'Les catégories du récit littéraire,' *Communications* 8 (1966): 126.

19 Kerbrat-Orecchioni, *L'énonciation,* 170.

20 Benveniste, *Problems in General Linguistics,* 208.

21 Benveniste, *Problèmes de linguistique générale,* 2:82. Here I have taken the liberty of 'adapting' Benveniste's ideas to narrative phenomena, which I have indicated in brackets.

22 Lubbock, *The Craft of Fiction,* 113.

23 The reader will have probably noticed the following gradation, which goes from the most to the least mimetic: *quoting, showing, telling, talking.* We could, moreover, apply this 'graduated scale' to figure 5.1 above by placing *quoting* and *showing* under the heading 'story' on the left and *telling* and *talking* under the heading 'discourse' on the right.

24 Jean Lallot, 'La "*Mimèsis*" selon Aristote et l'excellence d'Homère,' in Roselyne Dupont-Roc et al., *Écriture et théorie poétiques* (Paris: Presses de l'École Normale Supérieure, 1976).

25 We might adapt Genette's distinction between a narrative of events and a narrative of speech to remark that *quoting* is to the latter what *showing* is to the former.

26 Here I am speaking only of phrases that can be attributed to the narrator. As for 'quoted' phrases, which are quoted by the actors of the narrative (the characters), this is an entirely different matter.

27 Jaap Lintvelt, *Essai de typologie narrative* (Paris: Librairie José Corti, 1981), 50.
28 Ibid., 51.
29 Chatelain, 'Itération interne,' 389.
30 I say 'would seem' because, after clarifying my position, I will make a slightly different argument in the following chapter.

Chapter 6. Narration and Monstration

1 See note 8 in chapter 2 and note 10 in chapter 3.
2 *Oxford English Dictionary*, 2nd ed., vol. 10 (London: Oxford University Press, 1989), 220; *Le Grand Robert de la Langue Française*, vol. 4 (Paris: Dictionnaires le Robert, 2001), 1811.
3 Somewhat like Ferdinand Saussure's signifier and signified, which this linguist saw as being linked to each other like the front and back of a sheet of paper.
4 Not to mention that, in the field of cinema studies, an author as important and influential as David Bordwell, in his book *Narration in the Fiction Film* (Madison: University of Wisconsin Press, 1985), to a certain degree excludes the film narrator from his narrative system.
5 This is the title of the strictly narratological section of Genette's book *Narrative Discourse Revisited*, trans. Jane E. Lewin (New York: Cornell University Press, 1988 [1983]).
6 Ibid., 248.
7 This can vary, depending on the edition of the book. See the section in chapter 11 in which I discuss the *Arabian Nights*. The name appears as Sheherazade in some English translations.
8 Among other ways, by putting the name of the author in quotation marks, as was fashionable at one time.
9 In chapter 11 in particular.
10 This is a temporary name which we will soon abandon.
11 For me, any narrator other than the underlying narrator is a *delegated narrator*. Note that in the original French edition of this book I borrowed the expression *narrateur fondamental*, translated here as underlying narrator, from Danielle Candelon, who uses it in her unpublished dissertation 'L'auteur implicite dans le discours du récit: Une analyse de l'oeuvre de Jean Simard,' Université Laval, 1977.
12 Naturally, what I mean to say here is that we must give it a *generic* name and not at all – on the contrary in fact – a proper name.
13 I borrow these expressions from Wayne C. Booth, in his article 'Distance and Point-of-View: An Essay in Classification,' in *Essays in Criticism*, vol. 11 (Oxford: Basil Blackwell, 1961), 64.

14 Patrice Pavis, *Dictionary of the Theatre: Terms, Concepts, and Analysis*, trans. Christine Shantz (Toronto: University of Toronto Press, 1998 [1996]), 271 (the entry for 'playwright').

15 Ibid.

16 Thus Anne Ubersfeld's comment: 'The word representation, as imprecise as it may be for designating a stage production, is so commonly used that it would be difficult to dispense with it.' 'La couronne du Roi Lear ou Pour une poétique de l'objet théâtral,' *Pratiques* 24 (August 1979): 43.

17 First of all in my doctoral dissertation, which I defended in 1983, and later in my articles 'Narration and Monstration in the Cinema,' *Journal of Film and Video* 39 (1987): 29–36, and 'Film, Narrative, Narration: The Cinema of the Lumière Brothers,' in Thomas Elsaesser and Adam Barker, eds, *Early Cinema: Space, Frame, Narrative* (London: British Film Institute, 1990), 68–75.

18 I have borrowed this term from Betty Rojtman, who writes that 'the theatre is mimetic and offers the audience-recipients the "monstration" of a language that bears *directly* upon the characters.' 'Désengagement du Je dans le discours indirect,' *Poétique* 41 (1981): 106. In cinema studies, the term is also extensively employed by Xavier de France, but in another sense. See his book *Éléments de scénographie du cinéma* (Paris: Université de Paris X, 1982).

19 This term's usefulness seems to be increasingly accepted, but the meanings imparted to it can make you shiver. Thus, André Gardies uses it as a substitute for François Jost's term *ocularisation*, which he rejects. See André Gardies, 'Le pouvoir ludique de la focalisation,' *Protée* 16, nos. 1–2 (Winter–Spring 1988): 139–45; and François Jost, *L'oeil-caméra: Entre film et roman* (Lyon: Presses Universitaires de Lyon, 1987).

20 Anne Ubersfeld, *Reading Theatre*, trans. Frank Collins (Toronto: University of Toronto Press, 1999 [1996]), 94.

21 Here I distance myself from some of my earlier work, in which I saw narration and non-mimetic diegesis, on the one hand, and monstration and mimetic diegesis, on the other, as commensurate.

Chapter 7. The Narrator and The Monstrator

1 Aristotle, *The Poetics*, trans. W. Hamilton Fyfe (Cambridge, MA/London: Harvard University Press / William Heinemann, 1982 [1927]), 1448a22.

2 'Confluence' (*foyer*) and 'target' (*cible*) are the two terms Christian Metz proposes to replace, in the case of film *énoncés*, the overly anthropomorphic 'enunciator' (*énonciateur*) and 'enunciatee' (*énonciataire*). See 'L'énonciation impersonnelle ou le site du film,' *Vertigo* 1 (1987): 13–34; reprinted in his book *L'énonciation impersonnelle ou le site du film* (Paris: Méridiens Klincksieck, 1991).

3 Tzvetan Todorov, *Qu'est-ce que le structuralisme?* (Paris: Seuil, 1968), 109.
4 Ibid., revised 1973 edition, 100.
5 Anne Ubersfeld, *L'école du spectateur* (Paris: Éditions sociales, 1981), 333.
6 Ross Chambers, 'Le masque et le miroir: Vers une théorie relationnelle du théâtre,' *Études littéraires* 13, no. 3 (December 1980): 400.
7 Patrice Pavis, *Dictionary of the Theatre: Terms, Concepts, and Analysis*, trans. Christine Shantz (Toronto: University of Toronto Press, 1998 [1996]), 234 (the entry for 'narration').
8 Ibid., 271 (the entry for 'playwright').
9 Chambers, 'Le masque et le miroir,' 400.
10 Pavis, *Dictionary of the Theatre*, 355 (the entry for 'stage directions').
11 Ibid., 234 (the entry for 'narrator').
12 What is more, this narrator doesn't have much in common with the intradiegetic and acted-out narrator of textual narrative either.
13 Pavis, *Dictionary*, 234 (the entry for 'narrator').
14 Patrice Pavis, *Voix et images de la scène* (Lille: Presses Universitaires de Lille, 1982), 68.
15 François Baby, 'Du littéraire au cinématographique: Une problématique de l'adaptation,' *Études littéraires* 13, no. 1 (1980): 26.
16 Unless, and this is sometimes the case, the theatrical monstrator downplays completely the staged aspect of its narrative and privileges verbal narration (oral narration, in point of fact). If an actor takes the stage in a theatre and *recites*, without any other element of acting involved, a textual narrative – let's say Albert Camus's *The Stranger* – which he thus transforms into a verbal narrative, it is clear that all the principles of monstration we have brought to light here are no longer valid. It is also clear that, despite the narrative's passing to the verbal realm, the principles that apply belong to the realm of textual narration, with a few adaptations. Note that these principles thus apply to *verbal* performance and not to *staged* performance.
17 They resemble each other, but they are not the same: there remains the entire distance that separates the textual from the verbal. In this sense, we might ask ourselves if the narrative found in written letters is not one way for textual narrative truly to function as a form of monstration.
18 Catherine Kerbrat-Orecchioni, *L'énonciation: De la subjectivité dans le langage* (Paris: Armand Colin, 1980), 148.
19 Gerald Prince, 'Le discours attributif et le récit,' *Poétique* 35 (1978): 313. Note in passing that the monstrator can do without attribution precisely because it *shows* the various sources of speech.
20 Groupe μ, *Rhétorique générale* (Paris: Larousse, 1970), 175.
21 Tzvetan Todorov, 'Les catégories du récit littéraire,' *Communications* 8 (1991): 127.

22 Metz uses this expression to describe oneiric or fantastic narrative. See *Le signifiant imaginaire* (Paris: U.G.E., 1977), 114.

23 Thus, in cinema, in Christian Metz's terms, 'the cinema is a language of reality – and … its specific nature is to transform the world into discourse, *but so that its "worldness" is retained.'* Christian Metz, *Film Language: A Semiotics of the Cinema*, trans. Michael Taylor (New York: Oxford University Press, 1974 [1971]), 143; my emphasis. Jean Mitry also remarks: 'The novel is a narrative organized into a world; the cinema is a world organized into a narrative.' Jean Mitry, *The Aesthetics and Psychology of the Cinema*, trans. Christopher King (Bloomington: Indiana University Press, 1997 [1968]), 333.

24 These faculties are refused to the monstrator as such. Nothing prevents it, however, from communicating this information through a secondary agent.

25 Seymour Chatman, *Story and Discourse* (Ithaca: Cornell University Press, 1978), 225.

26 It might be better to speak of '*narrational* faculties,' since these monstrative (or 'monstrational') faculties on the part of the monstrator, which we will discuss immediately below, also remain 'narrative' in the sense that they contribute to communicating a *narrative*.

27 Wayne C. Booth, *The Rhetoric of Fiction* (Chicago: University of Chicago Press, 1961), 200.

28 About this situation, Anne Ubersfeld concludes: 'The literary problem of theatrical writing thus lies in the manner in which the voice of the writing *I* is covered by the voices of those others who speak. This is corollary to the fact of not speaking one's self.' *Reading Theatre*, trans. Frank Collins (Toronto: University of Toronto Press, 1999 [1996]), 9.

29 Danièle Chatelain, 'Itération interne et scène classique,' *Poétique* 51 (1982): 374.

30 Todorov, 'Les catégories,' 118.

Chapter 8. Narration and Monstration in the Cinema

1 Christian Metz, *Essais sur la signification au cinéma*, vol. 2 (Paris: Klincksieck, 1972), 54.

2 Albert Laffay, *Logique du cinéma* (Paris: Masson, 1964).

3 Jean Mitry, *The Aesthetics and Psychology of the Cinema*, trans. Christopher King (Bloomington: Indiana University Press, 1997 [1968]).

4 Claude-Edmonde Magny, *L'âge du roman américain* (Paris: Seuil, 1948).

5 The expression is Magny's (ibid., 52).

6 Ibid., 31.

7 Jacques Aumont et al., *Aesthetics of Film*, trans. Richard Neupert (Austin: University of Texas Press, 1992 [1983]), 86–7.

8 This, in any event, is where this agent leaves the most visible signs of its passage.

9 A hypothesis I developed in my doctoral dissertation and in my principal articles on narratology.

10 In the strict sense, and not in the sense of 'narration in the cinema,' which can include various forms of *secondary* narration through the use of a voice-off or voice-over narrator.

11 Here I take up in large measure the ideas I developed in my article 'Narration and Monstration in the Cinema,' *Journal of Film and Video* 39 (1987).

12 Ivo Osolsobé, 'Cours de théâtristique générale,' *Études littéraires* 13, no. 3 (December 1980): 417.

13 Anne Ubersfeld, *L'école du spectateur* (Paris: Éditions sociales, 1981), 303–4.

14 Ibid., 304. Here a remark becomes necessary. There is no doubt that, by means of a few unusual techniques (such as spotlights and the use of film in particular), the theatrical monstrator can manage to 'impose' a specific gaze on the viewer. I have also thought that it may also be possible to identify elements of some sort of 'narratorial' activity in the theatre. But these, in the end, are relatively unusual practices.

15 I owe this idea to Michel Colin, who said, during a conversation on this subject: 'In order for there to be narration, there has to be a narrator outside the here and now of the enunciated. Now, if editing is present, there is necessarily an organizing agent whose activity comes after the filmed event.'

16 I should add that, if we take television into account, where 'editing' can be carried out immediately, simply by switching from one camera to another, my criterion does not fit as well. To this I would respond that the editing in question, although it is carried out *at the same time* ('now') as the utterance being put in the can, can be considered all the same to be the work of an agent other than the one responsible for this 'putting in the can.' This agent is located *elsewhere* (as opposed to 'here'), in another 'seat.'

17 In the case of the theatre, we assume that the events being reproduced happened elsewhere. In the case of the cinema, the same situation holds, in addition to the fact that the re-presentation by the actors took place at a moment prior to the events' re-presentation (their re-re-presentation) on the screen.

18 Gérard Genette, *Figures of Literary Discourse*, trans. Alan Sheridan (New York: Columbia University Press, 1982 [1966]), 136.

19 The quotes are used here to indicate that this is in fact an illusion.

20 And this is true, so it would seem, for other temporal means for expressing
    words. Thus, the narrator can resort to the conditional and the optative
    tenses – for example, the 'potential' sequence of the two heroes' flight in a
    car in Jean-Luc Godard's *Pierrot le fou* (France, 1965).

21 Metz, *Essais*, 73.

22 Jean-Paul Simon, 'Remarques sur le temporalité cinématographique dans les
    films diégétiques,' in Dominique Chateau, André Gardies, and François Jost,
    eds, *Cinémas de la modernité: Films, théories* (Paris: Klincksieck, 1981), 58.

23 Otto Ludwig, quoted by William Kayser in 'Qui raconte le roman?' in
    Roland Barthes et al., *Poétique du récit* (Paris: Seuil, 1977), 81.

24 Or 18 fps during the silent era. Or, in the end, any speed at all (any speed
    over 10 fps, below which there is no illusion of continuous movement), as
    long as this speed is reconstituted at the time of projection.

25 Émile Benveniste, *Problems in General Linguistics*, trans. Mary Elizabeth
    Meek (Coral Gables: University of Miami Press, 1971 [1966]), 227.

26 Francis Vanoye, *Récit écrit, récit filmique* (Paris: CEDIC, 1979; repr. Nathan,
    1989), 181.

27 Ibid.

28 *Quoting*, in fact, is a way of bringing a past event into the present. Every
    quote, whatever it is, is in fact a reproduction of a past moment.

29 In a discussion of the film *Mary Jane's Mishap* (Smith, 1903), Marie-Claire
    Ropars-Wuilleumier comments that 'when Smith cuts up a short fictional
    film such as *Mary Jane's Mishap* into different units, some of which, for
    example a close-up of Mary Jane's face, do not represent a chronological
    stage but rather a *position of the gaze*, the sequence of camera angles after
    which he decided to insert this image establishes a *comment on reality*, and
    not its reflection.' 'Fonction du montage dans la constitution du récit au
    cinéma,' *Revue de sciences humaines* 141 (1971): 34. My emphasis.

30 Jaap Lintvelt, *Essai de typologie narrative* (Paris: Librairie José Corti, 1981), 56.

31 I have borrowed this expresssion from Marie-Claire Ropars-Wuilleumier:
    'It is for lack of another term that we have kept the name of "[sovereign]
    speaker" to designate the origin of this non-phonetic voice, which is per-
    ceptible only in the organization of the editing and which plays a role
    similar to that of the implicit *I* that accompanies anything being narrated.'
    'Narration et signification,' in Raymond Bellour, ed., *Le cinéma américain*,
    vol. 2 (Paris: Flammarion, 1980), 12.

32 Román Gubern, 'David Wark Griffith et l'articulation cinématographique,'
    Les Cahiers de la Cinémathèque 17 (1975).

33 These mini-narratives have so much autonomy that a good 15 years were
    necessary, between 1895 and 1910, for filmmakers to cast the monstrator's

mini-narratives into a continuous flux and thereby to give birth to the narrator specific to the cinema. The notion that the shot was an autonomous unit (in fact an autonomous narrative), which dominated film practice throughout the period of early cinema (until at least 1910), had very serious consequences, as we saw in chapter 1, for the way film was conceived during this period. It was because each shot was seen as a kind of autonomous narrative that filmmakers were led to practise what we call 'repetitive editing of the action.'

Chapter 9. The Film Narrative System

1 Gunning's initial terms, found in his unpublished doctoral dissertation, differed slightly from these, which appear in the published version of his dissertation, *D.W. Griffith and the Origins of American Narrative Film: The Early Years at Biograph* (Urbana/Chicago: University of Illinois Press, 1991), 19–20.
2 In book 10 of the *Republic*.
3 David Bordwell, *Narration in the Fiction Film* (Madison: University of Wisconsin Press, 1985), 325. Note however that Bordwell only views film as a palimpsest when a filmmaker literally transforms the subject matter and leaves *visible* signs of rewriting.
4 Here I deliberately neglect the entire process of writing a film (in a literal sense in this case): the script, continuity, treatment, etc. It would, however, be a sound idea to develop a narratological 'treatment' of film scripts. This is what Isabelle Raynauld proposed in her unpublished doctoral dissertation, 'Le scénario de film comme texte,' Université de Paris VII, 1990. See also her article 'Le point de vue dans le scénario,' *Protée* 16, nos. 1–2 (Winter–Spring 1988): 156–60.
5 I say 'agent,' but the reader will realize that in some cases it really is a 'sub-agent.'
6 My apologies to François Jost, who remarks: 'I don't see the merit in endlessly multiplying the number of narrative agents.' See *L'oeil-caméra: Entre film et roman* (Lyon: Presses Universitaires de Lyon, 1987), 62.
7 Tom Gunning, letter to the author, 9 July 1983. It was in this long, seven-page letter that my U.S. colleague pushed me, through his judicious comments, to develop my theoretical framework, helping in large part to give it its present stature. For this I give him my warmest and heartiest thanks.
8 I will not take into account here the rather rare film practice of 'doubling' the image, an interesting example of which is found in the film *Forty-Deuce* (Paul Morrissey, U.S., 1982).

9   *Etc.* because the list could be endless: quality of the emulsion, trick camera effects, and so on.

10   Pretty much everything that I have said about the inherent conditions of discourse in theatrical monstration can be applied, with slight modification, to profilmic monstration.

11   There exists, however, a way of making a match completely invisible, that has been used for a very long time – by the Edison studios as early as 1894 for a kinetoscope film, *Mary Queen of Scots* (Edison, 1894). This is the technique commonly known as the 'stop-motion effect' (and which should rightfully be known as the 'stop-*camera* technique'), whose glory days were in the period 1898–1905, in the hands of Georges Méliès in particular. In order to make an object appear or disappear, or to substitute one object for another, the filmmaker would stop the camera and carry out his 'little machination,' making sure that neither the camera nor the 'moving' decor or characters changed their initial position. The filming was then resumed and the action followed its course. What we have here then was a cut (a *jump cut*) that, if carried out well, went completely unnoticed (even if, logically, the viewer could assume its presence). Such cuts are made for 'magical' purposes and only rarely, properly speaking, have narrative ends. Note also that from a diegetic point of view these cuts do not constitute a change of shot. And, on a strictly technical level, they are a change of shot only on a temporal level: they create an 'ellipsis' in the temporal sequence (one that is not indicated at the level of the diegesis). They thus affect the duration of the shot. Spatially, however, they do not involve any 'movement' of the camera nor, as a result, do they affect the framing of the shot.

12   Except in the case of an express by contrary desire on the part of the monstrator (use of fast and slow motion, for example) or in the case of a mishap while shooting or projecting the film: if it becomes poorly lodged in the film track, the film can proceed too rapidly or with jerky movements.

13   At a conference on D.W. Griffith in Paris, Tom Gunning remarked: 'This movement towards the constitution of a *story* was maintained and even intensified by the classical American cinema which followed, while moments of *discourse* in cinematic style became, on the contrary, increasingly attenuated and dissimulated (if not completely eliminated).' 'Présence du narrateur: L'héritage des films Biograph de Griffith,' in Jean Mottet, ed., *David Wark Griffith* (Paris: Publications de la Sorbonne / L'Harmattan, 1984), 143.

14   Michel Colin, 'Film: Transformation du texte du roman,' unpublished doctoral dissertation (École Pratique des Hautes Études, 1974), 134.

15   The reader should not read any moral connotation into this judgment.

16 Alain Bergala, *Initiation à la sémiologie du récit en images* (Paris: Ligue française de l'enseignement et de l'éducation permanente [1977]), 34.
17 Michel Marie, 'Analyse textuelle,' in Jean Collet et al., eds, *Lectures du film* (Paris: Albatros, 1976), 24.
18 Except, perhaps, in the paradoxical case of slow and fast motion. But even here the monstrator remains riveted to a kind of temporal isomorphism: it is unable to skip a segment of the action, except by directly manipulating it. This, as we will see later on, is the only kind of temporal modulation afforded monstrative agents.
19 We don't know when the first editing activities took place. Until about 1902, most films were punctiliar, or made up of a single shot. We can assume that four early Lumière strips that, as Georges Sadoul remarks, 'form a coherent whole' (*Louis Lumière* [Paris: Seghers, 1964], 45), must have been glued end to end. The films in question are *Sortie de la pompe*, *Mise en batterie*, *Attaque du feu*, and *Sauvetage*. Clearly, at a certain moment the Lumière brothers (or their employees) began to glue their films end to end, if only for reasons of pure convenience.
20 Is it completely immaterial that the filmographic narrator came to take centre stage precisely when the star system was born?
21 See Jon Gartenberg's important article 'Les mouvements de caméra dans les films Edison et Biograph,' *Les Cahiers de la Cinémathèque* 29 (1979): 58–70.
22 In the very beginning segments of the action that were deemed of lesser importance were dropped from the film. Or the profilmic monstrator arranged things so that the action remained a captive of the imposed field of vision, even if this meant, in the event of any inclination to stray outside of this field, that the profilmic monstrator made sure, by means of a character if necessary, that the action was brought back into place. This is exactly what happened in *Waterer and Watered*. After committing his misdeed, the young scamp, no doubt unaware that in 1895 it was still not possible to make a 'real' chase film, takes off towards the off-screen space to the left. If it hadn't been for the dispatch (and severity) of the (heretofore) kind gardener, who, as a good lackey of the mise en scène, dragged the practical joker back to the centre of the frame in order to give him a spanking in front of the 'stupefied' camera, the film might have fizzled out then and there, especially since the length of the film stock was extremely limited.
23 Gartenberg, 'Les mouvements de caméra,' 65–6.
24 We should perhaps say 'almost ineluctably,' for reasons we will see immediately below.
25 This shot, moreover, is startling on a formal level: there is really nothing comparable to it before 1910. In my view, this is owing to questions of the

coherence of the 'script.' The mega-narrator probably felt the need to emphasize the kidnappers' departure to ensure that the viewer didn't succumb to the same confusion as the characters, who take the *burglars* in shot 5 to be the *kidnappers* of shot 3. This is a fine example of complicity between the narrative agents and the viewer, to the detriment to some of the film's characters.

26 The film was produced in 1902.

27 André Gaudreault, 'Temporality and Narrativity in Early Cinema, 1895–1908,' in *Film before Griffith*, ed. John L. Fell (Berkeley: University of California Press, 1983), 311–29.

28 As shot 9 in fact shows us: this shot repeats the temporality of shot 8 *in its entirety*. This time, the action is shown from outside the house in flames.

29 Among other possible examples, we could look at the film *The Firebug* (Biograph, 1905), in which this intervention is even *more* marked. See my article 'Temporality and Narrativity,' 320.

30 Even if it may not be voluntary in this case. Shot 8 was shot in a studio interior (whereas the view from the window is real) and we can assume that the true 'terra firma' for this decor of the bedroom's interior was 'really' situated just a few feet from the window that was supposedly one floor up.

31 When we look at these more closely, however, we can see that this was not at all the case! Indeed, the film contains an 'anomaly' that until now has apparently never been reported. No one has ever noticed that the exhibition copy for the United States (which was copyrighted by Biograph) is in fact *another* version, a *remake*, of the one that circulated (and still circulates) in Europe. The anomaly in question is, precisely, the product of the existence of these two versions. Examining the film closely, we can in fact see that in one of the versions an extra (found in an upper balcony) suddenly disappears, like magic, *by means of* the cut that joins, as I have pointed out, two segments with continuous framing and action. In the other version, meanwhile, this extra suddenly *appears*, by means of a cut at the some point in the action! This is a discovery that Jacques Malthête and I made in the late 1980s. Our (very summary) hypothesis is this: Méliès produced two different versions in order to have two original negatives and thereby facilitate distribution on two continents – and he switched the final segments. In one of the stagings, there is an extra extra, which explains his appearance/disappearance in the different versions. Bloody Méliès, who made substitutions even in his probably most 'realist' film! See Jacques Malthête, 'Les actualités reconstituées de Georges Méliès,' *Archives* 21 (March 1989).

32 The newspaper *The Era* of 21 June 1902 described this situation quite well: 'For this view, we chose the most characteristic moments of the ceremony,

which is thus shorter in length than the ceremony itself. We showed the ceremony in linking tableaux, acted out in an impressive way that conveys all the dignity of the ceremony.' Quoted in *Essai de la reconstitution du catalogue français du Star-Film*, followed by *Analyse des films de Georges Méliès recensés en France* (Paris: Centre National de la Cinématographie, 1981), 105. (Because parts of the original documentation are inaccessible to me, this quotation has been translated back into English using the author's French translation – Trans.)

Chapter 10. The Origins of the Film Narrator

1 Trans. Ian Patterson (London: Penguin, 2002). (Translation modified slightly – Trans.)
2 See Christian Metz, *Film Language: A Semiotics of the Cinema*, trans. Michael Taylor (New York: Oxford University Press, 1974 [1971]). If the reader will allow me to express my personal opinion, I would say that Metz went to a good school. On this topic, see my article 'Les aventures d'un concept,' in *Christian Metz et la théorie du cinéma* (Paris: Méridiens Klincksieck and *Iris* 10 [April 1990]), 121–31.
3 Most of the documents quoted in this chapter come from the Edison National Historic Site (West Orange, NJ), where I was able to carry out research thanks to the support of the Social Sciences and Humanities Research Council of Canada (SSHRC) and the Institut québécois du cinéma. This research was carried out as part of the project 'Un pionnier: Edwin S. Porter,' which I led from 1979 to 1982 at Université Laval, in collaboration with David Levy. Some of these documents were provided by Charles Musser, who was conducting research into Porter at the same time for his book *Before the Nickelodeon: Edwin S. Porter and the Edison Manufacturing Company* (Berkeley: University of California Press, 1991). Please note also that a good portion of this chapter is adapted from my article 'The Infringement of Copyright Laws and Its Effects (1900–1906),' *Framework* 29 (1985): 2–14.
4 Or the opinion of their lawyers, because we must remember that even when a film person is speaking directly these are 'interested' declarations.
5 On this topic, here is the legal opinion of a lawyer writing to a production manager at Edison: 'The Pathé films are not copyrighted, and therefore you can make and sell as many copies thereof as you desire without molestation from him, just as copies of uncopyrighted books can be made in this country without infringement.' F.L. Dyer to W. Gilmore, 22 January 1904.
6 A more detailed discussion is found in my article cited in note 3 above and in the article by David Levy cited in note 12 below.

7 Interested also in that the 'opinion' he sets forth has as its goal to deny the artistic aspect of shooting a film, so that it would be impossible to copyright it in any way, thus undermining the plaintiff's claim.

8 Affidavit by John J. Frawley, 24 June 1902.

9 There is no value judgment implied in the use of this term. The second layer is superior to the first in that it is applied *on top of it*.

10 Affidavit by James H. White, 9 June 1902.

11 Quoted from the Lubin case in the other case that will be discussed below. See *American Mutoscope and Biograph Co. v. Edison Mfg Co.*, Defendant's Brief on Demurrer to Bill, 18 April 1905, 5–6. We can also well imagine the problems that this verdict would have created if it had not been overturned: would it have become necessary to pay 50 cents per photogram to copyright a film?

12 David Levy, 'Edison Sales Policy and the Continuous Action Film, 1904–1906,' in John Fell, ed., *Film before Griffith* (Berkeley: University of California Press, 1983), 212–13, in which the author is summarizing the information found in *119 Federal Reporter*, 993–4 and in *122 Federal Reporter*, 240–3.

13 Defendant's Rejoinder to Complainant's Brief in Reply, 24 December 1904. This document concerns the second court case (around the film *Personal*), but it draws on the lessons learned in the first case (relating to *Christening*). The quoted passages are from documents concerning the first case.

14 The description of the film preserved at the Edison National Historic Site, seemingly in Porter's own hand, indicates that the film's original title was *Personal*. No doubt the author had a sudden change of heart, because this title is crossed out and is replaced by the other, much longer one.

15 We should point out that this new kind of 'pirating,' which would take the place of mere duping, was very widespread. *Personal*, for example, gave rise to at least two other pastiches (figures 10.2 and 10.3 here): *Meet Me at the Fountain* (Lubin, 1904) and, *Personal*'s reputation having already crossed the Atlantic, *Dix femmes pour un mari* (Pathé, 1905).

16 Defendant's Rejoinder, 2. This was a double-edged sword that could cut both ways. Indeed, if the judge accepted such an argument, *every* pluri-punctiliar film *already copyrighted* by Edison (and by every other producer, moreover) would fall into the public domain. This is when, out of prudence, the company began copyrighting its films *shot by shot*. This, we might mention in passing, had an effect on the development of the film mega-narrator. A film such as *The Ex-Convict* (Edison, 1904), for example, has often been singled out by film historians as representing the first use of intertitles containing a line of dialogue ('That man saved my life'). It has also been remarked that the dialogue in question appeared well before the diegetic moment when the heroine is supposed to have uttered it. It is not clear, however, if this insert

was a true intertitle or whether it was even present in exhibition copies. The only thing we know with certainty is that it was at the very least a *title*: a title for the tableau shot in question that, in order to be copyrighted as an autonomous film, had to have a title of some kind. This practice may have had an influence on the introduction of inserted intertitles. On this topic, see Yves Bédard, 'Images écrites: Étude de l'écriture dans le cinéma de 1895 à 1912,' unpublished master's thesis, Université Laval, 1987. Or, on the contrary, it may have favoured retaining the conception of the shot as an autonomous unit (so autonomous that each shot was entitled to its own title).

17 As an example, here are a series of statements by Porter in his affidavit of 3 December 1904 (for the same court case): 'Such a series of scenes, however, is really an aggregation of several series of negative impressions, each series constituting one photograph and each scene is generally sold separately ... [C]omplainant's film was in no sense a single photograph, since the view points are not the same in all the views. It is an aggregation of several views of scenes ... Furthermore, as it takes considerable time to arrange such pantomimes, some of the views were probably taken on different days and on different films from others of the views.'

18 In the same case, Defendant's Brief on Demurrer to Bill, 18 April 1905, 3. Emphasis in original.

19 Ibid., 5.

20 Ibid., 6.

21 Ibid. Emphasis in original.

22 A gap the same text acknowledges a little further on: '[T]here are seven points in the film where there is a rupture, a wide and total difference in character, light, position, background, etc., between one picture and that immediately following it.'

23 Defendant's Brief, 3.

24 See on this topic Levy, 'Edison Sales Policy.'

25 Complainant's Brief in Reply, 22 December 1904, 15. My emphasis.

26 Ibid., 14.

27 Quoted by Levy, 'Edison Sales Policy,' 218. Taken from *137 Federal Reporter*, 262–8. My emphasis.

28 An untitled and undated document from the same court case (*A.M. & B. v. Edison*), found in the Edison National Historic Site, p. 9. Further research should show whether this is a copy of the definitive version of the verdict, which was unfavourable to Edison.

29 Recall that the film *Christening and Launching* contained a panoramic shot that the camera operator J.B. Smith described in the following manner: 'As the boat moved in the launching I revolved my camera so as to follow the boat, and took continuous pictures of it.' J.B. Smith, Affidavit, 28 May 1902, 1.

Chapter 11. Narrator(s)

1 This has given rise to a whole series of new and quite legitimate meanings. It would in fact be more precise to say that the word 'narrator' already contained several meanings before narratological theory got hold of it. Here, as an example, are two uses of the word taken from the same issue of a newspaper (*Le Soleil*, Quebec City, 10 December 1985) on two consecutive pages: 'The new "Challenge" [in reference to the television series "World Challenge" (Défi mondial), based upon the work of Servan-Schreiber] will concern the children of the planet, based upon a book the world-famous actor and playwright Peter Ustinov is launching in Montreal ... Mr Ustinov is the *narrator* of the French Version of World Challenge' (p. B-13); and 'A Montreal group even intends to draw upon the dramatic story [of the singer Alys Robi] to launch a new musical comedy. As the *narrator* of the show [at the Théâtre de la Bordée] remarks, their aim is to "correct an entire people's blank memory."' My emphasis.

2 *Oxford English Dictionary*, 2nd ed., vol. 10 (Oxford: Clarendon Press, 1989), 220.

3 *Le Grand Robert de la Langue Française*, vol. 4 (Paris: Dictionnaires le Robert, 2001), 1810.

4 The words '*in praesentia*' and 'touch' should not be taken literally. Everything I say here about verbal narrative would be true even if it were delivered from the other side of a wall or by telephone. In such cases, there is still a level of 'presence' involved, and they presuppose protagonists who can 'touch each other,' even if this is only by means of an intermediary broadcast.

5 Thus these properly narrative words of Telemachus in a tirade nearly twenty lines in length: 'But now storm winds have carried him off as though nameless. He's gone, unseen and unheard of, leaving me mourning and smarting.' Homer, *The Odyssey*, trans. Edward McCrorie (Baltimore: Johns Hopkins University Press, 2004), 1.240–3.

6 A rapid calculation as to how many pages these four books take up shows that Odysseus monopolizes the 'microphone' for more than 18% of 'air time' in this instance alone.

7 I will not consider here the possibilities that arise when the bard is called upon to gradually become a veritable theatrical performer. Clearly, if we were to put several bards together on a stage, with each one playing a role (this is theatre), the one with Odysseus's narrative speech could be considered the real *narrator* of this speech (thus, in this case, Odysseus the character is the narrator). But here we would be leaving the realm of mere

verbal narration, which is being studied here, and entering into the realm of theatrical monstration, which presupposes an *underlying agent* other than the mere 'speakers,' other than the mere verbal narrators, an agent responsible for this other way of *telling* in which the viewer is placed before the actors, who *act out* a story in order, precisely, to tell it. This agent is the *theatrical monstrator*.

8 This agent is, in fact, the 'author of the *performance*.' Here I am following Aristotle who, we should recall, said of these performers, these theatrical actors, that they 'represent the characters as carrying out the whole action themselves' (1448a22).

9 The situation is entirely different in the case of textual narration. There, the narrator is *alive* (and thus *autonomous*) only because this life has been *breathed into it* by the author and subsequently *restored* by the reader.

10 These beings exist only in the sense that the verbal narrator's speech causes them to exist. They are no more living than the 'paper beings,' including the narrator(s), of textual narrative.

11 This has been well understood by Jean Châteauvert, who wrote a doctoral dissertation on these questions. In his master's thesis he writes: 'The narrator is a product of the narration and, like its source, is presented in a rhetorical manner.' See 'Prolégomènes à une lecture essayistique des quatre premiers "Comédies et proverbes" d'Éric Rohmer,' unpublished master's thesis (Université Laval, 1987), 34. Châteauvert's doctoral thesis was eventually published in revised form as *Des mots à l'image: La voix* over *au cinéma* (Paris/Quebec City: Méridiens Klincksieck / Nuit blanche, 1996).

12 *The Book of the Thousand Nights and a Night* (*The Arabian Nights*), vol. 1, trans. Richard F. Burton (London: Burton Club, [1885]), 27–8. Despite the debates around Burton's translation, it remains the standard translation into English of the *Arabian Nights*. In any event the choice of edition matters little, because the book exists, and I care little whether the author of the narrative in question is such and such an Arab storyteller(s) or purely and simply Burton himself.

13 Ibid., 27. Burton complains that the English word 'genie' is an unpardonable Gallicism (French *génie*) and employs the word 'Jinni' in its place.

14 Sheherazade in other English translations.

15 Shahrayar or Shayriyar in other English translations, including the translation of Proust found in the epigraph to the present chapter.

16 Narratologists familiar with Burton's book will think my comments here a lot of fuss over nothing, because they will have understood right from the first reading that Shahrazad is a character-narrator who comes to us by means of another narrator (a relatively omniscient narrator, to use a

somewhat out-of-date term). But this long propaedeutic discussion also functions as a sort of maieutic intended, first of all, for the newcomer, but also later, as we shall see, for the less 'disadvantaged.' What we have here, if the reader will permit me to quote Plato one more time, is a 'Socratic' activity: "'As a teacher," I said, "I seem to have a laughable inability to make my meaning clear. I'd better do what people who are no good at speaking do – avoid generalisations, take a particular example, and try to use that to show you what I mean."' Plato, *The Republic*, trans. Tom Griffith, ed. G.R.F. Ferrari (Cambridge: Cambridge University Press, 2000), 392e.

17 *Arabian Nights*, vol. 1, 2.

18 Ibid., vol. 2, 147.

19 Most of the time, its attributions conform to the model given. Sometimes, however, they are 'embellished' with the narration of certain events. In the end, the underlying narrator of the framing story intervenes only once every two or three pages.

20 Gerald Prince, *A Dictionary of Narratology* (Lincoln: University of Nebraska Press, 2003), 313.

21 Any such identification could not be easily done in the present case because the author (or authors) is (are) unknown. Here it would seem we are in the presence of the clearest example of 'collective authorship,' because the secondary narratives that make up this collection of stories were written down at a late date, long after they were first 'conceived' and after having undergone numerous – and inevitable – transformations within a very long oral tradition.

22 I wish to be perfectly clear here. I'm not expressing any form of contempt for the author, whom narratology may nevertheless question. Rather, I view the author as an *author* and not a *narrator*. I must repeat that Proust and Griffith are not *narrators* (despite what the dictionaries quoted at the beginning of this chapter would have us believe). The former is a *writer*, the latter a *filmmaker*. The only concession we might make would be to say that they were, in a sense, narrators at the *moment* (or rather moments) when they picked up their pen and camera respectively to compose their work. When this work is consumed, it is *no longer* the author who is *speaking* to me. The proof (I hope this does not appear facile): Yesterday I read *In Search of Lost Time* after watching *The Birth of a Nation* (what a busy day!) and yet Proust and Griffith are quite dead.

23 Oswald Ducrot, *Le dire et le dit* (Paris: Éditions de Minuit, 1984), 208.

24 We might even say that verbal narration is a kind of narration that allows the author to retain a significant presence (although as a narrator) within the sphere of narratology's concerns. As I said above, all storytellers are also

more or less authors (at least of the performance): the degree of their artistic creation may well be minimal, but it still plays a primary role on the level, for example, of the inflection of voices, pauses, the choice of words, etc. This, at bottom, is what Paul Zumthor refers to when he writes: 'In any verbal performance of poetry, the role of the performer is greater than that of the author(s). The performer does not completely eclipse the author, but, as the performance makes clear, the performer contributes more to determining the audience's auditory, corporeal, and affective reactions and the nature and intensity of its pleasure. The author, prior to the performance, creates a still-virtual work.' *Introduction à la poésie orale* (Paris: Seuil, 1983), 210.

25 Marcel Proust, *In Search of Lost Time: The Way by Swann's*, trans. Lydia Davis (London: Penguin, 2002), 7.

26 Albert Camus, *The Stranger*, trans. Stuart Gilbert (New York: Knopf, 1981 [1946]).

27 Bruno Bettelheim, Introduction to *Les Mille et Une Nuits* (Paris: Seghers, 1978), 12.

28 While my 'scenario' concerning Camus is pure fantasy, the one about Proust has a grain of truth in it. See Gérard Genette, *Narrative Discourse: An Essay in Method*, trans. Jane E. Lewin (Ithaca: Cornell University Press, 1972 [1972]), esp. 247–52, where he explains that, between *Jean Santeuil* and *In Search of Lost Time*, Proust switched from 'he' to 'I' (without the latter work being necessarily more autobiographical than the former).

29 Even if this story is, of course, largely autobiographical. The same would hold true even if it was '100%' autobiographical.

30 This implicit author has recently been revived by Paul Ricoeur under the name 'implied author' (see in particular chapter 7, volume 3 in *Time and Narrative*, trans. Kathleen Blamey and David Pellauer [Chicago: University of Chicago Press, 1988 (1985)]). Unlike Booth's 'implicit' author and Ricoeur's 'implied' author, my 'underlying narrator' is more a narrative category than a mere function, and thus remains completely disembodied.

31 Writing in French, I have suggested that we seek a more neutral term than 'narrateur' (narrator) and return to the word's Latin roots and refer to this underlying narrator as the 'narrator.' Obviously, this solution does not hold in English, so I will continue here to call this agent, which I describe in my work published in French as a 'narrator,' the 'underlying narrator.' See André Gaudreault, '*Narrator* et narrateur,' *Iris* 7 (Spring 1986): 29–36; repr. in *Le cinéma aujourd'hui: Films, théories, nouvelles approches*, ed. Michel Larouche (Montreal: Guernica, 1988), 173–84.

32 I owe this observation and Stendhal quotation to Danielle Candelon: 'If we were to manufacture telling machines or analysing machines in Birmingham

or Manchester using good English steel, machines which would function all by themselves by unknown dynamic processes, they would work just like Mr Flaubert.' *Le Pays*, 6 October 1857, quoted in Danielle Candelon, 'L'auteur implicite dans le discours du récit: Une analyse de l'oeuvre de Jean Simard,' unpublished doctoral dissertation (Université Laval, 1977), 69.

33   André Gardies, 'Le su et le vu,' *Hors cadre* 2 (1984): 47.

Chapter 12. A Monstrative Entertainment

1   This chapter takes up in large part the ideas found in my article 'Showing and Telling: Image and Word in Early Cinema,' trans. John Howe, in Thomas Elsaesser and Adam Barker, eds, *Early Cinema: Space, Frame, Narrative* (London: British Film Institute, 1990), 274–81.

2   Norman King, 'The Sound of Silents,' *Screen* 25, no. 3 (May–June 1984): 15.

3   Here I will quickly pass over experiences using sounds other than the lecturer's voice. For more detail, see my article cited in note 1 above. Another article of great interest is Charles Musser, 'The Nickelodeon Era Begins: Establishing the *Framework* for Hollywood's Mode of Representation,' *Framework* 22–3 (Fall 1983): 4–11.

4   Michel Chion, *The Voice in Cinema*, trans. and ed. Claudia Gorbman (New York: Columbia University Press, 1999 [1982]), 18–19.

5   The narrative aspect of the magic lantern show was not always at the forefront, however, because slides were sometimes used to illustrate lectures. In some cases, this was even true of the cinema: in order to give their work a nobler quality, some film showmen sometimes seemed to give precedence to their commentary over the moving pictures they were projecting. Such a move could be important in a society such as French Canada's, for example, where the *nihil obstat* of the Catholic Church was necessary in order to confer longevity on moving picture shows given by the cinematograph, that 'invention of the devil.' Here is how one of the pioneers of film exhibition in Quebec, who was originally from Brittany, announced his show in 1901: 'Illustrated lectures. The Comtesse de Grandsaignes d'Hauterives ... offering her illustrated lectures in support of all religious works, requests everyone who ...' *La Presse*, 22 April 1901, quoted by Germain Lacasse (in collaboration with Serge Duigou), *L'historiographe (Les débuts du spectacle cinématographique au Québec)* (Montreal: Cinémathèque québécoise, 1985), 29.

6   'In part' because there were many other factors. Since many of the first film showmen had seemingly first been magic lanternists, it seems natural that the lecturer was retained. Even more so when we view cinema as a technological improvement on the magic lantern (note that the apparatus used in

film projection included a magic lantern as its light source) and consider
that the first film shows (over a period of several years) were often 'multimedia' in nature, in the sense that they readily alternated between films
and magic lantern slides, in addition to other forms of entertainment.

7 According to Martin Sopocy, this was the case in particular with most of
James Williamson's films. See 'Un cinéma avec narrateur: Les premiers
films narratifs de James A. Williamson,' *Les Cahiers de la Cinémathèque* 29
(Winter 1979): 108–26. See also Sopocy's more recent work, *James A.
Williamson: Studies and Documents of a Pioneer of the Film Narrative*
(Madison/Teaneck, NJ: Fairleigh Dickinson University Press, 1998).

8 Tom Gunning, 'D.W. Griffith and the Narrator System: Narrative Structure
and Industry Organization in Biograph Films,' doctoral dissertation, New
York University, 1986. This sentence is taken from page 34 of the draft
version, to which I had access, but does not appear in the final version.

9 This is even truer when we consider, as David Levy remarks, that 'with the
arrival of nickelodeon exhibition, the need for a major modification in the
mode of commercial display required of the manufacturers a lecturer-
independent experience based on a stricter codification of spatio-temporal
convention and a tighter sequential arrangement of focused visual detail.'
'Edwin S. Porter and the Origins of the American Narrative Film, 1894–
1907,' unpublished doctoral dissertation (McGill University, 1983), 333–4.

10 Gunning, 'D.W. Griffith and the Narrator System,' 117 of the draft version.
My emphasis.

11 *Views and Film Index*, September 1906, 10. Quoted in Musser, 'The Nickelodeon Era Begins,' 6.

12 Van C. Lee, 'The Value of a Lecture,' *Moving Picture World*, 8 February 1908.

13 *Moving Picture World*, 22 February 1908. The reference in question is to a
'Letter to the Editor' written by a certain W.M. Rhoads in response to the
article by Van C. Lee published a few weeks earlier (note 12 above).

14 Gunning, 'D.W. Griffith and the Narrator System,' 304–5 of the published
version.

15 I refer here to an article by Roger Odin entitled 'L'entrée du spectateur
dans le fiction,' in Jacques Aumont and Jean-Louis Leutrat, eds, *La théorie
du film* (Paris: Albatros, 1980), 198–213.

16 This is often how the lecturer was seen, as illustrated by this description of
film screenings from the period: 'A band of juxtaposed photographs passes
rapidly in front of a bright light, produced by two incandescent carbons,
and a lens, which blows them up. Add to this a long murmur arising from
the assembly, eyes wide open, heads more or less stretched out from the
neck, and, in a word, a bored man explaining to you what you are seeing,
to whom you don't listen and who imperturbably recites his lecture right

to the end!' Quoted in Lacasse, *L'historiographe*, 26. Let's hope for the lecturer's sake that this viewer in the year 1900, visibly fascinated by the images, would pay more attention to the lecture at any future screening he might attend!

17 I allude here to one of the first models of the film genre in question, Sacha Guitry's 1936 *The Story of a Cheat*. (The film's original French title, *Le roman d'un tricheur*, conveys better the author's play on words here, as *roman*, translated as 'story,' actually means 'novel' in French, while *tricheur* means something of a 'trickster,' not a 'cheat' – Trans.)

Chapter 13. Delegated Film Narrators

1 Except in Japan, where 'benshi' remained popular until the end of the 1930s. See Noël Burch, *To the Distant Observer: Form and Meaning in the Japanese Cinema* (London: Scolar, 1979). See also Hiroshi Komatsu and Charles Musser, 'Added Attraction: Benshi Search,' *Wide Angle* 9, no. 2 (1987): 72–90.

2 Syncretic in the sense, to borrow Greimas and Courtés's expression, that it 'implements several manifestation languages.' A.-J. Greimas and J. Courtés, *Semiotics and Language: An Analytical Dictionary*, trans. Larry Crist et al. (Bloomington: Indiana University Press, 1982 [1979]), 326.

3 Émile Benveniste, *Problèmes de linguistique générale* vol. 2 (Paris: Gallimard, 1974), 68.

4 There are at least two other factors that cause a variation in the status of all film narrators, because these factors change the 'nature' of the place in which the narrator speaks and tells the story. This is the case, for example, when a narrator allows itself to go through the 'cloakroom' of the profilmic visual field, which is to say to anchor its speech in a visible, living body. This is also the case when the narrator allows itself to speak directly to me, the viewer, rather than simply to the actors in the narrative. The next step in my research into this topic will be to apply the system I propose here for the cinema to the analysis of films with verbal narrators (this work has already begun: see André Gaudreault and François Jost, *Le récit ciné-matographique* [Paris: Nathan, 1990], as well as my article, published in Spanish only, 'Sistema del relato de un film con narrador verbal: *Citizen Kane* de Orson Welles,' *Archivos de la Filmoteca* 27 [October 1997]: 128–41).

5 François Jost, 'Narration(s): En deçà et au-delà,' *Communications* 38 (1983): 205.

6 François Jost, *L'œil-caméra: Entre film et roman* (Lyon: Presses Universitaires de Lyon, 1987), 31–2.

7 I refer here to narrators such as Camus's Meurseault and Proust's Marcel, who appear to be primary narrators because the underlying narrator has made itself invisible to the highest degree (see chapter 11 above).

8 Homer, *The Odyssey*, trans. Edward McCrorie (Baltimore: Johns Hopkins University Press, 2004), 9.2 and 37–8.

9 Bergman, quoted without a source given in the 1980 program guide 'Ciné-matographe' of the ciné-club of the Collège de Sainte-Foy in Quebec City.

10 Plato, *The Republic*, trans. Tom Griffith, ed. G.R.F. Ferrari (Cambridge: Cambridge University Press, 2000), 393a.

11 In Mikhalkov's film, these two narrative strata appear perfectly commensurate. Some films, however, present opposite situations: this is the case with the opening sequence of *Singin' in the Rain* (Gene Kelly and Stanley Donen, U.S., 1952), in which Don Lockwood (Kelly) reminisces about his early days in the film business. The audio-visuals (which show the hero in grotesque situations) contradict Kelly's speech, in which he states on numerous occasions that he had always preserved his dignity.

12 Unless the film narrator uses, *diegetically*, other means to tell the story, such as moving pictures.

13 Jost, 'Narration(s),' 206.

14 This 'nothing leads us to believe' might appear exaggerated to those who believe in placing certain 'instructions to the viewer' in a commanding role. It is true that in some cases – in point of fact quite a few – the audio-visualization is clearly meant to be read as being distilled directly by the delegated narrator, without any intermediary, as, for example, in Akira Kurosawa's *Rashomon* (Japan, 1950). These instructions to the viewer are based on conventions whose importance is not at all negligible and to which I intend to return in the follow-up I plan on writing to the present volume. My position here may seem extreme, but I have decided to start from a clean slate in order to clearly distinguish the essential differences between the narrative dislocation created by delegating in textual narratives and that found in the simplest film narratives.

15 We mustn't forget that Romano-the-storyteller is at the same time Romano-in-the-story-told. The narrative structure of this film is as follows: the film mega-narrator (the great image-maker = the storyteller) tells (by means of a film narrative involving a film mega-monstrator and a filmographic narrator) that Romano (who is also part of the story told) tells (becoming a storyteller, in fact a sub-storyteller) a story about some of his life's adventures. Whew!

16 This paradox is similar to the one described by Jost (in 'Narration(s): En deçà et au-delà,' 206): 'If the character is in external focalization, then we

are in the presence of that "paradoxical situation" Genette speaks of with respect to Proustian narrative, of a "first-person" yet omniscient narrator. This paradox is accentuated in cinema by the fact that the character telling the story is also seen from outside. We must therefore acknowledge either that the character splits into two in order to look at itself or that the character is looked at by another, a higher-level agent, the filmmaker. When the character is in internal focalization, the situation is "coherent" in literature but odd in cinema, because the person is still *seen* from without.' I have two remarks to make about this. My proposals here are in harmony with Jost's to the extent that he too establishes a higher-level agent, an agent that I am unable to see as identical, for reasons I have explained, to the *filmmaker*. As for the paradox of the first-person yet omniscient narrator (similar moreover to any other case of paralipsis), this seems to me simple enough to resolve once we establish, as I have done, an intermediary agent, the *underlying narrator*, between the narrator who speaks with 'I' (Marcel) and the author (Proust).

17 And, monstration having demands of its own, in ample detail.

Conclusion

1 In book 10 of the *Republic*.

2 Marcel Proust, *In Search of Lost Time: The Way by Swann's*, trans. Lydia Davis (London: Penguin, 2002), 43. How can we avoid thinking of Jean-Luc Godard's comment on the television program *Apostrophes* in the early 1980s to the effect that what people see when they watch a film on television is no longer a film but a *reproduction* of a film?

3 Jean-Claude Dumoncel, 'Deleuze, Platon et les poètes,' *Poétique* 59 (1984): 371.

4 John Harkness, 'Nightworld: Interview with James Cole and Holly Dale,' *Cinema Canada* 108 (June 1984): 12.

Afterword

1 This Afterword was written under the aegis of GRAFICS (Groupe de recherche sur l'avènement et la formation des institutions cinématographique et scénique) at Université de Montréal, which is funded by the Social Sciences and Humanities Research Council of Canada (SSHRC) and the Fond québécois de recherche sur la société et la culture (FQRSC).

2 This work includes the following books, which were published shortly

before the first edition of my own book: Edward Branigan, *Point of View in the Cinema* (Berlin/New York/Amsterdam: Mouton Publishers, 1984); David Bordwell, *Narration in the Fiction Film* (Madison: University of Wisconsin Press, 1985); Francesco Casetti, *Dentro lo sguardo: Il film e il suo spettatore* (Milan: Bompiani, 1986 – later published in English translation as *Inside the Gaze: The Fiction Film and Its Spectator*, trans. Nell Andrew and Charles O'Brien (Bloomington: Indiana University Press, 1998); and François Jost, *L'oeil-caméra: Entre film et roman* (Lyon: Presses Universitaires de Lyon, 1987).

3 In particular by bringing my ideas face to face with those of François Jost when we co-authored a book that attempted to define the concept of narrative in the cinema on the basis of our respective views on narratology. While these views were certainly different, we did not completely disagree. See André Gaudreault and François Jost, *Le récit cinématographique* (Paris: Nathan, 1990).

4 The term intermediality, I believe, was first used by Jürgen E. Müller in the late 1980s. See his article *'Top Hat* et l'intérmédialité de la comédie musicale,' *Cinémas* 5, nos. 1–2 (Fall 1994): 211–20, in which the author provides a bibliography of his previous work on intermediality (219 n. 6) and comments: 'If we understand by "intermediality" that media have variable relationships among themselves as media and that the way they operate is born among other things of the historical evolution of these relationships, this implies that the concept of "monads," or "isolated" media, is untenable' (213). See also his book *Intermedialität: Foren moderner kultureller Kommunikation* (Münster: Nodus, 1995). The reader may wish to consult another German-language source, Franz-Josef Albersmeier's *Theater, Film, Literatur in Frankreich: Medienwechsel und Intermedialität* (Darmstadt: Wissenschaftliche Buchgesellschaft, 1992). Jürgen Müller reviews this book in the same issue of *Cinémas* cited above.

5 The rest of this Afterword is made up of three sections. The first, 'The Origins of a Concept: Narrativity,' takes up and extends some of the research I carried out for a conference in honour of Christian Metz (see André Gaudreault, 'Les aventures d'un concept,' in *Christian Metz et la théorie du cinéma* (Paris: Méridiens Klincksieck and *Iris* 10 [April 1990]): 121–31). The second and third parts, 'Early Cinema's Intermedial Meshing' and 'Giving Wings to Film Narrative: Literariness,' were in part the subject of two lectures, the first presented at Coimbra University in Portugal in October 1997 (at the Encontros do Cinema conference) and the second at Université de Paris I – Panthéon-Sorbonne in June 1998, where I was a guest professor. Some of the ideas presented here were also sketched out in André

Gaudreault, 'Les *vues cinématographiques* selon Georges Méliès, ou: Comment Mitry et Sadoul avaient peut-être raison d'avoir tort (même si c'est surtout Deslandes qu'il faut lire et relire),' in Jacques Malthête and Michel Marie, eds, *Georges Méliès, l'illusionniste fin de siècle?* (Paris: Presses de la Sorbonne Nouvelle / Colloque de Cerisy, 1997), 111–31. The underlying questions in this Afterword are the subject of a recent book of mine in French, *Cinéma et attraction: Pour une nouvelle histoire du cinématographe* (Paris: CNRS, 2008). An English translation of this volume is currently in preparation.

6 Albert Laffay, *Logique du cinéma* (Paris: Masson, 1964), 73, 76.

7 Metz is often credited with coining the expression *grand imagier,* which his translators translate as 'grand image-maker,' but which I prefer to translate as 'great image-maker,' although in fact he borrowed it from Albert Laffay. In my article 'Les aventures d'un concept' cited in note 5 above I discuss numerous instances when Metz may have been influenced by Laffay's work.

8 Christian Metz, 'Le cinéma: Langue ou langage?' *Communications* 4 (1964), published in translation as 'The Cinema: Language or Language System?' in *Film Language: A Semiotics of the Cinema* (1971), trans. Michael Taylor (New York: Oxford University Press, 1974). Metz wrote this article before he read Laffay's book, which appeared the same year and reprinted articles written in the 1940s (and with which Metz was unfamiliar). Note also that the term 'narrativité' appears in an article by Claude Bremond in the same issue of *Communications* that appears to have been written after Metz's. On this topic, see my article 'Les aventures d'un concept.'

9 The 1975 edition of *La Grande Larousse de la langue française* (7 vols.) informs us that the origin of this 'scholarly term derived from narrative' dates from Greimas's article 'Éléments d'une grammaire narrative' published in 1969 in the July–September issue of the journal *L'Homme*. The *Grand Robert de la langue française*, in its most recent edition (2001), also traces this word's origins to Greimas, citing the same article but in a version reprinted in the book *Du sens* published in 1970. We might add that in addition to appearing a great number of times in Metz's work before 1969 (in volume one of the *Essais*, published in 1968, which was an anthology of articles published since 1964), the term narrativity was also used on numerous occasions by other authors in another famous issue of *Communications*, no. 8, in 1966 (three years before Greimas's article) in articles by Claude Bremond ('La logique des possibles narratifs') and Jules Gritti ('Un récit de presse: Les derniers jours d'un "grand homme"'), and, as we shall see further on, in a book by Jean Mitry (*Histoire du cinéma*, vol. 1 [Paris: Éditions universitaires, 1967]).

10 Metz, *Film Language*, 45.

11 Ibid., 98. (Translation modified slightly – Trans.)

12 This article initially appeared in the *Revue d'esthétique* 19, nos. 3–4 (July–December 1966) and was published in translation in Metz, *Film Language*.

13 *Film Language*, 26.

14 Jean Mitry, *Histoire du cinéma*, vol. 1 (Paris: Éditions universitaires, 1967), 370.

15 I have borrowed the expression 'cultural series' from Louis Francoeur, in his book *Les signes s'envolent: Pour une sémiologie des actes de langage culturels* (Sainte-Foy: Presses de l'Université Laval, 1985), 69–70. However, I alter its meaning significantly without, I believe, contradicting Francoeur's principles. On this topic, see Gaudreault, 'Les *vues cinématographiques*.'

16 Denis Saint-Jacques, in a paper given at the 'Littératures populaires: Mutations génétiques, mutations médiatiques' conference in Limoges in May 1998, subsequently published as 'Brève histoire d'une paisible révolution populaire,' in Jacques Migozzi, ed., *De l'écrit à l'écran. Littératures populaires: Mutations génétiques, mutations médiatiques* (Limoges: PULIM, 2000), 151–65.

17 Metz, *Film Language*, 94.

18 Rick Altman develops similar ideas in his article 'Penser l'histoire du cinéma autrement: Un modèle de crise,' *Vingtième siècle* 46 (1995): 65–74.

19 Anciens Établissements Pathé Frères, *Catalogue no. 4* (March 1902). Since the film dates from 1901, I presume this notice accompanied its release.

20 For a discussion of my hypothesis concerning Pathé, see the paper I gave at the 1996 Domitor conference in Paris, 'Les *vues cinématographiques* selon Pathé, ou: Comment la cinématographe embraye sur un nouveau paradigme,' in *La firme Pathé frères (1896–1914)*, ed. Michel Marie (Paris: Association française de recherche sur l'histoire du cinéma, 2004), 237–46.

21 Quoted in Francis Lacassin, *Louis Feuillade* (Paris: Seghers, 1964), 115.

22 Gérard Genette, *Fiction and Diction*, trans. Catherine Porter (Ithaca: Cornell University Press, 1993 [1991]), vii.

23 On the question of the importance of intertitles in the history of editing and their influence on the 'literary-ization' of the film medium, see the work of Claire Dupré la Tour, in particular her article 'Les intertitres réduits au silence, aperçus et remises en perspective,' in Francesco Pitassio and Leonardo Quaresima, eds, *Scrittura e immagine: La didascalia del cinema muto* (Udine: Università degli Studi di Udine, 1998).

24 André Gaudreault, 'Récit itératif, récit singulatif: *Au bagne* (Pathé, 1905),' in *Les premiers ans du cinéma français* (Perpignan: Institut Jean Vigo, 1985), 233–41.

25 One day we will have to define such a term in a way that takes into account the way narration effects monstration, thereby avoiding, as Paul Ricoeur suggests in the Preface to this book, 'any subordination of the filmic to the literary,' so that we may one day definitively pass from the literary to the filmic ...

Bibliography

Note: Entries for translated works give the date of the original-language edition in parentheses following the title.

Abel, Richard. *The Ciné Goes to Town: French Cinema, 1896–1914*. Berkeley: University of California Press, 1994.

Adam, Jean-Michel. *Le récit*. Paris: Presses Universitaires de France, 1984.

– *Le texte narratif*. Paris: Nathan, 1985.

Albera, François, and Roland Cosandey. *Cinéma sans frontières 1896–1918 / Images across Borders*. Lausanne and Quebec City: Éditions Payot Lausanne and Nuit blanche éditeur, 1995.

Albersmeier, Franz-Josef. *Theater, Film, Literatur in Frankreich: Medienwechsel und Intermedialität*. Darmstadt: Wissenschaftliche Buchgesellschaft, 1992.

Altman, Rick. 'Penser l'histoire du cinéma autrement: Un modèle de crise.' *Vingtième siècle* 46 (1995).

Aristotle. *The Poetics*. Edited Hamilton Fyfe. Cambridge and London: Harvard University Press and William Heinemann, 1982 (1927).

Poetics. Introduction, commentary, and appendices by D.W. Lucas. Oxford: Clarendon Press, 1968.

Aubert, Michelle, and Jean-Claude Seguin. *La production cinématographique des frères Lumière* (accompanied by a CD-ROM). Paris: Éditions Mémoires du cinéma and Bibliothèque du Film, 1996.

Aumont, Jacques. 'L'image filmique de film?' *Revue d'esthétique* 7 (1984).

– *Montage Eisenstein*. (1979.) Translated by Lee Hildreth, Constance Penley, and Andrew Ross. London and Bloomington: British Film Institute and Indiana University Press, 1987.

– *L'œil interminable: Cinéma et peinture*. Séguier: Paris, 1989.

Aumont, Jacques, et al. *Aesthetics of Film*. (1983). Translated by Richard Neupert. Austin: University of Texas Press, 1997.

Aumont, Jacques, André Gaudreault, and Michel Marie, eds. *Nouvelles approches de l'histoire du cinéma.* Paris: Publications de la Sorbonne, 1989.

Aumont, Jacques, and Jean-Louis Leutrat, eds. *La théorie du film.* Paris: Albatros, 1980.

Baby, François. 'Du littéraire au cinématographique: Une problématique de l'adaptation.' *Études littéraires* 13, no. 1 (April 1980).

Bal, Mieke. *Narratology: Introduction to the Theory of Narrative.* (1977.) Translated by Christine van Boheemen. Toronto: University of Toronto Press, 1985.

Baron, Anne-Marie. *Balzac cinéaste.* Paris: Méridiens Klincksieck, 1990.

Barthes, Roland. *Critical Essays.* (1964.) Translated by Richard Howard. Evanston: Northwestern University Press, 1972.

– 'Introduction à l'analyse structurale des récits.' *Communications* 8 (1966).

Barthes, Roland, et al., eds. *Poétique du récit.* Paris: Seuil, 1977.

Bédard, Yves. 'Images écrites: Étude de l'écriture dans le cinéma de 1895 à 1912.' Unpublished master's thesis. Université Laval, 1987.

Belloï, Livio. 'Poétique du hors-champ,' *Revue belge du cinéma* 31 (1992).

Bellour, Raymond, ed. *Le cinéma américain.* Vols. 1 and 2. Paris: Flammarion, 1980.

Benveniste, Émile. *Problems in General Linguistics.* (1966.) Translated by Mary Elizabeth Meek. Coral Gables: University of Miami Press, 1971.

Bergala, Alain. *Initiation à la sémiologie du récit en images.* Paris: Ligue française de l'enseignement et de l'éducation permanente, [1977].

Bessalel, Jean, and André Gardies. *200 mots-clés de la théorie du cinéma.* Paris: Éditions du Cerf, 1992.

The Book of the Thousand Nights and a Night (The Arabian Nights). Vol. 1. Translated by Richard F. Burton. London: Burton Club, [1885].

Booth, Wayne C. 'Distance and Point-of-View: An Essay in Classification.' In *Essays in Criticism*, vol. 11. Oxford: Basil Blackwell, 1961.

– *The Rhetoric of Fiction.* Chicago and London: University of Chicago Press, 1961.

Bordwell, David. *Making Meaning: Inference and Rhetoric in the Interpretation of Cinema.* Cambridge, MA, and London: Harvard University Press, 1989.

– *Narration in the Fiction Film.* Madison: University of Wisconsin Press, 1985.

– 'Textual Analysis, etc.' *Enclitic*, Fall 1981 / Spring 1982.

Bordwell, David, Janet Staiger, and Kristin Thompson. *The Classical Hollywood Cinema: Film Style & Mode of Production to 1960.* New York: Columbia University Press, 1985.

Bourneuf, Roland, and Réal Ouellet. *L'univers du roman.* Paris: Presses Universitaires de France, 1975.

Bowser, Eileen. *The Transformation of Cinema 1907–1915.* Berkeley, Los Angeles, and London: University of California Press, 1990.

Branigan, Edward. *Narrative Comprehension and Film*. London and New York: Routledge, 1992.

– *Point of View in the Cinema*. Berlin, New York, and Amsterdam: Mouton Publishers, 1984.

Bremond, Claude. *Logique du récit*. Paris: Seuil, 1973.

Bremond, Jules. 'La logique des possibles narratifs.' *Communications* 8 (1966).

Burch, Noël. 'Porter, or Ambivalence.' *Screen* 19, no. 4 (Winter 1978–9).

– *Life to Those Shadows*. Translated and edited by Ben Brewster. Berkeley and Los Angeles: University of California Press, 1990.

– *To the Distant Observer: Form and Meaning in the Japanese Cinema*. London: Scolar, 1979.

Burgoyne, Robert. 'Le narrateur au cinéma.' *Poétique* 87 (1991).

Burgoyne, Robert, Robert Stam, and Sandy Flitterman-Lewis. *New Vocabularies in Film Semiotics*. London and New York: Routledge, 1992.

Camus, Albert. *The Stranger*. Translated by Stuart Gilbert. New York: Knopf, 1981.

Candelon, Danielle. 'L'auteur implicite dans le discours du récit: Une analyse de l'oeuvre de Jean Simard.' Unpublished doctoral dissertation. Université Laval, 1977.

Carcaud-Macaire, Monique, and Jeanne-Marie Clerc. *Pour une lecture sociocritique de l'adaptation cinématographique*. Montpellier: L'Institut de sociocritique, 1995.

Casetti, Francesco. *Inside the Gaze: The Fiction Film and Its Spectator*. Translated by Nell Andrew and Charles O'Brien. Bloomington: Indiana University Press, 1998.

Chambers, Ross. 'Le masque et le miroir: Vers une théorie relationnelle du théâtre.' *Études littéraires* 13, no. 3 (December 1980).

Chateau, Dominique. *Le cinéma comme langage*. N.p.: Éditions AISS-IASPA, Publications de la Sorbonne and Atelier de Création et d'Études Vidéographiques, 1986.

– 'La sémiologie du cinéma: Un bilan.' *Degrés* 64 (Winter 1990).

Chateau, Dominique, André Gardies, and François Jost, eds. *Cinémas de la modernité: Films, théories*. Paris: Klincksieck, 1981.

Châteauvert, Jean. 'Confusions et dissensions autour du narrateur en voix off.' *Protée* 19, no. 1 (1991).

– *Des mots à l'image: La voix over au cinéma*. Paris and Quebec City: Méridiens Klincksieck and Nuit blanche éditeur, 1996.

– 'Narrer et ne pas narrer.' *Poétique* 93 (1993).

– 'Prolégomènes à une lecture essayistique des quatre premiers "Comédies et proverbes" d'Éric Rohmer.' Unpublished master's thesis. Université Laval, 1987.

Chatelain, Danièle. 'Itération interne et scène classique.' *Poétique* 51 (1982).

Chatman, Seymour. *Coming to Terms: The Rhetoric of Narrative in Fiction and Film*. Ithaca and London: Cornell University Press, 1990.

– *Story and Discourse*. Ithaca and London: Cornell University Press, 1978.

Cherchi Usai, Paolo. *Burning Passions: An Introduction to the Study of Silent Cinema*. London: British Film Institute, 1994.

Chion, Michel. *The Voice in Cinema*. (1982.) Translated and edited by Claudia Gorbman. New York: Columbia University Press, 1999.

Clerc, Jeanne-Marie. *Écrivains et cinéma*. Paris: Presses Universitaires de Metz, 1985.

– *Littérature et cinéma*. Paris: Nathan, 1993.

Colin, Michel. 'Film: Transformation du texte du roman.' Unpublished doctoral dissertation. École Pratique des Hautes Études (Paris), 1974.

Collet, Jean et al. *Lectures du film*. Paris: Albatros, 1976.

Cordesse, Gérard. 'Narration et focalisation.' *Poétique* 76 (1988).

– 'Notes sur l'énonciation narrative.' *Poétique* 65 (1986).

Cosandey, Roland. *Cinéma 1900: Trente films dans une boîte à chaussures*. Lausanne: Éditions Payot Lausanne, 1996.

Cosandey, Roland, André Gaudreault, and Tom Gunning, eds. *Une invention du diable? Cinéma des premiers temps et religion / An Invention of the Devil? Religion and Early Cinema*. Sainte-Foy and Lausanne: Presses de l'Université Laval and Éditions Payot Lausanne, 1992.

Crane, R.S., ed. *Critics and Criticism*. Chicago: University of Chicago Press, 1952.

De France, Xavier. *Éléments de scénographie du cinéma*. Paris: Université de Paris X, 1982.

Deutelbaum, Marshall. 'Structural Patterning in the Lumière Films.' *Wide Angle* 3, no. 1 (1979).

Dubois, Jean, et al. *Dictionnaire de linguistique*. Paris: Larousse, 1973.

Ducrot, Oswald. *Le dire et le dit*. Paris: Les Éditions de Minuit, 1984.

Dumoncel, Jean-Claude. 'Deleuze, Platon et les poètes.' *Poétique* 59 (1984).

Dupont-Roc, Roselyne. '*Mimēsis* et énonciation.' In Dupont-Roc et al., *Écriture et théorie poétiques*. Paris: Presses de l'École Normale Supérieure, 1976.

Dupré la Tour, Claire. 'Les intertitres réduits au silence, aperçus et remises en perspective.' In Francesco Pitassio and Leonardo Quaresima, eds, *Scrittura e immagine: La didascalia nel cinema muto*. Udine: Università degli Studi di Udine, 1998.

Eisenstein, Sergei. *Towards a Theory of Montage. Selected Works*, vol. 2. Translated by Michael Glenny, edited by Michael Glenny and Richard Taylor. London: British Film Institute, 1991.

Elsaesser, Thomas, and Adam Barker, eds. *Early Cinema: Space, Frame, Narrative*. London: British Film Institute, 1990.

Ertel, Evelyne. 'Éléments pour une sémiologie du théâtre.' *Travail théâtral* 28 (Summer–Fall 1977).

Fell, John, ed. *Film before Griffith*. Los Angeles: University of California Press, 1983.

Francoeur, Louis. *Les signes s'envolent: Pour une sémiotique des actes de langage culturels*. Sainte-Foy: Presses de l'Université Laval, 1985.

Garcia, Alain. *L'adaptation du roman au film*. Paris: Éditions I.F. Diffusion, 1990.

Gardies, André. *L'espace au cinéma*. Paris: Méridiens Klincksieck, 1993.

– 'Le pouvoir ludique de la focalisation.' *Protée* 16, nos. 1–2 (Winter–Spring 1988).

– *Le récit filmique*. Paris: Hachette, 1993.

– 'Le su et le vu.' *Hors Cadre* 2 (1984).

Gartenberg, Jon. 'Les mouvements de caméra dans les films Edison et Biograph.' *Les Cahiers de la Cinémathèque* 29 (Winter 1979).

Gaudreault, André. 'Les aventures d'un concept.' In *Christian Metz et la théorie du cinéma*. Méridiens Klincksieck and *Iris* 10 (April 1990).

– 'Bruitage, musique et commentaires aux débuts du cinéma.' *Protée* 13, no. 2 (Summer 1985).

– 'Detours in Film Narrative: The Development of Cross-Cutting.' In Roger Holman, ed., *Cinema 1900–1906: An Analytical Study*, vol. 1. Brussels: International Federation of Film Archives, 1982.

– 'Film, Narrative, Narration: The Cinema of the Lumière Brothers.' In Thomas Elsaesser and Adam Barker, eds, *Early Cinema: Space, Frame, Narrative*. London: British Film Institute, 1990.

– 'L'histoire du cinéma revisitée: Le cinéma des premiers temps.' *CinémAction* 47 (1988).

– 'Histoire et discours au cinéma.' In *Le Cinéma: Théorie et discours*. Montreal: La Cinémathèque québécoise, *Les Dossiers de la Cinémathèque* 12, 1984.

– 'The Infringement of Copyright Laws and Its Effects (1900–1906).' In Elsaesser and Barker, eds, *Early Cinema*.

– '*Mimēsis* et *diēgēsis* chez Aristote.' *Cahiers des études anciennes* 24 (1990).

– '*Mimēsis, diēgēsis* et cinéma.' *Recherches sémiotiques / Semiotic Inquiry* 5 (1985).

– '*Mimēsis* et *diēgēsis* chez Platon.' *Revue de métaphysique et de morale* 1 (1989).

– 'Narration and Monstration in the Cinema.' *Journal of Film and Video* 39 (1987).

– 'Narrator et narrateur.' *Iris* 7 (1986). Reprinted in Michel Larouche, ed., *Le cinéma aujourd'hui: Films, théories, nouvelles approches*. Montreal: Guernica, 1988.

– 'Récit scriptural, récit scénique, récit filmique: Prolégomènes à une théorie narratologique du cinéma.' Unpublished PhD dissertation. Université de Paris III (Sorbonne Nouvelle), 1983.

- 'Showing and Telling: Image and Word in Early Cinema.' Trans. John Howe. In Elsaesser and Barker, eds, *Early Cinema.*
- 'Singular Narrative, Iterative Narrative: *Au Bagne* (Pathé 1905).' *Persistence of Vision* 9 (1991).
- 'Sistema del relato de un film con narrador verbal: *Citizen Kane* de Orson Welles.' *Archivos de la Filmoteca* 27 (October 1997).
- 'Temporality and Narrativity in Early Cinema, 1895–1908.' In John L. Fell, ed., *Film before Griffith*, Berkeley: University of California Press, 1983.
- 'Theatricality, Narrativity and "Trickality": Reevaluating the Cinema of Georges Méliès,' *Journal of Popular Film and Television* 15, no. 3 (Fall 1987).
- 'Les *Vues cinématographiques* selon Georges Méliès, ou: Comment Mitry et Sadoul avaient peut-être raison d'avoir tort (même si c'est surtout Deslandes qu'il faut lire et relire).' In Jacques Malthête and Michel Marie, eds, *Georges Méliès, l'illusionniste fin de siècle?* Paris: Presses de la Sorbonne Nouvelle and Colloque de Cerisy, 1997.
Gaudreault, André, ed. *Ce que je vois de mon ciné … La représentation du regard dans le cinéma des premiers temps.* Paris: Méridiens Klincksieck, 1988.
- *Pathé 1900. Fragments d'une filmographie analytique du cinéma des premiers temps.* Paris and Sainte-Foy: Presses de la Sorbonne Nouvelle and Presses de l'Université Laval, 1993.
- In collaboration with Germain Lacasse and with the assistance of Jean-Pierre Sirois-Trahan. *Au pays des ennemis du cinéma … Pour une nouvelle histoire des débuts du cinéma au Québec.* Quebec City: Nuit Blanche éditeur, 1996.
Gaudreault, André, and Tom Gunning. 'Early Cinema as a Challenge to Film History.' Translated by Joyce Goggin and Wanda Strauven. In Wanda Strauven, ed., *The Cinema of Attractions Reloaded.* Amsterdam: Amsterdam University Press, 2006.
Gaudreault, André, and François Jost. *Le récit cinématographique.* Paris: Nathan, 1990.
Genette, Gérard. *The Architext: An Introduction.* (1979.) Translated by Jane E. Lewin. Berkeley: University of California Press, 1992.
- *Figures III.* Paris: Seuil, 1972.
- *Fiction and Diction.* Translated by Catherine Porter. Ithaca: Cornell University Press, 1993.
- 'Frontiers of Narrative.' In *Figures of Literary Discourse.* (1966.) Translated by Alan Sheridan. New York: Columbia University Press, 1982.
- *Narrative Discourse: An Essay in Method.* (1972.) Translated by Jane E. Lewin. Ithaca: Cornell University Press, 1980.
- *Narrative Discourse Revisited.* (1983.) Translated by Jane E. Lewin. New York: Cornell University Press, 1988.

Gili, Jean, et al., eds. *Les vingt premières années du cinéma français: Actes du colloque de la Sorbonne.* Paris: Presses de la Sorbonne Nouvelle, 1996.

Girard, Gilles, Réal Ouellet, and Claude Rigault. *L'univers du théâtre.* Paris: Presses Universitaires de France, 1978.

Greimas, Algirdas-Julien. *Structural Semantics: An Attempt at a Method.* (1966.) Translated by Daniele McDowell, Ronald Schleifer, and Alan Velie. Lincoln: University of Nebraska Press, 1983.

Greimas, A.-J., and J. Courtés. *Semiotics and Language: An Analytical Dictionary.* (1979.) Translated by Larry Crist et al. Bloomington: Indiana University Press, 1982.

Gritti, Jules. 'Un récit de presse: Les derniers jours d'un "grand homme."' *Communications* 8 (1966).

Groupe µ. *Rhétorique générale.* Paris: Librairie Larousse, 1970.

Gubern, Román. 'David Wark Griffith et l'articulation cinématographique.' *Les Cahiers de la Cinémathèque* 17 (December 1975).

Gunning, Tom. 'The Cinema of Attractions: Early Film, Its Spectator and the Avant-Garde.' *Wide Angle* 8, nos. 3–4 (1986).

– 'D.W. Griffith and the Narrator System: Narrative Structure and Industry Organization in Biograph Films.' Doctoral dissertation. New York University, 1986.

– *D.W. Griffith and the Origins of American Narrative Film: The Early Years at Biograph.* Urbana and Chicago: University of Illinois Press, 1991.

– 'The Non-Continuous Style of Early Film 1900–1906.' In Roger Holman, ed., *Cinema 1900-1906: An Analytical Study,* vol. 1. Brussels: International Federation of Film Archives, 1982.

– 'Présence du narrateur: L'héritage des films Biograph de Griffith.' In Jean Mottet, ed., *David Wark Griffith.* Paris: Publications de la Sorbonne and L'Harmattan, 1984.

– '"Primitive" Cinema: A Frame-Up? Or, The Trick's on Us.' In Thomas Elsaesser and Adam Barker, eds, *Early Cinema: Space, Frame, Narrative.* London: British Film Institute, 1990.

Hamon, Philippe. 'Pour un statut sémiologique du personnage.' In Roland Barthes et al., *Poétique du récit.* Paris: Seuil, 1977.

Hansen, Miriam. *Babel and Babylon: Spectatorship in American Silent Film.* Cambridge, MA and London: Harvard University Press, 1991.

Harkness, John. 'Nightworld: Interview with James Cole and Holly Dale.' *Cinema Canada* 108 (June 1984).

Helbo, André. *L'adaptation: Du théâtre au cinéma.* Paris: Armand Colin, 1997.

Holman, Roger, ed. *Cinema 1900-1906: An Analytical Study.* Vol. 1. Brussels: International Federation of Film Archives, 1982.

Homer. *The Odyssey*. Trans. Edward McCrorie. Baltimore: Johns Hopkins University Press, 2004.

Jenny, Laurent. 'Le poétique et le narratif.' *Poétique* 28 (1976).

Jost, François. *Un monde à notre image: Énonciation, cinéma, télévision*. Paris: Méridiens Klincksieck, 1992.

– 'Narration(s): En deçà et au-delà.' *Communications* 38 (1983).

– *L'œil-caméra: Entre film et roman*. Lyon: Presses Universitaires de Lyon, 1987.

– 'Où en est la narratologie cinématographique?' *CinémAction* 20 (1982).

– *Le temps d'un regard: Du spectateur aux images*. Paris and Quebec City: Méridiens Klincksieck and Nuit blanche éditeur, 1998.

– 'Vers de nouvelles approches méthodologiques.' In Dominique Château et al., eds, *Cinémas de la modernité: Films, théories*. Paris: Klincksieck, 1981.

Kayser, William. 'Qui raconte le roman?' In Roland Barthes et al., *Poétique du récit*. Paris: Seuil, 1977.

Kerbrat-Orecchioni, Catherine. *L'énonciation: De la subjectivité dans le langage*. Paris: Armand Colin, 1980.

King, Norman. 'The Sound of Silents.' *Screen* 25, no. 3 (May–June 1984).

Komatsu, Hiroshi, and Charles Musser. 'Added Attraction: Benshi Search.' *Wide Angle* 9, no. 2 (1987).

Kozloff, Sarah. *Invisible Storytellers: Voice-over Narration in American Fiction Film*. Berkeley and Los Angeles: University of California Press, 1988.

Lacasse, Germain, with Serge Duigou. *L'historiographe* (*Les débuts du spectacle cinématographique au Québec*). Montreal: La Cinémathèque québécoise, *Les Dossiers de la Cinémathèque* 15, 1985.

Lacassin, Francis. *Louis Feuillade*. Paris: Seghers, 1964.

Laffay, Albert. *Logique du cinéma*. Paris: Masson, 1964.

Lagny, Michèle. *De l'histoire du cinéma: Méthode historique et histoire du cinéma*. Paris: Armand Colin, 1992.

Laillou Savona, Jeannette. 'Narration et actes de parole dans le texte dramatique.' *Études littéraires* 13, no. 3 (December 1980).

Lallot, Jean. 'La "*Mimēsis*" selon Aristote et l'excellence d'Homère.' In Roselyne Dupont-Roc et al., *Écriture et théorie poétiques*. Paris: Presses de l'École Normale Supérieure, 1976.

Larouche, Michel, ed. *Le cinéma aujourd'hui: Films, théories, nouvelles approches*. Montreal: Guernica, 1988.

Lee, Van C. 'The Value of a Lecture.' *Moving Picture World*, 8 February 1908.

Levy, David. 'Edison Sales Policy and the Continuous Action Film, 1904–1906.' In John Fell, ed., *Film before Griffith*. Los Angeles: University of California Press, 1983.

– 'Edwin S. Porter and the Origins of the American Narrative Film, 1894–1907.' Unpublished doctoral dissertation. McGill University, 1983.

Lintvelt, Jaap. *Essai de typologie narrative*. Paris: Librairie José Corti, 1981.

Lotman, Yuri. *The Semiotics of Cinema*. (1973.) Translated by Mark E. Suino. Ann Arbor: University of Michigan Press, 1976.

Magny, Claude-Edmonde. *L'âge du roman américain*. Paris: Seuil, 1948.

Malthête, Jacques. 'Les actualités reconstituées de Georges Méliès.' *Archives* 21 (March 1989).

– *Méliès: Images et illusions*. Paris: Exporégie, 1996.

Malthête, Jacques, Madeleine Malthête-Méliès, and Anne-Marie Quévrain. *Essai de reconstitution du catalogue français de la Star-Film, suivi d'une analyse catalographique des films de Georges Méliès recensés en France*. [Bois d'Arcy]: Publications du Service des Archives du Film du CNC, 1981.

Malthête-Méliès, Madeleine. *Méliès l'enchanteur*. Paris: Hachette, 1973.

Malthête-Méliès, Madeleine, ed. *Méliès et la naissance du spectacle cinématographique*. Paris: Klincksieck, 1984.

Marie, Michel. 'Analyse textuelle.' In Jean Collet et al., eds, *Lectures du film*. Paris: Albatros, 1976.

– 'Découpage.' In Collet et al., eds, *Lectures du film*.

Marion, Philippe. *Traces en cases: Travail graphique, figuration narrative et participation du lecteur. Essai sur la bande dessinée*. Louvain-la-Neuve: Academia, 1993.

Masson, Alain. *Le récit au cinéma*. Paris: Éditions de l'Étoile, 1994.

Mazon, Paul. *Introduction à l'Iliade*. Paris: Les Belles Lettres, 1942.

McKeon, Richard. 'The Concept of Imitation in Antiquity.' In R.S. Crane, ed., *Critics and Criticism*. Chicago: University of Chicago Press, 1952.

Metz, Christian. 'Le cinéma: Langue ou langage?' *Communications* 4 (1964). Published in translation as 'The Cinema: Language or Language System' in Metz, *Film Language*.

– 'L'énonciation impersonnelle ou le site du film.' *Vertigo* 1 (1987).

– *L'énonciation impersonnelle ou le site du film*. Paris: Méridiens Klincksieck, 1991.

– *Film Language: A Semiotics of the Cinema*. (1971.) Translated by Michael Taylor. New York: Oxford University Press, 1974.

– *Language and Cinema*. (1971.) Translated by Donna Jean Umiker-Seabeok. The Hague and Paris: Mouton, 1974.

– *Le signifiant imaginaire*. Paris: U.G.E., 1977.

Meusy, Jean-Jacques. *Paris-Palaces ou le temps des cinémas (1894–1918)*. Paris: CNRS Éditions, 1995.

Milot, Louise, and Fernand Roy, eds. *La littérarité.* Sainte-Foy: Les Presses de l'Université Laval, 1991.

Mitry, Jean. *The Aesthetics and Psychology of the Cinema.* (1968.) Translated by Christopher King. Bloomington: Indiana University Press, 1997.

– *Histoire du cinéma.* Vol. 1. Paris: Éditions universitaires, 1967.

Mottet, Jean, ed. *David Wark Griffith.* Paris: Publications de la Sorbonne and L'Harmattan, 1984.

Müller, Jürgen E. *Intermedialität: Formen moderner kultureller Kommunikation.* Münster: Nodus, 1995.

– '*Top Hat* et l'intermédialité de la comédie musicale.' *Cinémas* 5, nos. 1–2 (Fall 1994).

Musser, Charles. *Before the Nickelodeon: Edwin S. Porter and the Edison Manufacturing Company.* Berkeley, Los Angeles, and Oxford: University of California Press, 1991.

– 'The Early Cinema of Edwin Porter.' *Cinema Journal* 13, no. 1 (Fall 1979).

– *The Emergence of Cinema: The American Screen to 1907.* New York: Charles Scribner's Sons, 1990.

– 'The Nickelodeon Era Begins: Establishing the *Framework* for Hollywood's Mode of Representation.' *Framework* 22–3 (Fall 1983).

Musser, Charles, and Carol Nelson. *High-Class Moving Pictures.* Princeton: Princeton University Press, 1991.

Odin, Roger. *Cinéma et production de sens.* Paris: Armand Colin, 1990.

– 'L'entrée du spectateur dans la fiction.' In Jacques Aumont and Jean-Louis Leutrat, eds, *La théorie du film.* Paris: Albatros, 1980.

– 'Du spectateur fictionnalisant au nouveau spectateur: Approche sémio-pragmatique.' *Iris* 8 (1988).

Osolsobé, Ivo. 'Cours de théâtristique générale.' *Études littéraires* 13, no. 3 (December 1980).

Pavis, Patrice. *L'analyse des spectacles.* Paris: Nathan, 1996.

– *Dictionary of the Theatre: Terms, Concepts, and Analysis.* (1996.) Translated by Christine Shantz. Toronto: University of Toronto Press, 1998.

– *Problèmes de sémiologie théâtrale.* Montreal: Presses de l'Université du Québec, 1976.

– *Voix et images de la scène.* Lille: Presses Universitaires de Lille, 1982.

Plato. *The Republic.* Vol. 1, translated by Paul Shorey. 1930. Cambridge, MA, and London: Harvard University Press and William Heinemann, 1963.

– *The Republic.* Translated by Tom Griffith, edited by G.R.F. Ferrari. Cambridge: Cambridge University Press, 2000.

Prince, Gerald. *A Dictionary of Narratology.* Lincoln: University of Nebraska Press, 2003.

– 'Le discours attributif et le récit.' *Poétique* 35 (1978).

Proust, Marcel. *In Search of Lost Time: The Way by Swann's.* Translated by Lydia Davis. London: Penguin, 2002.

– *In Search of Lost Time: Finding Time Again.* Translated by Ian Patterson. London: Penguin, 2002.

Raynauld, Isabelle. 'Le point de vue dans le scénario.' *Protée* 16, nos. 1–2 (Winter–Spring 1988).

Récanati, François. *La transparence et l'énonciation.* Paris: Seuil, 1979.

Ricoeur, Paul. *Time and Narrative.* (1985.) Translated by Kathleen Blamey and David Pellauer. Chicago: University of Chicago Press, 1988.

Rojtman, Betty. 'Désengagement du Je dans le discours indirect.' *Poétique* 41 (1981).

Ropars-Wuilleumier, Marie-Claire. 'Fonction du montage dans la constitution du récit au cinéma.' *Revue des sciences humaines* 141 (1971).

– 'Narration et signification.' In Raymond Bellour, ed., *Le cinéma américain,* vol. 2. Paris: Flammarion, 1980.

Sadoul, Georges. *Louis Lumière.* Paris: Seghers, 1964.

Salt, Barry. *Film Style and Technology: History and Analysis.* London: Starword, 1993.

Schaeffer, Jean-Marie. *L'image précaire: Du dispositif photographique.* Paris: Seuil, 1987.

Simon, Jean-Paul. 'Remarques sur la temporalité cinématographique dans les films diégétiques.' In Dominique Chateau, André Gardies, and François Jost, eds, *Cinémas de la modernité: Films, théories.* Paris: Klincksieck, 1981.

Simon, Jean-Paul, and Marc Vernet. 'Avant-propos.' *Communications* 38 (1983).

Sopocy, Martin. *James A. Williamson: Studies and Documents of a Pioneer of the Film Narrative.* Madison and Teaneck, NJ: Fairleigh Dickinson University Press, 1998.

– 'A Narrated Cinema: The Pioneer Story Films of James A. Williamson.' *Cinema Journal* 18, no. 1 (Fall 1978).

Souriau, Étienne. 'La structure de l'univers filmique et le vocabulaire de la filmologie.' *Revue internationale de filmologie* 7–8 (1951).

Souriau, Étienne. *L'univers filmique.* Paris: Flammarion, 1953.

Thérien, Gilles. 'Le cinéma québécois: Une recherche sur la voie de l'écriture.' *Revue des sciences humaines* 173 (1979).

Todorov, Tzvetan. 'Les catégories du récit littéraire.' *Communications* 8 (1966).

– *Les genres du discours.* (1971.) Paris: Seuil, 1978.

– *The Poetics of Prose.* Translated by Richard Howard. Ithaca: Cornell University Press, 1987.

– *Qu'est-ce que le structuralisme?* Paris: Seuil, 1968.

– *Qu'est-ce que le structuralisme?* Rev. ed. Paris: Seuil, 1973.

Toulet, Emmanuelle. *Cinématographe, invention du siècle.* Paris: Gallimard, 1988.

Tsivian, Yuri. *Early Cinema in Russia and Its Cultural Reception.* London: Routledge, 1994.

Ubersfeld, Anne. 'La couronne du Roi Lear ou Pour une poétique de l'objet théâtral.' *Pratiques* 24 (August 1979).

– *L'école du spectateur.* Paris: Éditions sociales, 1981.

– *Reading Theatre.* (1996.) Translated by Frank Collins. Toronto: University of Toronto Press, 1999.

Vanoye, Francis. *Récit écrit, récit filmique.* Paris: CEDIC, 1979; reprinted by Nathan, 1989.

Vernet, Marc. *Figures de l'absence.* Paris: Éditions de l'Étoile and Cahiers du Cinéma, 1988.

Vicaire, Paul. *Platon critique littéraire.* Paris: Klincksieck, 1960.

Zumthor, Paul. *Introduction à la poésie orale.* Paris: Seuil, 1983.

Index

PREVIOUS PUBLICATIONS

Du littéraire au filmique: Système du récit. Paris and Quebec City: Méridiens Klincksieck and Presses de l'Université Laval, 1988. Preface by Paul Ricoeur. Revised edition, with new postface, published in 1999 by Armand Colin and Nota Bene (Paris and Quebec City). Also published in Italian and forthcoming in Spanish and Chinese.

Le Récit cinématographique. Paris: Nathan, 1990. Co-authored by François Jost. Also published in Spanish, Korean, Chinese, and Portuguese.

Pathé 1900: Fragments d'une filmographie analytique du cinéma des premiers temps. Paris and Quebec City: Presses de la Sorbonne Nouvelle and Presses de l'Université Laval, 1993. Co-authored by Tom Gunning and Alain Lacasse.

Au pays des ennemis du cinéma … Pour une nouvelle histoire des débuts du cinéma au Québec. Quebec City: Nuit Blanche, 1996. Co-authored by Germain Lacasse and Jean-Pierre Sirois-Trahan.

Cinema delle origini. O della 'cinematografia-attrazione.' Milan: Il Castoro, 2004.

Cinéma et attraction. Pour une nouvelle histoire du cinématographe. Paris: CNRS Éditions, 2008.

EDITED VOLUMES

Ce que je vois de mon ciné … La représentation du regard dans le cinéma des premiers temps. Paris: Méridiens Klincksieck, 1988.

Histoire du cinéma. Nouvelles approches. Paris: Publications de la Sorbonne, 1989. Co-edited by Jacques Aumont and Michel Marie.

Une invention du diable? Cinéma des premiers temps et religion / An Invention of the Devil? Religion and Early Cinema. Lausanne and Quebec City: Payot Lausanne and Presses de l'Université Laval, 1992. Co-edited by Roland Cosandey and Tom Gunning.

La Transécriture: Pour une théorie de l'adaptation. Quebec City and Angoulême: Nota Bene and Centre national de la bande dessinée et de l'image, 1998. Co-edited by Thierry Groensteen.

Le Cinéma au tournant du siècle / Cinema at the Turn of the Century. Quebec City and Lausanne: Nota Bene and Payot Lausanne, 1999. Co-edited by Claire Dupré la Tour and Roberta Pearson.

Le Cinéma en histoire: Institution cinématographique, réception filmique et reconstitution historique. Paris and Quebec City: Méridiens Klincksieck and Nota Bene, 1999. Co-edited by Germain Lacasse and Isabelle Raynauld.

Arrêt sur image, fragmentation du temps: Aux sources de la culture visuelle moderne / Stop Motion, Fragmentation of Time: Exploring the Roots of Modern Visual Culture. Lausanne: Payot Lausanne, 2002. Co-edited by François Albera and Marta Braun.

Le Cinématographe, nouvelle technologie du XXe siècle / The Cinema, A New Technology for the 20th Century. Lausanne: Payot Lausanne, 2004. Co-edited by Catherine Russell and Pierre Véronneau.